First published in Australia in 2021
by Jacqueline Bawtree

This edition published in 2022

The Urban Gypsy - Storyteller
ABN 998 4089 2638
Jacquelinebawtree.com
Brisbane, Queensland Australia

© Jacqueline Bawtree 2021

The right of Jacqueline Bawtree to be identified as the author of this work has been asserted by her in accordance with the Copyright Amendment (Moral Rights) Act 2000.

This work is copyright. Apart from any use as permitted under the Copyright Act 1968, no part may be reproduced, copied, scanned, stored in a retrieval system, recorded or transmitted, in any form by any means, without the prior permission of the publisher.

A catalogue record for this book is available from the National Library of Australia.

ISBN 978-0-6452982-0-8 (paperback)
ISBN 978-0-6452982-1-5 (e-book)

Cover Design by Taylor-Jayne Wilkshire
Author Photo by Kris Ashpole
Design by Jordan Bariesheff

Printed and bound in Australia by Ingram Spark
www.ingramspark.com

LIFE TAKES YOU UNEXPECTED PLACES.
LOVE BRINGS YOU HOME.

Coming Home

JACQUELINE BAWTREE

Ai miei nipoti
Joelle, Naomi, Maria, Jemima, Alex,
Bonita, Lucia, Andrew, Aviva and Serafina

♥

"Vedi Napoli... e poi muori"
See Naples and then Die

*~ **Neapolitan saying** ~*

PROLOGUE

Napoli, Italia
Ottobre 2009

Flying. Air rushed around me as I soared towards the sky.

Falling. The ground hurtled towards me. Disorientated.

NO! NO! NO! Mum will kill me if I go like this. A scream tore through every fibre of my soul as my body slammed down on the cobblestones of via Santa Teresa degli Scalzi. My left arm flung out in desperation.

Grasping. Anything. *STOP! MAKE IT STOP!*

I rolled once. Twice. I felt like I was about to go over a cliff. I dug my fingers down onto the surface of stones. Trying to find a grip. Trying to bring my momentum to a halt before my body was flung around further.

Stop.

There was no cliff. I opened my eyes to see traffic roaring around the corner from Piazza Museo, veering past the spot where I lay.

I felt no pain. But neither did I feel inclined to move.

There had been no escape as I took two steps onto the pedestrian crossing of the busy thoroughfare outside Museo Archeologico Nazionale. One hundred and ten kilograms of metal in the form of an iconic Italian moped had appeared from nowhere, slammed into my left thigh and propelled me unknown meters through the air. It had taken only seconds for the pull of gravity to bring me back down. My landing point much further along the road.

It was early afternoon on a sunny, autumn day in southern Italy.

The shadows and light cascading between the buildings of Via Toledo filtered into my dazed eyes. I felt an aura of twilight closing in around me.

"Aiuto..." I gasped, inaudible to anyone other than myself... and God.

Help me.

PART 1

~ *La Principessa* ~

THE PRINCESS

"Infinito cielo stellato ti guardo e subito mi domando…
"Cos' altro io sono altre a quello che gia' sa di essere?"

Infinite starry sky, I look at you and ask…
"Who am I other than that which
I already know myself to be?"

~ Filo ~

(Alessandro Valenti di art Alvalenti a Siena)

1

Sydney, Australia
January 2009

The tiny bottle of limoncello lay cool in my hand. Relaxing back into a deck chair on my Sydney balcony on the balmy January evening, I twisted the cap off. The sweet smell of citrus swept me back to the side streets of Sorrento, where I had bought the memento on my holiday in Italy, the year before.

Floating in the cool ripples of Coogee Bay as the sun rose earlier in the day had been the perfect start to my birthday. The workday had ended with a meeting to do a final review of plans for delivery of the first Grand Final of Australian football's new W-League, scheduled for later that week. Elise, Jane and I had dashed from the boardroom to meet the rest of my urban family, waiting outside the Football Federation Australia (FFA) office on Hyde Park, to walk down to Mrs Macquarie's Chair.

A picnic of chicken salad, and bottles of rosé to sip on as we gazed across to the Sydney Opera House and Harbour Bridge at sunset had marked communal celebrations this year. Low key but classy. As well as Elise and Jane, other former colleagues—who had become both friends and a substitute family to me in the city I had called home for ten years—had come out tonight. Laura, Helen, Kris, Pete, Amie, Eugenie, Jules. And in addition, a wild card called Maxence. I had met Max in a Paddington pub one night after I finished work at the Sydney Football Stadium. The Socceroos had been playing Ghana and we all turned up for an after-work drink at the Paddington Arms hotel around midnight. There was a fleeting sense of romantic possibility in the chance meeting with the endearing Frenchman. But after one brunch date a week later, it instead evolved into an unexpected and fabulous friendship that had now lasted more than six months. Catching up weekly and messaging daily, I helped him adjust to life in Australia, while he fed my emerging dream of moving to Europe for an indefinite period.

As we cracked open the rosé, I had announced to everyone that the idea planted in my imagination nine months earlier, on a hilltop just outside the city walls of Siena in the centre of Tuscany, was officially set to shape my thirty-fifth year. I was leaving my life in Sydney to learn Italian in the Tuscan town of Siena, then travel around Italy with my anticipated new-found language skills for as long as it took to find new direction for my future: or the money I had begun to scrupulously save ran out. The conversation erupted with recommendations of everyone's favourite European countries to visit. My travel interests beyond Italy, were more in the direction of north Africa, with Egypt, Tunisia, Morocco and Spain top of the list. But with Italy my primary focus, I simply wanted to see where the road would take me without too much pre-planning.

"Perhaps you'll buy a house in Tuscany," Kris laughed, knowing my go to escape from the reality of my own divorce was to watch the film, *Under the Tuscan Sun*.

"With that spare pool of cash I have tucked away for such a purchase?" I mocked my own financial reality with a laugh. There had been no assets to divide after my own marriage of more than eight years had ended. In the two years following, I had however managed to save enough to fulfil a long-held dream of visiting France and Italy on a three-week holiday, with the flights subsidised by a friend with an excessive number of frequent flier points, who wanted to contribute to see my unrequited dream of visiting Europe become a reality.

The idea of following in the footsteps of Francis Mayer—who bought and renovated a villa in Tuscany and created a new life for herself as told in *Under the Tuscan Sun*—had sprung to mind as the tour bus moved through the region. However, after I bounced back from the unplanned excesses of the trip, my next financial goal had been to attempt to get into a property market far less romantic and potentially harder to enter than the one in Tuscany. Sydney.

With the stability of the emotional home once shaped by a happy marriage gone, I thought perhaps bricks and mortar might be a way to fill something of the loss I still acutely felt. A sensible next step as I sought to stabilise my future.

The thing is though, *'once you have tasted flight you will walk the earth with your eyes turned skywards, for there you have been and there you will long to return'*. Leonardo da Vinci once articulated the inspiring impact a change in perspective can create. I had flown back to Sydney devoid of desire to tie myself to the financial commitment of a mortgage after tasting the freedom of being somewhere different. The burden of having to pursue a high enough salary to keep up payments on a home that would be empty, absent of the family I had envisioned we would one day have, held no appeal. And while I still enjoyed my current job, as the dust settled in my personal life, I recognised it may not suffice to satisfy my non-financial needs long term.

Laura bounced with excitement as I opened my present from her.

"It's like your trip!" She wasn't the first person to exclaim this, after hearing about my plans. I didn't like to tell her I had recently succumbed to reading *Eat, Pray, Love* as I pulled the popular travel memoir from the wrapping. My own trip had been mapped before I read it. And so, had my judgement of Elizabeth. After three years sorting through her own post-divorce haze, Elizabeth funded her international sabbatical from everyday life, after landing a book deal to open her heart and head to readers with confronting honesty. I would pick up the bestselling book each time I was in the travel section of my favourite bookstore as I searched for memoirs by independent female travellers. But as I read the synopsis on the back cover yet again, the book would be quietly returned to the shelf. I found no connection to the personal journey of Elizabeth. I had finally read the copy Jane had leant me when she first heard about the journey I was thinking of making. The story was engaging, even brave. But I struggled to reconcile with the woman whose justification for stepping out of her marriage re-opened the wounds of abandonment I was still healing from, in the aftermath of the collapse of my own.

"Did you finish reading *See Naples and Die*?" Elise asked, as everyone finished exclaiming over the poignant choice of gift from Laura. The favourite of my travel writers was Australian journalist and author Penelope Green, who made friends from around the world in Perugia while learning the language, lived and worked in Rome as a waitress then written her first memoir *When in Rome*. From there she found work in the complex southern city of Naples from which came *See Naples and Die*, a book which—as I immersed myself in it morning and evening, swinging from the hand grip of the 373 bus between Randwick and the Sydney CBD—had left me with a deep fascination for the political and social complexity of Southern Italy. She had fallen in love with a bass guitarist in a band who she met through a work assignment. Now they lived on the picturesque island of Procida in the bay of Napoli and she was reportedly working on a third book. The start of her journey sounded much more like my own scraped together self-funded plan. I felt a connection as she wrote about her explorations of both place and self. And if I eventually found myself living on an Italian island with a new love as an outcome of my own adventures, I would be more than happy to embrace that outcome too.

"I bet YOU write a book out of all this," Jane nudged my shoulder with hers. I gave a non-committal shrug. Unlike the memoir writers I aspired to follow in the travel footsteps of, beyond the long emails home to friends and family while I was away, I wasn't a writer.

My language school destination of Siena, the start point of my adventure was confirmed and the flights booked. While the global financial crisis saw job losses around the world, I began putting away every dollar I could, fervently preparing to cast off the bowlines and leave my safe harbour of Sydney and the security of a job that still made me happy. I had six months to prepare to leave Sydney. But before then, there was an A-League Finals Series and three international Socceroos matches to deliver around the country alongside my colleagues.

FFA had announced plans to bid for the 2015 AFC Asian Cup as well as the 2018 and 2022 FIFA World Cups. Staff were moving into new roles and newly formed teams. Part of me wanted to stay for the next chapter in the evolution of Australian football, but the stronger pull was to explore another chapter of my own volition.

The life I had expected to continue leading, had vanished three years earlier. The man I had been married to for eight years, and who I had expected would be the father of my children, was gone. The future I had envisioned by his side, in shards.

As the worst of the grief passed, I worked to let go of the life I had thought was ahead of me. In doing so though, I was left with a big, empty void. I had no idea what I was aiming for. I finally recognised that I needed to create space to spark new hopes and dreams and find fresh fuel to embrace new goals.

I needed to take some time to pause and take a breath.

As my birthday came to a close, I lifted the bottle of limoncello up to the light-polluted Sydney sky. Stars twinkled dimly behind the haze. I hoped all that was written there but yet unseen, would become clearer as I entered the year ahead.

2

Siena, Italia
Luglio 2009

"Piazza... Gram-skee... ?" I tentatively requested into my phone. "Ahhh si. Piazza Gramsci," the operator at the taxi company articulated sprightly. Promptly switching to English at my tentative response, he assured me that he knew where I could be found. I nodded farewell to my fellow passengers milling around the coach stop where we had alighted after arriving from Rome and clambered into the taxi that appeared a few minutes later.

"Kwaah-tr-oh PiAhhzza SAan Fran-ses-cOH, per favore," I emphasized the vowels of the address for the driver in the hope he would understand.

He nodded cheerfully in acknowledgement.

A high arch appeared over the road, the distinctive medieval city walls of Siena rolled out from either side providing me with reassurance that I was in the right place. The taxi slipped through the opening of the ancient rampart taking us into the inner city, the narrow cobblestoned streets quiet in the mid-afternoon of a Sunday, as we bumped steadily uphill.

I had booked my accommodation through the school—a shared

apartment, along with other language students attending summer classes at Scuola di Leonardo da Vinci. I envisioned myself in the coming weeks, tucked away in a gothic residence within the UNESCO World Heritage listed historic centre, high above the narrow passageways of ancient cobblestoned city streets.

We took a hairpin turn up the hill and passed under a false window embedded in a corner wall—framing the sculpture of a topless woman coquettishly peering from around marble curtains—before pulling through a narrow archway, coming to a stop under some trees to the side of a sunny piazza in front of a towering five-hundred-year-old Franciscan Basilica.

"Allora. Abbiamo arrivata a Piazza San Francesco, Signora," the driver announced.

Doorways lined the flat-faced buildings extending off either side of the entrance arch that had welcomed us into the spacious piazza. Shaded by large leafy trees, a young mother with a baby in a pram sat on a park bench, keeping a watchful eye on her toddler son, busy trying to keep up with bigger children chasing a football around the communal space.

"Il numero quattro è laggiù," the driver directed me to where my new front door was with a nod of his head.

I inhaled sharply in surprise. A large villa, painted a cheery yellow with green shutters, lay right beside the towering Basilica. This was where I would call home for the next six weeks.

Home. Back in Sydney, the household items from my rented apartment that hadn't been sold in the two garage sales, or sent off to the Salvos, were locked away in storage for if and when I returned... *If I returned...* The thought played on my mind constantly as I imagined where the road might take me in the next twelve months.

~ * ~

Marrying an actor had never been part of my plan, and although we had arrived together from Brisbane ten years earlier, I had left Sydney alone.

We had spoken for the first time when we both turned up at our church drama group around the age of eighteen. The thing though that had drawn us together in the months that followed, was our common interest in helping other people. I had wanted to study behavioural science out of high school, but after not getting into my preferred course I deferred for a year, and started working as the receptionist for our large Baptist Church as I took time to consider my options. He had spent a year away in the army reserve after high school, but now as our romance blossomed, he was set to begin a social sciences degree. As a new couple, we started going out on the Drug Arm Street Van together to get some frontline experience helping others from different walks of life to our own.

He performed in amateur theatre as he returned to study, and after performing in a Shakespearean comedy with Harvest Rain Theatre Company in Brisbane, he gained the interest of a local talent agent. All who knew him could see that performing was his passion. He soon landed a lead role in an iconic Australian play, performing at the old La Boite Theatre in Paddington and with that, decided to drop out of university and take the unexpected chance to follow his love of the stage.

I appreciated his talent and supported his decision, but not without questioning what this shift in career path meant for my future. As I contemplated how this new career choice would impact me and the life we were considering building together, I didn't favour a journey that was likely to be framed by financial insecurity and uncertainty. Nor could I imagine having to deal with the romantic roles he was likely to have to play with other women on stage or screen. Many a tense conversation followed as we worked through some of the things that concerned me. But, I knew by then that I loved him, that I wanted to be in his life and have him in mine. I felt sure I would regret not marrying him and seeing where life took us.

After returning from a two-month trip to England to visit extended family I had contemplated returning to study: my interest by then though had shifted to journalism, with travel prompting a curiosity in me about the world at large and a love of hearing stories from people from different walks of life. But returning in the middle of the academic year, I instead focused on getting a job and settled into a role as a personal assistant to the general manager of a four-star hotel in Brisbane's inner city. With plenty of administrative positions in the job market, I knew I could ensure we had at least one stable income coming in, as we began our life together as a married couple and he began to carve out his career.

We had been married for just over a year when we arrived in Sydney: just the two of us, taking on the world together. We packed up our 1985 Ford Telstar and drove all our goods and chattel down the New England Highway into Australia's largest city. He had landed a place at the prestigious National Institute of Dramatic Art (NIDA) and there was no question that we would make the move for his talent to be further cultivated. We settled into our accommodation in a room above the Olympic Sports Bar in Paddington for the first two weeks. I started my new job as a sales and marketing coordinator with a luxury hotel group while he began the hunt for somewhere for us to live.

On my meagre salary we struggled to pay the rent on our mouldy one-bedroom unit, with little to no disposable income beyond covering our bills. But, with his access to free tickets to shows around town—from student performances at NIDA to performances at the Opera House—and discounts I could source on tourism activities and restaurants through my work, we managed to find ways to make the most of life in our new city.

After eighteen months, I landed a job as an account coordinator in an international public relations agency. A significant increase in my salary with this professional move made life on one wage marginally less strenuous. As I leapt into the heady world of PR I relished being involved with communications professionals, though now with a twinge of regret that I hadn't returned to university to study journalism: a decision which would prove a limiting factor to future career opportunities I began to aspire to.

As his talent and profile grew during his years of study, our social connections diversified as we met and were hosted by high profile supporters of the creative sector. From a catered dinner in the home of the art dealer who provided a scholarship which helped fund my husband's final year of formal training, to a day out on a boat on the Hawksbury River with the Director of NIDA who came full of stories to regale us with of past graduates like Cate Blanchet and Hugo Weaving. Or a dinner under a beautiful arbour in the harbourside garden of a local film director and producer and his wife at their Darling Point home, as they gathered a small group of actors at different stages of their careers to meet and connect. I timidly entered these social settings feeling very much an outsider, but appreciating the chance to observe the community we were set to become a part of.

With a strong stage presence and good looks, he landed several lead roles in the NIDA student productions, including in their graduating show. Family and friends flew in from Brisbane to see his final performance as his studies came to an end. Immensely proud of his achievements, I went four times. On the last night, Baz Luhrmann and Nicole Kidman, in town for the launch of *Moulin Rouge*, had even been a part of the audience. He graduated in a blaze of glory with a strong selection of agents offering to represent him. The path he had chosen looked to be the right one, as the world seemed set to become his oyster.

The work began to come through. Relatively regular but not consistent. Stage and screen. I remained the primary breadwinner keeping a roof over our head, but as he landed roles and began bringing in some money, we began to improve our day-to-day living standards. Over the next three years, we upgraded to a two-bedroom rental—relatively mould free—rental, bought a couch and dining room table, adopted a kitten, and traded in our old car. After years of holidays focused around visiting family back home in Brisbane, we finally took an overseas holiday together, to Sabah on Malaysian Borneo. The upgrades to our circumstances provided a degree of luxury to our life after years of just getting by.

A big professional break loomed on the horizon for him not long after we returned from Sabah. A lead role in a new TV show to be filmed in Melbourne. We moved south later that year. I had been ready for a job change. While it took longer than I expected to land work in a new city, I enjoyed having a break to settle into our new home after rushing straight into work when we made the move to Sydney. Together we enjoyed attending opening nights for film festivals, musicals and other events as invitations came through. Eventually I started work in the marketing team in the head office of World Vision. Though not as fast paced a role as the long, intense hours at the PR agency in Sydney, I relished having such meaningful employment as I learnt about international development work through my day-to-day role.

The new show barely survived the first season with a new model of entertainment—reality tv—increasingly being commissioned and programmed instead of funding going to local dramas. We moved back to Sydney a year later. I was sad to leave World Vision, but also glad to return to friends and the familiarity of life in Sydney.

His Sydney-based agent introduced him to some representatives from the U.S. not long after we returned. With these new connections, we decided the time was right for him to head over to the States for pilot season to see if any doors might open in the larger international market. As he headed off to try his luck, I continued in a temporary role I had taken on—supporting a professor at a medical research institute—while continuing to assess my next career move.

He didn't land a role in America. And though he returned to Australia three months later, he never came home. To me anyway.

When we decided to marry, we knew his career choice would throw up unusual challenges. We had always managed to work through them, though not always easy. But not this time. His decision to leave was soul crushing. I didn't expect to have to go back to the beginning and start again at the age of thirty-one. But that it seemed, was exactly what I needed to do.

My oldest friends from Brisbane, parents and sisters made dashes to Sydney over the following months to check on me. Many assumed I would move home to Brisbane. But we had only been back in Sydney for six months. I couldn't imagine changing cities again so soon. Besides which, I was excited about my new job in the sponsorship team of Football Federation Australia that I had finally locked in while he was away.

The opportunity in football had taken me by surprise in the midst of my search for a permanent role after our return from Melbourne.

"We need you Jacq! There might be a job for you in our team," Elise had first exclaimed on the phone to me in November 2005.

Australia was still tingling from the excitement of the match-winning penalty kick by Socceroo John Aloisi, that had clinched our place in the finals of the FIFA World Cup to be played in Germany the following year. Bringing the nation to a standstill, beating Uruguay 4—2, the heart stopping penalty shootout had followed one-hundred-and-twenty minutes of hard-fought play and would take the Australian men's soccer team to the World Cup for the first time in thirty-two years.

They needed extra help in the commercial team. A systems person. An organiser. Those things I could offer, despite my lack of knowledge about the industry of sport. It took some time to receive a firm offer, and it was late February by the time I started, right in the midst of the hectic activity of an office preparing for the first ever A-League Grand Final in only six days' time. It was an unexpected door that had opened to me after never having much interest in sport. I quickly realised that I loved the work I had been brought in to do and appreciated the sense of belonging I found in my new job as I stepped up into a more dynamic role.

The wonderful group of strong women who formed my friendship group—most of whom I had met while working in the PR agency—surrounded me, drew me into their homes and extended families, listened to my heartbreak, and most importantly, took me dancing. Elise who had given me the lead that saw me land the job at FFA had introduced me to Jane in our events team—who proved a levelling confidant—and Eugenie, our legal counsel, who kept things matter-of-fact. Eugenie would eventually witness my divorce papers over dinner on a Friday night—then ensure we went dancing to shake the tragedy of the moment off. I dubbed them my "urban family" as Bridget Jones had described her London friends.

After twelve years with my husband, I had been ready to start a family. Not to start dating again. I had no idea where to begin. Fighting to stay sane through the emotional apocalypse, I threw myself into my work.

The World Game was on the rise in Australia. My role expanded quickly as we made our way through the 2006 FIFA World Cup campaign, while preparing to kick-off the second season of the A-League. An addictive adrenaline stimulated by the pace at which we operated and my desire to escape into work, drove me in a dynamic and exhausting job.

I did everything I could to avoid spending too much time alone in the empty shell I had once called home, clinging to the life raft that work afforded me as I moved day-by-day through the thick fog of heartbreak. I worked long hours and embraced the opportunity to travel. Delivering sponsor activations in venues around Australia and New Zealand provided me with new motivation and excitement after a professional journey that had until then seen me more often than not, sitting behind a desk in an office, day in, day out. Organising match day functions, I drew from my experience on the sidelines of celebrity circles, to now play host to football mad A-listers and corporate guests. The glamour and excitement that surrounded his career, lost when he left, was replaced by the exhilarating world of sporting superstardom as I immersed in a revitalised sporting code that had captured the nation's collective imagination.

I indulged in many flirtations in my search for validation after his rejection, quickly discovering the hazards of post break-up vulnerability. I made bad choices—usually under the influence of too many Friday night drinks—and wept through my regrets. It was a season of deep, dark shadow and despair as my personal life continued in freefall, contrasted by hope-raising light as my career blossomed.

Three years later, during the fourth season of the A-League, I found myself standing alone beside the field in the rain, at Hindmarsh Stadium in Adelaide. In the early years a greater cohort had travelled together to help implement the requirements of the new league. But tonight, I was travelling with only one other colleague from the office. I was there to support the agency team of our major sponsor as they rolled out the half-time activation for the tenth time in a few weeks. I found a spot in the stands to sit alone and watch the second half of the match once our work was done, then ducked into post-match drinks with my teammate before we took a cab back to the hotel. I had begun to wonder if I had spent enough Saturday nights this way.

I was still enjoying my work, but I wasn't sure where it was leading me long-term. After three years of taxi - airport - hotel - stadium - hotel - airport - taxi - home, I realised I wanted the chance to see and experience more of the world myself—beyond the confines of work-related travel.

When we married in our early twenties, we had had plans to explore Europe together one day. We had never found a big enough window of time to take that trip, instead opting for our shorter holiday to Borneo. I had been to England at the age of twelve with my parents and again at the age of twenty-one to visit extended family. Obsessed with art, I still longed to visit France, Italy and beyond.

I started saving towards a trip once I had found a flatmate to start sharing the rent. I took basic Italian lessons in a tiny language school in York Street after work, spurring my dream of visiting the galleries and eating gelati in the romantic piazzas. The musicality of the new words I was learning seeped into my soul each week, providing a regular antidote to divert me from the frenetic activity of work and loneliness of home.

Debbie—my best friend since the age of seventeen—had sent me a little quote book called *Do What You Love* before I flew out on that first trip. As I sat on the plane to Paris for my much dreamed of holiday to France and Italy, I began flicking through the quotes about following your passion from people like Steven Spielberg and Danny Kaye, Ella Fitzgerald and D.H. Lawrence. I was overwhelmed by the realisation that beyond this trip, I had absolutely no idea what I wanted out of life anymore. I had no goals, no hopes, no dreams – professional or personal, of my own.

Do what I love? I didn't even know what that phrase meant. For so long everything that mattered to me had been intertwined with his life. After his departure I filled the void with the new career path which offered me so much professionally, and also provided a new identity to define myself with. I was beginning to realise that I was afraid of committing to someone else's dreams for the future again, before taking the chance to identify what really mattered to me and what it was I wanted out of life.

I had provided the support underpinning other people's dreams and achievements throughout both my career and personal life. The excitement of travel, the perceived glamour of working with and being around famous people and high achievers in their fields—creative performers or sports stars—no longer provided me with the validation or fulfillment it once had.

I could continue in the slipstream of life as I had been doing. Or I could take the risk to stop and take audit. I knew it was time for me to pause and take time to develop a clearer picture of the life I wanted to lead in the years to come.

I watched my final match day unfold in the same venue as my first. The first had been the Socceroos in a match against Greece at the Melbourne Cricket Ground (MCG) the day before they stepped on the plane to Europe in May 2006 on their way to the World Cup in Germany. Three years later I was there for the last of the 2010 FIFA World Cup qualification matches which Australia had won against Japan.

As I inhaled the refreshing scent of the evening dew covering the now silent field of the MCG on a crisp winter's night in Melbourne, I felt a chapter in my life tangibly coming to a close. The goal nets had been pulled off the posts by the ground staff. Taking a slow jog across the famous field in my navy match day suit and silver ballet flats to pick them up, I lugged them back to the operations room. As the lights went down around me, I savoured my last moments in the job that had given me a reason to keep going when the rest of my life had fallen apart. I had worked hard and played hard, as I sought to build some sort of version of a new life. The opportunity had reshaped my life, given me an identity within the football tribe, and provided me with a bold new confidence to take on the world alone.

After flying back home to Sydney the morning after the match, there had been a whirlwind forty-eight hours of farewells as I wrapped up my job and prepared to fly out. Finalising things at work, lunches, dinners, drinks, dancing on the bar of the Mars Lounge in Surry Hills until the wee hours... In a delirious, sleep deprived haze, I faced up to all I was leaving behind as I dragged my suitcase down the stairs from my apartment. I clutched a mass of tissues to contend with the flood of emotion still chasing me as I made my way down to Laura, who was waiting to take me to the airport.

Laura was always there when I needed her. She was one of the stayers sitting with me by the water in Darling Harbour well after midnight after my farewell drinks when I left the agency for our move to Melbourne. She had appeared at my front door the day after he had told me he was leaving the marriage and whisked me off to a quiet bar for the evening, watching me cry into my drink as I tried to process the rupture in my reality. Laura was calm, practical and pragmatic—and outrageously fun—as she walked with me through the highs and lows in the years that followed. And here she was again, busy trying to work out how to squeeze my luggage into her tiny Toyota Yaris, while giving me a motivational talk, reminding me of all I had to look forward to as I closed the door on yet another chapter of my life. With the handing over of car keys to a new owner, passing of home keys to my flat mate, and returning my Sydney high-rise office pass, the only belongings I had access to were now in a suitcase and small backpack. I waved goodbye in the rear vision mirror to a life, a city, friends, colleagues, a career, financial security, and perhaps most traumatically, my beloved cat.

Heading into the departure lounge of Sydney airport alone, it felt peculiar not to bump into any colleagues or acquaintances. For three years I had often been travelling with familiar faces—another staff member, contractor, player or media representative who was transiting to the match I was also on the road for. This was going to be it going forward. Just me. No guest passes into the business class lounges with colleagues. No cab charges to get me home from the airport after a big day of travel. Just me, what I had managed to save in the past year and what it could afford me. And my own determination.

I had visited my middle sister and her family in Hervey Bay three months earlier to say goodbye, but had only two days in Brisbane with my parents and eldest sister and her family before leaving the country. I was used to living in a different city, but this time I was flying across the world. I realised too late it wasn't long enough with them given I was leaving without certainty about when I would be back.

I travelled to London first for a whirlwind visit around England visiting Aunts, Uncles, and cousins spread out across the country. I indulged in a quick weekend in Paris with Alexis—my friend, flatmate and colleague from FFA—who had moved to London a year earlier.

~ * ~

Three weeks after leaving Australia, I had finally arrived in Italy. A few days were spent with an old friend from Brisbane and her family in their home in the Roman port town of Ostia Lido, before I spent a few days staying on my own in the centre of the Eternal City.

Between packing up a home, leaving a job, visiting extended family and taking short sojourns with friends, I was relieved to be now bumping my suitcase over the pavers towards the front door of my Sienese villa where I could unpack for the next six weeks.

At last I had reached the start line, to begin again.

3

Siena, Italia
Aprile 2008

The tour group had stopped in Siena during my holiday the year before for only a few hours. The medieval city was enchantingly peaceful as we wandered the city streets. More than fifty years earlier, Siena had been the first European city to limit vehicle access through the city centre, helping to preserve the ancient fabric of the **UNESCO** World Heritage site. We visited the exquisite Duomo, lunched in a nearby cafe, and indulged in gelato while wandering around the Piazza del Campo before we departed for Rome and our last night together as a group.

Mesmerised by the hazy afternoon light rolling over the Tuscan hills as we waited for our coach at the meeting spot outside thirteenth century Porta San Marco, the seed that prompted me to take a pause in my life and return here a year later had been planted.

'The best advice I ever had about travel was to not hesitate—see everything... do everything... taste everything', Elise had written in a card to me as I left on my long-anticipated holiday.

As well as bringing me into the fold of football with a job, Elise as my friend, was a trusted advisor, constant encourager, work travel buddy and the lead activities coordinator in our group of friends. From beach volleyball lessons on Maroubra beach, hula hooping classes in an inner west dance studio, hip hop classes with the Sydney Dance Company, football club memberships that would ensure we saw each other at home games once a fortnight, theatre performances, concerts, and discovering new and old dining venues around town, Elise ensured our group of friends caught up regularly and were always experiencing new things. *See everything... do everything ... taste everything...* Elise's travel advice was something she had clearly embraced for her everyday life as well.

I had done my best to follow her lead. Travelling as if in a dream, I had indulged in the romanticism of both the past and present of the places I found myself in over the three weeks, making the most of every opportunity.

I had dreamt of visiting Paris since I was twenty-one. An exhibition from and about the magical city had come to the Queensland Art Gallery and I had fallen madly in love with the allure of the city and the stories of the impressionist painters who had haunted her streets and garret studios a hundred years earlier, and I was determined to visit one day.

When I arrived in Paris over a decade later, I had moved through the streets as if still in that dream. I walked the Avenue des Champs-Élysées and climbed to the top of the Arc d'Triomphe. I spent two days lost in the history and stories captured within the thirteen kilometres of galleries in the Louvre. I was captivated by the collections of the Musee d'Orsay before dwelling in the Musee de l'Orangerie surrounded by Monet's expansive Water Lilies cycle. I walked the streets of Montmartre and found two of her remaining windmills and passed by homes inhabited at various times by Renoir, Van Gogh, Picasso and Toulouse Lautrec, before taking pause above the city from Place du Parvais du Sacré-Coeur. Catching the train out to Versailles I explored the lives of French Kings and Queens—including the infamous Marie Antoinette—and visited the Hall of Mirrors where the Treaty of Versailles was signed. In the upmarket Galleries Layfette I tried on designer outfits—that I had no hope of affording—before buying a ham and cheese baguette for lunch, consumed as I perched under the busts of Beethoven and Mozart on the steps of the Palais Garnier, home of the Paris Opera. I splashed out to join a tour group for dinner on the first floor of the Eiffel Tower followed by a boat trip down the Seine, before being bused from the dock to a late-night revue at the Moulin Rouge.

I flew on to Rome to join the two-week art and history focused coach tour mostly around the northern regions of Italy. A friend had once sent me a postcard from Florence, years earlier, writing descriptions of the sights and sounds around her as she sat in a central piazza, her words so captivating that it took me right to where she was. A desire to visit had stayed with me since.

The sound of the Italian words coming through the announcements on my AirItalia flight from Paris made my heart beat a little faster, though I couldn't understand what they were saying. With pride, I began to roll out my *'buongiornos'* and *'grazies'* to the air hostess and the customs official, then the coach driver and our tour guide, to the hotel receptionist and the restaurant staff. The ten beginner classes taken the year before had enabled me to at least engage through general courtesies and order gelato fairly effectively.

Astounded by the ruins of the Colosseum and the Roman Forum on our first night, I blinked back the tears as I tried to quash the reminder that my husband wasn't there with me. I knew he also would have loved the view into the ancient world from where I stood looking out over the ruins from behind Piazza Venezia. Sadness that our plans to explore Europe together one day had never been realised crept in briefly, as instead, I found myself standing with a group of strangers I had met only a few hours earlier. I shoved the broken dream away, determined not to have anything taken from me in that moment, as my eyes absorbed the remaining architectural wonders of a world long lost.

Our experienced guide ensured we beat the crowds with an early start the following morning. As the first of the many tour groups that pass through the Vatican Museum and the Sistine Chapel daily, we had a few moments of space to enjoy the rich collection as the first group to enter for the day. I left the Sistine Chapel with a crick in my neck from gazing at Michelangelo's biblical frescos, reaching down from the ceiling toward us, before standing in front of his Pieta masterpiece of Mary and Jesus, carved from a single slab of white Carrara marble, housed in a chapel in Saint Peter's. The Pantheon's architectural majesty inspired awe as I stood under the oculus of the former Roman Temple first commissioned by Marcus Agrippa and completed by the Emperor Hadrian—where he often held the Senate—before it was converted in the seventh century to a Christian church.

Travelling down to Sorrento on Good Friday, the group emerged from our restaurant following a gluttonous dinner, only to be swept to the sidelines of a mysterious procession of men in black hoods silently walking the main streets of the town in tribute to the Passion of the Christ. I suffered on the ill-tempered seas of early spring to spend a few hours on the Isle of Capri—recovering from the hydrofoil journey with a leisurely walk to take in the fresh air from the heights of Tiberius's gardens—before sipping shots of locally prepared limoncello in the glamorous Piazzetta.

We explored the excavation of mystical Pompeii still lying in the shadow of Vesuvius, the volcano whose eruption had buried the Roman city for nearly two thousand years. Artefacts from Pompeii are held in the *Museo Archeologico* in Napoli. Our tour guide urged us to visit Napoli to see the collection if we ever had the opportunity. In the next breath though she warned us to take care if we were to visit, with issues of petty street crime and mafia infiltration in local government allegedly rife. After reading Penelope Green's memoir 'See Naples and Die' I had some understanding of the political complexities of the city lying half-an-hour north of Pompeii. But the memoir had also left an imprint on me about the deeper layers of colour and character of a city once romanticised by ancient writers and poets. I gazed at the outskirts of the city as we drove past on the highway, my curiosity growing. I wondered how and when I might be able to pass by this way again and satiate my increasing interest in the dark jewel of Italy's south.

Easter Sunday took us north to Umbria to reflect in the churches of Assisi. I discovered pizza in a cone, after spending a morning marvelling at the beauty of the richly coloured Byzantine mosaics in the Basilica of San Vitale in Ravenna.

Lounging in a gondola as our boatman brought us gliding into Venice, I clutched a glass of champagne under bright blue skies on a cool but pristine afternoon, along with the boatful of strangers who had become friends, as we briskly toured the country together.

I popped into Verona to visit Juliet's balcony, and rugged up to walk along the foreshore of Lake Como while the icy Italian Alps loomed in the distance. With every other tourist, I posed awkwardly for photos that were supposed to make it look like I was pushing the leaning tower over in Pisa, before heading to Florence. Dazzled by the works in the Uffizi, I saw David in all his glory at the Galleria dell Accademia, before lashing out and buying a leather trench coat from Florentine artisans, a memento of what I then thought would be my once-in-a-lifetime trip.

As I waited for the coach to pull up on that Sienese hillside at the end of my holiday, and the cool Spring air tingled against my skin, I felt a subtle restlessness. After traversing the heart wrenching trauma that had turned my world upside down two years earlier, I felt an odd sensation returning—a strengthening heartbeat. I had indulged in three weeks of cultural gluttony and felt utterly satiated in that moment. But with this shift of perspective, I knew that once I had digested this journey, I would be left wanting for more. I thought it would be the elegance of France that would enrapture me. And it had. But something in the raw, at times uncouth, passion of Italy, experienced through everything from the traffic chaos of Rome to sweeping landscapes in the regions, from the depth of her history to the character of her architecture, and the feast of art and rich layers of storytelling at every turn, compelled my desire to return here to spend more time. It felt clichéd. I clearly wasn't the first broken person to flee overseas to search for something that had been lost in them along the way.

As I settled into my seat on the coach, I relegated the wistful thoughts of returning for an extended period of time to an unlikely dream. But within weeks of my return to Sydney, I knew the chance had to be taken. I needed to find out what mattered to me. To find what I loved. Whatever that first trip had unearthed became a relentless tug at my heart in the months that followed, demanding to be further explored.

~

Siena, Italia
Luglio 2009

Another taxi pulled up as I approached the front door of the villa. Miriam, a schoolteacher from Switzerland, had travelled all day by train from her home just near Basel. She was the only other new arrival at the apartment today, as resident students came and went each week. We exchanged pleasantries while waiting downstairs for our new landlord, Signor Pagetti, to let us in.

A short, blond-haired man with leathery tanned skin in his early fifties opened the dark wooden door from inside.

"Avanti! Avanti!" he gestured to follow him into the recess. He led the way up a marble staircase crowned with a kitsch angelic fresco on the ceiling above, leading to our front door on the second level. Miriam turned around to look at me with her eyes wide, a thrill of shared excitement passing between us as we took in the charm of the old villa.

Entering a corridor, we passed a small lounge-room off to the left. Signor Pagetti showed Miriam into a small room on the right. Through her bedroom window—which faced the wall of the Basilica—voices drifted up as people made their way along via di Sinitraia down below, entering through the city walls and heading into the centre of town. A large family table sat in the centre of an adjacent dining room, with large rustic sideboards running along both walls, full of crockery, pots and pans. French doors flung open wide, invited us out to the balcony.

Miriam and I slipped a glance to each other, struggling to mask our excitement.

"It's beautiful," she mouthed with eyes wide as we took it all in. I nodded in delight as I stepped outside.

The city walls curved around the slope below the villa, a collection of modern apartment blocks lay on the outskirts just before the green hills rolled back upwards, dotted with church towers, olive groves and umbrella pines. With the apartment set up high on the hill, sweeping views beyond the walls of the city transported us into the countryside.

We crossed back through the small living room, furnished with an antique sideboard and couch. Landscape paintings adorned the walls and a skylight bordered with a floral fresco edging around the opening allowed light to pour into the centre of the home. We glanced into the larger of the two bathrooms, as we passed it on the way to my room. An enormous bathtub sat under high ceilings from which an ostentatious glass light fitting hung. The toilet, perched beside an open window, offered spectacular views out across the city.

"You are here longest so you have best room," Signor Pagetti informed me convivially in his heavy accent. The other students—in residence since the previous week—had the room at the front, off the main balcony, and the small room at the end of the hall next to mine. There was no sign they were at home.

Leaving us to settle in, Signor Pagetti departed for his home near Florence, promising to return mid-week to collect rent and help with anything we needed.

"I think perhaps we unpack and take a small rest," Miriam suggested. "Then we can go explore, try and find somewhere to buy food?"

I closed my door quietly and paused to take in my new residence. A single bed sat at the centre of the room with a sky-blue coverlet, a framed picture of white daisies hanging above. An enormous old wooden wardrobe painted cream took up most of one wall and against the other a wooden dressing table rested under one of the two gilt framed mirrors in the room. Over the bed hung a wonky replica chandelier with gold paint peeling off it. Later that night, it would be lit up by six, haphazardly placed light bulbs. Floor length taffeta curtains in shimmering azure were clasped open along each side of the doorway to a small balcony. Through the doorway bright light spilled into the room across the red and white tiled floor. The views from the balcony to the left were resplendent with a terraced landscape of Sienese homes cast in rosy, ochre and cream hues. Vibrant in the afternoon sun they swept up and across one of the sloping hills of the city. Far below to the right, the road weaved out of a city gate and towards the outer communes of Siena. The sound of cars and buses outside the walls floated up from a distance, the distinctive sirens of the Carabinieri police vehicles only occasionally piercing through the overall serenity.

I took another slow turn as I re-entered the room. And finally let go. Jumping up and down in the soft rubber of my black thongs, I leapt around the room like I was on a jumping castle, waving my arms, punching the air, and making ridiculous faces as I took in my new palazzo. There may even have been a moment when I rushed to the balcony doorway, clasping a hand to each side of the doorframe and raised my face to the sky as I leant out to drink in the air. I could have been on Broadway with the moves I was rolling out in this red and white tiled Tuscan bedroom.

The same magic that had enveloped me when I arrived in Paris and Venice the year before found me here in this room. I felt like a bona fide principessa as I took in my new quarters. I had done it. I had scrimped and saved and taken risks and travelled across the world and now... now I was here. I had no idea what I was doing here. But I was here.

Refreshed after a short rest, Miriam and I passed back under the arch, on foot this time, winding our way out of the sunshine in the piazza, into the shaded passage of via dei Rossi, animatedly discussing the charm of our new abode and what had brought each of us to town.

Miriam explained to me that her primary language was Swiss-German, "At school we learn German, French and Italian as they are all our national languages. Of course, we also have to learn English."

She had decided to spend two weeks of her summer holiday in Italy improving her Italian. I felt overwhelmed by the talent of my multi-lingual friend. I had studied Japanese in early high school, but twenty years later I remembered only how to greet, count to ten, ask for milk and tell someone they were nice. Ashamed after arriving in Paris on my first trip a year ago and realising I couldn't even order a coffee at the airport, I had taken ten weeks of French lessons to compensate. From those classes I could now order coffee, as well as greet and farewell people, tell them they made me laugh… and ask if they were drunk. Our young teacher had deemed this question particularly useful vernacular for travellers.

Miriam and I turned onto the circular thoroughfare of Banchi di Sopra, running the curve of il Campo, which lay behind the buildings lining the street. Ten minutes from our new home, we found the local 'Conad Supermercato'.

Reconvening at the checkout after twenty minutes, we both bore baskets filled with fresh bread, pasta, tomatoes, cheeses and pesto. I proudly held up a small pot plant I had picked up.

"Basilico!" Miriam nodded approvingly, "Now we are Italian no?"

Our flatmates—Katharina from Germany and a Miami-based Mexican called Franco—had returned home while we were out. We joined them on the balcony with our contributions to dinner, before Franco left to meet some friends at the outdoor cinema in the local Medici Fortress. I returned to my room to conduct a quick revision of the few notes I still clung to from my basic language classes in Sydney.

I hoped and prayed as I rolled into bed, that my limited knowledge would help me to grasp enough to get by initially, as I took on classes that would be conducted solely in Italian.

Waking up to a hot July morning, I dressed for my first day of school and headed to the kitchen where I found the girls making breakfast. There was no sign of Franco yet.

"He went to see 'The Curious Case of Benjamin Button' dubbed in Italian" Katharina told me, "but I'm pretty sure he went out to the bars afterwards. We don't wait for him."

Katharina guided us to our school in via Paradiso—the way of heaven. I hoped the spirituality of the street address would bode well for the miracle I was starting to think I might require to get through the day. It had been a long time since I had been a student. Making my return to the classroom in a foreign country, to learn a new language was daunting. The butterflies in my stomach were going crazy.

We joined morning commuters walking up from the carparks located outside the city, strolling the cobblestoned passageways, enjoying the gentle pace of morning peak hour in Siena. As we reached the obscure entrance to our schoolrooms, a tall priest with kind eyes behind rimless glasses held the door open behind him to let us enter.

"Is he a teacher?" I whispered to Katharina as we followed him into the building. She shrugged as she disappeared up the hall to her classroom.

Speaking confidently to the receptionist, Miriam demonstrated she had an existing strong grasp on Italian. I had listened to her chatting easily with Signor Pagetti the day before, lapsing into English only as needed or to involve me in the conversation. Taking her entry exam into a side room to complete, she began the test which would establish the level of class she should join.

I introduced myself at the desk.

"Buongiorno. Mi chiama Jacqueline."

The friendly girl behind the counter handed me a sheet of papers rattling off instructions in Italian. Like a kangaroo caught in the headlights, I stared back at her blankly.

"You do exam. Bring to me," she explained in English as a worried frown creased her brow. Taking a deep breath, I took the papers and joined Miriam. She looked up with a smile as I sat down.

"It is difficult!" she whispered.

My eyes widened with fear. What on earth was I thinking not starting in a beginner's week!

I looked down at the paper. 'Nome' was the only word I recognised, although I could make a fair guess at some of the other personal details required at the top of the sheet. I slowly ran my eyes down the page. Everything was in Italian. Not a scrap of English providing me a hint of what I was supposed to do. *Grammatical questions? Grammar? We didn't do grammar in the Sydney classes. I can barely remember the rules of English grammar. What on earth is a preposizioni! In Italian or English!* My head was racing as I scribbled some rough answers against the few questions I could comprehend thanks to the words similar to English. Dragging myself humbly back to the counter, I handed my sheet in. The receptionist placed it straight onto a pile without looking up.

"Jacqueline?" a teacher holding my papers called my name from the hall. Taking me to a side room it seemed I needed to do a listening and speaking test. She spoke briefly in Italian to me, then waited expectantly for my response. I managed to introduce myself before fading back to an expression of blank alarm. She paused, studying me carefully.

"Why have you not answered more questions on your test?" she asked.

"I... I... don't understand what I am supposed to do," I stuttered in mortification.

She pulled my papers together, imperceptibly shaking her head in despair, without the hint of a sympathetic smile. "There is no beginners class this week," she sighed, looking at me with a worried expression. "We will put you in the class that started last week and see how you go. If you are no good, we will put you back in the beginner's class that starts next week."

I smiled weakly, kicking myself under the table. Apparently being able to meet and greet people, rattle off the days of the week and count to ten, didn't quite qualify me with having basic Italian language skills.

We had to wait for the morning break before joining the classes we were allocated to. Having done well in her 'difficult' test, Miriam vanished into one of the higher-level classes. I crept into my classroom and found a spare seat while everyone was out in the hall getting their morning fix from the espresso machine.

The priest I had followed into the school was the first to enter the room. I looked up and smiled as he took his seat beside me. Padre Rick was just a year older than me at thirty-five, hailed from Oklahoma but grew up in New Jersey, and was part of the Dominican order. He was based down the road staying in the local monastery, while learning the language before heading to Rome to study philosophy.

The room gradually refilled with mainly young American and German women in town on their summer break, chattering loudly as they returned. A quiet young Japanese man slipped in behind the crowd, nodding in greeting as he sat down opposite me.

"Buongiorno. Mi Chiama Jacqueline. Sono Australiana."

Trying to tap back into the over-confidence, that made me think

I could forego the beginner's week classes, I proudly took my turn as we went around the room introducing ourselves.

So far so good! I thought triumphantly as everyone nodded in understanding.

I peered over to the Padre's workbook to see what page we were on as the class commenced. Every word spoken and every word written really, truly was all in Italian. *Intensivo* or intensive teaching. We were there to learn Italian after all, not English. But I had nothing. *Niente!* My heart was sinking as I began to get an idea of what I was up against.

Relying instead on non-verbal cues, I tried to follow what was being discussed. There was hope inspired by words that were recognisable due to their similarity to English. But I spent most of the lesson lost in translation, attracting the kindly but disapproving frown of mia insegnante—*my teacher*—every time I whispered queries to my English-speaking desk buddies.

This is going to be impossible, I thought as panic began to rise.

I was concentrating with every ounce of focus I had on the content of the lesson. I pinned my gaze on Liccia. An attractive blonde woman around her mid-fifties, our insegnante occasionally laughed so hard at our errors that she snorted through one nostril. I watched her mouth move, trying to pick up her mannerisms, absorbing the reactions of my classmates to what was being discussed in an effort to comprehend. Something. Anything. She was kind and patient, but I knew she could see through my false bravado, as she in turn assessed where her new student was at.

With my mind exhausted from the exertion of trying to understand, I exited the classroom after midday, re-joining my housemates in the entry hall of the school to wander back through the sun-drenched streets.

"How did you go?" Miriam asked kindly.

I shook my head despondently, "It was a disaster," I moaned. "I should have started last week as a beginner. I had no idea what was going on."

"It's only day one," she tried to hose down my melodrama as she patted my arm. "I speak some Italian, but it was very hard to follow the lesson today for me too. It takes time."

I smiled gratefully appreciating her solidarity. But I knew things were far direr for me. I loved jumping in the deep end, but this time I feared I was more likely to sink than swim.

Crowds of tourists and locals filled our path, all pushing in as close as possible to capture some of the shade cast by the buildings, as we tried to avoid the heat of the midday sun. Sienese architecture sports slim awnings at best and shade was at a premium as we walked home. A bevvy of young girls from the school caught up to Franco beseeching him to join them for lunch. With a wave of farewell to us, he vanished into the crowd.

After a light lunch on the balcony, I went to my room to burrow into my textbook for the afternoon. There had to be a way to miraculously absorb the basics of grammar instruction that had been covered the week before.

My book was no help. All in Italian. I tried to piece together the sections we had been going through that morning and make sense of it all. I read the notes in the back of my dictionary, but it seemed I didn't have the natural ability to amalgamate grammatical theories of Italian after one lesson.

As the western sun blazed into my room, I began wilting at the faded green plastic table that I had dragged inside from the balcony to work at. There were no fans in the villa, and the airflow in my room was limited to the doorway. I abandoned study for the day. My flatmates, who had completed their assigned homework within half-an-hour, were reclining on the balcony enjoying the relief of the light breeze flowing in over the hills. Franco had returned bearing a bottle of cheap wine from the local store. We figured all Italian wine would be good, but it turns out cheap wine is cheap wine, no matter where it comes from. We drank it anyway.

The tops of the trees swayed below. From somewhere under the canopy of leaves a drum beat reverberated. "They are practicing," Katharina advised us, "EVERY afternoon you will hear them."

"What are they doing?" I peered through the foliage to try and identify the source.

"Practice for *il Palio*," she said.

On the second of July and sixteenth of August each year, two annual bareback horseraces, dating back to the twelfth century, take over the paved amphitheatre of *Piazza del Campo*. The second of the races was due to happen in a few weeks, while I was in town.

With races and festivities marking religious or civic occasions and celebrations common across medieval Europe, the Sienese event had evolved over the centuries from bull fights and competitions involving other competitive animals to eventually become a horse race.

Unlike Australia where sport is almost a form of secular religion, in Siena these races hold a more profound connection to spiritual ritual, with both events intertwined with religious traditions connected to Catholic feast days.

The date of the first race—Palio di Provenzano—was firmly established in the Sienese calendar in 1656, falling on the religious Feast of the Visitation which recognises the visit of Mary, soon to be mother of Jesus, to her cousin Elizabeth, mother of John the Baptist. It also coincides with the veneration of the Madonna di Provezano, a fourteenth century terracotta icon of the Madonna that is said to have been the source of many miracles now housed in the church of Santa Maria di Provenzano in Siena.

The second race—il Palio della Madonna Assunta held on the sixteenth of August—was locked into the Sienese calendar in 1802 and is held on the Feast of Assumption.

Every so often, what looked like a broomstick, would fly into the air. I leant over the balcony railing, straining to see the flag throwers practicing to the drum beat.

"Part of the Palio festival includes a parade that takes place ahead of the race," Katharina continued to explain. "The two drummers we can hear and the flag thrower will represent our contrada in four-weeks' time."

Seventeen contrade make up the competitors of the Palio. Originally thought to be military groupings numbering up to forty, they defended the free Republic of Siena in the Middle Ages. Now the seventeen areas are the established suburban districts of Siena.

The drumbeats eventually faded, along with the light. In the cool of the early evening, we wandered up to meet other students relaxing in il Campo. The shell shaped outdoor piazza had played centre stage to Sienese life for generations. The natural shape in the landscape it had been built into is thought to have been an ancient volcanic crater. Paved in the first half of the fourteenth century in red brick, the piazza sectioned into nine is divided by ten lines of travertine, a form of limestone, running down to a centre point.

With a population of just fifty-five thousand residents, the city attracts more than one-hundred-and-sixty thousand international visitors every year. I was conscious already of the number of different accents and languages I had heard so far in the streets.

Sitting on the sloping brickwork, I ran my gaze up the warmly lit façade of the Palazzo Publicco and adjoining four-hundred-and-forty-four-metre-tall Torre del Mangia. A magnificent curtain of royal blue draped the buildings as dusk faded away. I sipped my Peroni, listening quietly to the conversations of the students around me. Some were from our school, others were language students at the local university. From countries across the world, everyone selected parts of the languages they knew and felt most comfortable communicating in, interchanging with their native tongue when they ran out of words in their second and third languages. I already felt out of my depth after one class. Hearing such a range of language speakers communicating with one another despite limitations, I hoped tomorrow would bring me more optimism about how my own language journey would go.

Spellbound, I watched the early evening sky deepen further and across the ephemeral fabric of deep nightfall, a swathe of bright shining stars emerged.

4

Siena's streets were silent as I pulled the huge wooden front door of the villa closed. I padded quietly across the piazza. Rounding the curve of via dei Rossi, I set off at a brisk walk. The sound of vehicles rumbling slowly along Banchi di Sopra announced the approach of early morning deliveries coming through the sleepy city streets to make drop-offs to local vendors. In the Middle Ages, Banchi di Sopra was occupied by money changers. One of the oldest streets in the city, its mercantile focus remained evident, the passage into the city centre now lined with banks.

"Buongiorno!" I sang out to a cleaner as she swept out the doorway of a shop.

Startled by my enthusiasm at the early hour, she glanced up from under thick eye lashes. "Buongiorno," she muttered in return, before her eyes dropped back down to the back-and-forth sweep of her brush.

I bounded down the slope of the empty Piazza del Campo, pausing on the bottom corner, inhaling deeply. The concave of ancient buildings gave off a slightly damp, earthy smell, as the sun warmed the masonry. The nine sections divided by the travertine lines, disrupted by the crowds splayed across them the evening before, were clear and distinct. Sunlit buildings quietly courting the edges, glowed orange in the early morning light. Silent restaurants, bars and gelato stores, that would quickly fill later in the morning and remain busy with trade well into the evening, had their shutters pulled down tight. The only sound was water spraying from the hose of the cleaner rinsing spilt gelati from the central brickwork, down to the modern front drains outside the Palazzo Publicco.

At the end of the thirteenth century, Piazza del Campo was the home of fairs and markets, a crossroad of important roads for trade in the region. I closed my eyes, imagining the scents and sounds of Siena past. The clatter of cart wheels and market bartering, the smell of flowers and fresh produce, and by the end of a long hot day, perhaps the less appealing smell of rotting produce and animal excrement. The clatter of hooves, the baying of cattle, the roar of the crowd, the smell of the livestock. The laughter of children, alongside the lively debates of men and women in this communal meeting place. The entire population of Siena would gather to attend events, tournaments, and buffalo and bull races – the events which had led to the establishment of today's Palio. The fulcrum of city life for so many centuries, this amphitheatre had encased every important event in the history of the city, from the time of the Republic, up until the Medici period—when Siena had come under the control of fierce territorial rival Florence, led by eventual Grand Duke of Tuscany, Cosimo I de'Medici—right up to the present.

The cleaner shut off his hose as the last of the diluted gelati vanished into the drain. I departed the sloping piazza to begin powering up and down the side-streets.

Passing under the gothic arches that bridged buildings together, I sought out the laneways offering the steeper climbs, pushing myself to burn more calories to justify a three-flavour serving of gelato later in the day. I wound my way around the streets to the piazza lying in front of Siena's elegant Duomo.

Sinking down onto a sun-warmed stone bench, carved into the exterior wall of Santa Maria della Scala, the museum of what was once the medieval city's hospital, I studied the marble carvings ornamenting the gothic architecture of the grand church opposite. This had become my daily indulgence. A moment of quiet on my own in this beautiful spot where swarms of tourists would soon descend upon until late evening.

The creak of a door opening drew my attention to the right. The night security guard emerged from the museum entrance. Glancing briefly in my direction he paid me no mind as he lit up a cigarette.

The beautiful zebra-like Duomo had captured my imagination on my visit the year before – the striking blocks of black, red and white marble defining her style both inside and out. After two weeks of visiting a plethora of cathedrals and churches across the country, it had been hard to choose a favourite. The layers of biblical stories in the richly coloured Byzantine mosaics decorating the presbytery of the sixth century Basilica di San Vitale in Ravenna had been breathtaking, and the beauty and serenity of the simple chapel of San Francesco di Assisi had inspired reverence, however Siena's Duomo stunned me with its aesthetics. The vibrant colours in the tapestry of patterns, colour and life woven through multiple materials, from the core architecture, to frescos, to sculptures, to mosaics. The decor inside was breathtaking with the striped pillars, a spectacular inlaid mosaic floor with bible stories laid out in black, white, green, blue and red marble. Visual storytelling was so important in these ancient venues, built and developed in a time when much of the population would have been illiterate. Looking up past the coffers of the dome—where three dimensional golden stars sparkled above on a sea of blue—you could see the hexagonal dome crowned with Bernini's gilded lantern. The *Libreria Piccolomini* off the left aisle of the main nave with displays of ancient musical scripts and beautiful, richly coloured frescos stimulated the soul.

The bells started to ring announcing the start of the seventh hour of the day. A rustle of movement drew my eyes up to the left. A nun of south-east Asian background was busy dusting the sill of the shuttered window she had pushed open from quarters beside the Duomo.

The sound of an engine turning over on the opposite side of the piazza broke the tranquillity. A carabinieri (military police) car rolled slowly out of a parking space beside the nearby headquarters.

Wandering between the Duomo and Carabinieri headquarters, heading down the stairs leading from Saint John the Baptist's Baptistery, I returned to the political and economic heart of the town.

It was hard to correlate the aesthetics of a weekday morning in Siena, with that of the many I had rushed through in Sydney. The very early hours in Sydney were the only time of day when the city wasn't moving at full pelt. I would be on my way by 5.30am for a brisk walk or run down to Coogee Beach, embracing the last moments of dawn. It was the tiniest window of time where I felt like the city wasn't on full throttle, I wasn't on full throttle, and I could take a moment to breathe. By 6.30am the streets of Australia's largest city would already be busy as the densely populated eastern suburbs began moving with people heading into work for long, relentless days in office towers around the harbour.

Ensconced in the serenity of my balcony looking to the Tuscan hills, eating breakfast at my plastic table an hour later, I offered up a few distracted prayers. There was a distinct plead within them for a miracle that would enable me to comprehend my new language as I contemplated the day ahead. I came from a family who all seemed particularly good at taking time out each morning to meditate and offer up the day ahead to God before launching into their day. I however had always been a little more erratic in managing my spiritual well-being. Though fairly routine with boot camps or gym and trying to eat well for good health, taking time to strengthen my spiritual muscles had tended to be a little more ad-hoc.

Faith in God however, was something that had been with me since I was a child. I was the daughter of English protestant missionaries, born after they moved out to Australia following ten years living and working in Nigeria. I had been raised in a community of faith in my home as well as through connection with our local church.

My father grew up in a protestant evangelical Christian family. Mum was sent to an Anglican Sunday school along with her sisters, though her parents rarely attended church themselves. As a teenager she made a personal commitment of faith in Jesus along with her younger sister. While studying nursing she heard about a need for nurses in Africa. She went on to specialise in midwifery, before heading off to theological college for two years. From there she stepped on to the MV Aureol, sailing for three weeks on the ship that would bring her into port in Lagos, Nigeria, where she joined the Sudan United Mission to work in the north-east of the country.

She was the last of the missionaries to travel by sea.

After several years working on a farm in Wales, Dad had gone on to study agriculture at a technical college before completing a Diploma to become a teacher. He took the plane to Nigeria six months after my mother stepped on the MV Aureol, heading to the same mission, to work in agricultural training. And that's where they met, married and started their family.

After ten years living in Nigeria, and a year back in England, they had been living in Australia for eighteen months with my two elder sisters when I arrived. They were among the last of the 'Ten-Pound-Poms', escaping miserable British weather and choosing to carve out the next chapter of their lives in the humid climes of the antipodes.

My parents dedicated me to God at the Church of Christ in Dalby, a small town on the Darling Downs of Queensland where they had made their first home in Australia. Dedication being different to infant Baptism, is a commitment of the parents to raise their child in the character of Jesus but leaves the personal choice of faith to the child to make a commitment of their own, as and when they may choose.

Moving to Brisbane when I was two, I grew up learning bible stories both at home, and in a little Anglican Church housed in the bones of a converted, wooden, army hall, devoid of high church ritualism and propriety, in the then sleepy outer suburb of Upper Mount Gravatt. In our humble surrounds, I was often impressed by the organist who still wore a very big hat and sang the hymns with great vibrato.

We started to attend a large charismatic Baptist Church when I was 14 where there were more young people. By then I was the only one left at home. My family instilled knowledge and understanding of the faith into which I was born, but the choice to make the faith actively my own was always left with me. At the age of sixteen I made the choice to commit to my faith publicly and be baptised.

A few months earlier, my cousin Elaine from England, who was living with us at the time, was killed in a car accident coming home from a youth group Christmas party held on the Gold Coast. Five years older than me, she had been staying with us during her gap year and became like another big sister to me. After eight months in Australia, she had been due to head home in time for Christmas only a week after the accident happened.

An excessively drunk driver swerved, hitting the car she was travelling home in on the highway, at around three in the morning. The collision killed her, along with another young man in the front passenger seat, and left the driver seriously injured. To see two young lives cut short so needlessly was confronting for all who knew them.

Life and death inevitably make you ask the big questions, and for me, what my faith really meant to me as I approached adulthood was laid squarely on the table in the weeks and months that followed losing Elaine.

After high school, I started work as receptionist at the large Baptist church. After hours I attended prayer group, bible study, dance group, youth group and took a Sunday school class. When I finished working there my participation lessened. Perhaps I had overdone it. Perhaps I knew I had needed to experience more of the wider world beyond the one I had grown up in.

When my husband and I moved to Sydney eight years after my

public declaration of faith, we found it difficult to find a church we both felt we could settle into. In Brisbane, a big part of the pull to attend each week was to see family and friends regularly, but without those established close connections in Sydney, we stopped attending.

I still prayed and read my bible from time to time, but neither of us were committed to investing in our faith or being involved in the associated community. We began to be Easter and Christmas church goers. The commonality of our faith had brought us together, our shared passion for his career path united us, but change and the unexpected pressures on the relationship had unravelled us.

As my life tumbled down around me with the end of my marriage, I was shocked to find the core of my soul limp, weakened by neglect. A soul crushing loss of personal moral agency had unleashed as I relinquished any capacity to deal with the pain of my heartbreak, and I found myself indulging in superficial ways to reaffirm my worth, after the devastation of a rejection that had run rampant into my very being.

Under the combined influence of deep heartache, and over-the-bar non-prescription beverages, I was haunted by the ever-present reminder of the life that had been shattered – the shards of which felt embedded in the soles of my shoes as I stomped across the broken glass of dance floors in the months that followed. Anaesthetising myself with inebriated nights and dancing up a storm with friends was a great way to unleash pent up emotion after struggling through the week. The rhythm of my body on the dance floor provided a mask for the erratic rhythm of my heart, at times seemingly barely beating as the ache of loss overwhelmed me in the sober hours.

My self-esteem, which had been chipped away over the years

as insecurities crept in, was officially in pieces. As my friends and I cheered the DJ to turn the music up in the midst of our fun, the boundaries that could preserve me came down, and I added to my existing pain by opening myself up to false intimacy.

I wanted love but had no capacity to give or receive it in the cycle of pain I was trapped in. In the depths of despair, I felt that I might never be able to truly love anyone or anything again, my heart bruised and beaten by the wounding.

A conflict of emotional turmoil embroiled me as I felt the fibres of my soul tearing with every ill-thought-out choice I made.

'My position is the more terrible in that I can find no foothold in myself or anywhere.' Tolstoy's character Alexei Alexandrovich—betrayed husband of Anna Karenina—captured the vacuous space also now haunting me. I was not the person I once knew myself to be. I no longer had the past, present or future life I had anticipated. Everything I had once hoped for, the stability of a great love and life-long marriage and all the associated hopes and dreams… gone.

I went back to church, alternating between Randwick Anglican Church (when feeling serious and morose) and Hillsong at Waterloo (when needing to hide in a crowd and let the emotion of the auditorium full of thousands of voices raised in song together overwhelm me).

Christine Caine, a pastor at Hillsong, spoke one week in her sermon about how we go to gym to work on our core to ensure our body is strong and centred, yet we don't invest as much in our soul. Christine's words struck home. I knew my life was not where I wanted it to be. I was reminded as I listened to Christine, that the one that is greater than anyone or anything in this world valued and loved me just the way I was and saw who I had the potential to become. I realised that my true centre had not been nurtured properly in a long time. In that moment I made the choice to commit more time to again growing my understanding of the nature of God, by exploring the life and teachings of Jesus and what they meant to me. But life was still busy and challenging. It was to be a gradual shift.

As I sat in the quiet of my balcony in Siena, I hoped some space from my everyday existence might help me to find a way to resolve the residual confusion about where my life had been, where I had thought it was going, and hopefully where I would find a new centre from where a new sense of purpose and direction could emerge.

As I entered week two of language school, I was relieved to avoid being dropped back into the beginner's group. Doing my best to present an adequate illusion of comprehension each day, I learnt to drop my face into my notebook, scribble madly, and nod sagely as if I was capturing the intricacies of Italian grammar far more effectively than my morose reality. I hoped to God this would start to make sense soon. Loving the Italian language that I had tasted in Sydney two years earlier, had done little to prepare me for the digestive complexities of learning a new language in-country as an adult.

I established that if I sat around the middle of the u-shaped class, I would never need to be the first to enter into a group discussion. This gave me time to work out what the question was, before plundering my disintegrating dictionary for key vocabulary to formulate an answer. Within days, the spine of my brand-new dictionary had started to split off under the duress of my frantic searches, both in class and while trying to get through *il compito*—homework.

Today we were discussing what everyone's occupations were in their home countries. I rushed to find the word for football before it was my turn—*Calcio*—and then how would I say *Sponsorship Manager*... I flicked hopefully to S in the English section... *How was I going to explain that?* I wondered.

"Hmmm... Sono attivita di commercio... hmmm... Calcio," I looked expectantly at my teacher hoping she would interpret successfully. Grammar and sentence structure aside, if I could remember enough vocabulary to stutter something out, I felt positively fluent. "Sponsors? Ummm. Commercial? Business?" I threw a few English words in hopeful one might be similar to an Italian equivalent to our non-English speaking teacher.

Julia paused. Studying me carefully, she tried to work out what I was trying to communicate. "Ahhhhh!" she exclaimed at last, "Sponsorazzione di Calcio! Va bene, va bene!"

I nodded enthusiastically, "Si! Si! Esatto!" It made life much easier when the English and Italian words were similar.

"Com'e si scrivere?"—*how do you write that*—I asked so I could make a note. Walking to the whiteboard she wrote it down for everyone. My classmates who had continued to look a little perplexed, took a moment to read the phrase, then turned and looked at me curiously.

Was I imagining it or did a few of them look a little impressed?

"Will you be working at the World Cup in South Africa?" Claire—a French girl—broke class protocol to ask me in English. Clearly, she had worked out we would be here all day if she asked me in Italian. Julia shot her a look of reprimand before turning back to me expectantly.

"Forse,"—*maybe*—I smiled, though it was unlikely given I had quit my job. With my self-confidence taking a beating as I struggled with classes, I felt myself tugging back on one of the bowlines that had given me so much self-confidence in the past three years. No one here cared what I had done before. They didn't need to. But now that they knew I had worked in elite football, I felt myself sit up a little straighter as they connected me with my enviable job.

"E conosce quindi, alcuni giocatori?"

I looked blankly at Claire, wishing she had ignored Julia's glare and stuck with English. The French and Spanish speakers in the class seemed better able to pick up the basics of the language more quickly, as speakers of a fellow romance language.

Padre Rick helpfully conferred with Claire before turning to me, "Do you know any players?"

"Ah si," I paused to work out which words I needed to use. "Hmmm, un Socceroo in Australia e anche... player?"

I leant over to the Padre again, "How do I say player again?"

"Giocatore."

"Si! Giocatore in Italia," I continued, "Mark Bresciano e Vincenzo Grella."

No-one recognised the names of the two Australian born players, who had carved out careers in the Italian league as well as playing for the Socceroos.

I didn't know any of the players when I started at FFA. I didn't come in star struck. I wasn't a jersey tugger just hanging to meet some of our national heroes. I was there to do my job. John Aloisi and Tony Vidmar's names and faces I remembered from the qualification match against Uruguay, but it was only as I worked with the teams that I began to understand the profile of the Tim Cahills and Lucas Neills, the Mark Schwarzers and the Harry Kewells. My appreciation for what they meant to the nation grew.

Latching back on to that bowline of identity as I saw my classmates impressed by my association with football, I wished I had the words to impress them further and tell them about some of the other moments of circumstantial privilege that I had enjoyed through my job, like the time I found myself on the edge of the training ground of the Argentinean soccer team while they were in Melbourne to play a friendly against the Socceroos.

Based in Melbourne for a week leading into the game in 2007 and with no commitments on the Sunday afternoon, my mate Adam (media manager for our national team) invited me to join him at the restricted access training ground for the Argentineans at a local private school. With avid fans hanging off fences in the distance, I stood sideline with their coaching staff and a handful of South American press watching Lionel Messi and Carlos Tevez and their teammates, going through their drills. When a ball had come flying towards me, I swept my leg out in my heeled boot, launching it perfectly back onto the field. I had limited skills on a football field (though I made tactically lacking contributions to our lunchtime football games in the Sydney Domain) but sheer luck presented me with my own moment of sporting glory. There were cheers from the press, and an impressed nod from the Argentinean player I returned it too. I had dined out on that story among friends at home for a while. But I didn't have enough words to tell those stories today.

Julia moved on to the next student before anyone could ask me any more questions.

Ban from Japan told us that he was in Italy to play professional calciatore (Futsal) an indoor five-a-side football competition for nearby Serie B team, U.S. Poggibonsi. We smiled across at each other realising the common connection between us thanks to football. While living and studying in Siena, he was commuting out to the nearby Sienese township for training with the team.

Padre Rick was up next. I already knew he was on his way to Rome to study philosophy after his three-month enrolment at the school.

With weekly enrolments, new classmates joined our group, replacing those who finished up the Friday prior. Ban and Padre Rick were my two consistent classmates staying on at the school during my own stay.

Next to share his story was Gunter from Germany. With white wispy hair, a bushy white moustache and glasses slipping down his nose, he peered over at us with kind eyes under rampant eyebrows. From the moment I laid eyes on him, he had reminded me of Geppetto, Pinocchio's father. A retired dentist, he was in Italy for six months to write a book.

Helios from Brazil sporting a white shirt and matching shorts, his dark hair slicked back stylishly leant back comfortably in his chair. He was here to improve his Italian. As a coffee exporter to Italy he needed to communicate better with his clients.

Tucked in the hot little room painted pastel green with dark green shutters, I slumped in my chair, feeling my reasons for wanting to learn Italian were frivolous compared to American priest's preparing to study philosophy in the Vatican library, Japanese football players carving out their career in the Tuscan countryside, German writers making Italy their home, and Brazilian coffee exporters ramping up their skills to build their business. The only reason for being here I had offered had been, 'I love learning the language'. And to be honest, since arriving I hadn't been loving it that much given the struggle to keep up in class. Of all the romance languages to choose, Italian was the least spoken anywhere outside of Italy. I stared out the window as I lost concentration. My classmates had all come here with purpose. I had come looking for purpose and I still wasn't sure how I was going to find it.

We closed the shutters to try and keep some of the heat out for the last hour of class. Despite the temperatures reaching the mid-thirties by the middle of the day, I was yet to come across a fan, let alone air-conditioning in Siena. By midday, all I wanted was a cool marble floor to lie on and rest my overheated, overextended brain.

Finishing my *compito* that afternoon, I took a walk to find the local football stadium to check if any pre-season games were coming up. Siena had been promoted to the Serie A in the 2003/2004 season, for the first time in the club's history. Originally the Società Studio e Divertimento—the Society for Study and Entertainment—the football section opened in 1908 as Società Sportiva Robur.

Stadio Artemio Franchi was just a short walk from the school on the edge of the city. I found a notice for an upcoming match in two weeks against U.C. Sampdoria, a club based out of Genoa. I peered through closed gates into an arena similar in size to one of my favourite stadiums to work at on the Central Coast at Gosford. Capacity here was only a little over fifteen thousand. Thinking about friends back in Sydney preparing for season five of the A-League,

I felt a slight pang looking at the empty venue. It still felt strange to have handed over the initial planning work I had been doing before departing, and no longer having ownership over the delivery of activities.

After today's chat, I wondered if perhaps I would in fact be back in the fold of football by the end of the year and find a way to be selected as part of the operational team that would travel to South Africa in 2010.

This pause from career had been purposeful, but I still felt resistant to fully embracing the open road I had cleared for myself. I stood at the gates, battling my unwillingness to completely let go, and considering possible end dates on the road of uncertainty I had chosen.

On Easter Sunday during my trip the year before, I had attempted to attend my first Catholic Mass in the Basilica of San Francesco in Assisi. The weather had been moody all morning as our coach travelled up from Sorrento, dark grey clouds with occasional bursts of sun drifting over the road in front of us. I was fascinated arriving in the birthplace of Saint Francis —Italy's patron saint alongside Saint Catherine of Siena—on Easter Sunday.

Slowly obliterating the view over the sun dappled Umbrian plains, a thick fog had crept up the hillside, rolling in over the city walls and enveloping the streets as we walked from our hotel to the church. A gentle drizzle accompanied the mist. Crowds of locals and tourists, wrapped in cloaks and scarves and clutching umbrellas, were pouring down the pathways into the Basilica for early evening services. By the time I had entered the sanctuary, my feet were wet and frozen through. I lingered at the back of the main nave as the service began. After fifteen minutes trying to meditate quietly whilst the mass was conducted in Italian, my cold, aching feet became too great a distraction. Realising the futility of trying to follow a service in a language I knew little of and a religious tradition I had no direct connection to, I had slipped back to the hotel.

Today with warmer feet, I padded down the marble stairs, crossing the path running between our front door and the piazza, and edged through the heavy wooden doors of my neighbourhood basilica of the same name. Passing quietly into the expansive building, a sudden fluttering of pigeon wings outside one of the stained-glass windows caused me to start. The cool air ensconced by the stone walls was refreshing. The tranquillity within the silent cavern, soothing.

Alone in such an enormous building, I felt that whatever concerns I had carried with me from outside the door could be left behind. Solitude. A leaving behind. A place that enabled disconnection from outside influences to allow thoughtful reflection.

Another pigeon cooed quietly somewhere up in the eaves far above me, gently interrupting the silence. *How did they even get in here?* I wondered.

A door catch clicked. A young monk pushed open a door on the left, revealing the monastery gardens that lay hidden behind the wall outside our kitchen window. Smiling at me briefly as the door closed behind him, he rustled across the stone floor in his long black robes, vanishing into a side chapel. Remaining in the middle of the basilica, I waited to see what would happen next. Where were the people? Was no one else planning to attend this morning? I was sure I had read a notice that indicated there was a service in English scheduled.

Examining the artworks in the main nave and side chapels and spectacular artistry in the lead lighting of the stained-glass windows, I spotted the young monk kneeling quietly in prayer. I wondered who was taking the service if the only padre I had seen was occupied with his own meditations.

Rounding a corner, I found a man and a woman, kneeling separately in a chapel area praying quietly. I slipped onto a pew nearby. Pulling out my pocket Bible, I began my own reading and reflection. I allowed my bible to fall open and found myself in the Gospel of Matthew.

For where your treasure is, there your heart will be also...

I closed my eyes trying to decide what my treasure was. God, friends, family, work?

'But what else,' I debated impatiently with God internally. *'What is it that motivates my heart?'*

Silence.

No idea. Nothing. Niente.

What was it that I was looking for that would provide the spotlight to guide me into a new direction?

... do not worry about your life, what you will eat or drink; or about your body, what you will wear. Is not life more than food, and the body more than clothes?...Therefore do not worry about tomorrow, for tomorrow will worry about itself. Each day has enough trouble of its own.

This verse had been reassuring as I prepared to take the leap and leave all my securities. Nearly two months into my trip, the lack of answers or sense of direction yet to materialise however, was playing heavily on my mind.

Look at the birds of the air; they do not sow or reap or store away in barns, and yet your heavenly Father feeds them. Are you not much more valuable than they? Can any one of you by worrying add a single hour to your life?

'Okay God,' I closed my eyes, '*Are you trying to tell me you've got this? That I just need to take one day at a time and trust in your timing to reveal the learnings of this journey?*'

A rustle beside me made me look up.

"Shuuk... shk shk...," wearing a black dress and beads, and with greying hair held at the nape of her neck in a thin scarf, the lady shooed at me with her hands. Hustling along the row from the spot I had been settled in on the aisle, I kept my eyes lowered to mask my smile.

"Mi scusi," I whispered, earning a hint of a smile along with a curt nod. Despite the rows of empty seats, I had obviously chosen her regular spot to sit down in.

Several other elderly women had arrived. Bowing a knee quickly in front of the statue of Jesus at the front, they crossed themselves before commencing a quiet but efficient hive of activity around the altars finally preparing for a service.

I closed my bible as I drew my meditations to a close.

Nearly an hour had passed since I walked in. I watched the elderly women take their seats, then decided to slip away before formalities commenced. The time of tranquil reflection on my own had sufficed. The message was both ambiguous yet clear.

Do not worry.

5

Signor Pagetti sat down for a glass of wine before he got started on some odd jobs around the villa one afternoon.

"I love to visit le belle ragazze," his green eyes sparkled between the creases of his sun worn face as he pulled up a chair. He had taken a particular shine to Miriam, as she negotiated basic conversations with him in Italian. Sipping my mid-afternoon wine quietly at the end of the table, I pretended to follow their verbal exchange. I nodded, rolled my eyes when it seemed appropriate, laughed when they laughed. I had been completely lost for a good ten minutes when Signor Pagetti, perhaps suspicious of my charade, turned to me.

"And you," he looked at my quizzically, "Can you speak Italian yet?"

Startled back into the conversation as he broke into English, I pouted and shook my head. "I feel like there is too much information. I can't make sense of it yet."

Putting a hand on my arm he looked at me with intense sincerity. "When you first learn the other language, your head is full."

He stood up from the table and walked into the kitchen. Picking up a pan from the sideboard he gestured, "You put words, grammar, all the information in," he demonstrated filling the pan with invisible ingredients, "and for a time, it is very difficult to make it into something beautiful. But soon, it will all together to start to make beautiful."

Seeing my downcast face, the frustration of my first few weeks apparent, he put the pan down in front of me. Leaning in, he held my gaze.

"Please. You must not give up. I would be very disappointed if you give up. A student last year give up and leave Siena. I was very sad."

Warmed by his sincerity alongside his Italian predilection to immediately incorporate food into his analogy, I lifted the corners of my sulky mouth into a smile and nodded obediently. "I will not give up," I assured him with more confidence than I felt.

Finishing off the last of his wine he declared, "I will help you! Piano piano. You know what piano piano means?" he asked.

I had heard it used, but it was a word with multiple meanings, including as reference to the musical instrument. I shook my head.

Signor Pagetti paused, looking at Miriam as he thought of the words in English to explain it to me. "Slowly," he said. "Step by step. Piano piano. Every time I visit we will speak in Italian! Piano piano."

As I nodded obediently, I hoped he wouldn't see the alarm in my eyes.

How exactly was that going to happen? I wasn't stringing anything together. I couldn't understand why I couldn't run before I could walk. Well, let's face it, crawl. I felt like my tongue had been cut out at the thought of attempting conversation in Italian. Even if it was *piano piano*.

Elise had told me about a friend of hers who had studied French intensely, and within a month, was dreaming in her new language. As things stood, the only dreams I was having in Italian consisted of verbs, and their conjugations swimming around in my head in a grammatical whirlpool. I was treading water in a giant ocean, grabbing desperately at life rings of irregular verbs, pronouns, adverbs and adjectives with a strong undertow of prepositions, present and future tenses, not to mention subjunctive something-or-others.

I was envious of the apparent progress Padre Rick seemed to be making. He was staying in the monastery of the nearby Basilica di San Domenico, where he needed to use the language day-to-day to get by. Torn between using English with fellow students and housemates, I had been trying harder to use some of the Italian I was learning socially. With everyone at different levels of comprehension however, it was often hard for a conversation to go too far in Italian. With most students reasonably fluent in English, we would inevitably abandon our attempts in Italian so the social conversations could continue with ease.

"Have you been to Follonica yet?" Signor Pagetti asked as he prepared to take his leave. Katerina had done a day trip to the beach near Grosseto and told me it had taken her nearly two hours by train from Siena. She had then paid thirty euros for a deck chair and umbrella to enjoy the small beach. That may have been exciting for a German, but for a girl who had lived half-an-hour's walk from the clean ocean waters and soft sands of Coogee in Sydney's eastern suburbs for ten years, I felt my weekends in central Tuscany would be better spent frequenting nearby towns to explore the history, art and food. This weekend instead of Follonica, I told him,

I would be heading out to the east of Siena on a guided day trip booked through the school, to the town of Cortona.

Waking up in a sweat with the sun pouring into my room at nine o'clock on Saturday, I leapt out of bed. I found my small travel clock lying on the floor nearby, where I had flung it an hour earlier in response to its offensive blast, before rolling back to sleep. Our group was due to depart from a piazza near the school in a little under thirty minutes. Racing to assemble myself, my plans to look exceedingly beautiful and molta eleganta should I encounter any would be suitors I might happen upon in the town of *Under the Tuscan Sun* fame, were unlikely to be realised. I raced through the streets with wet hair plastered to my back, clutching my jewellery, hoping I had my camera, and cross checking I had remembered to put a bra on as I ran. The last student to arrive pulled up short behind me, breathless, the clap of her brisk footsteps having tailed me through the last two streets.

Traversing across the countryside immersed in fields of sunflowers in full bloom, I listened idly to the driver and one of the students chattering in Italian during the hour-long journey. I overheard Ricardo, our guide for the day, say he was from Calabria in the south. Unshaven, his longish dark curls with flicks of grey, were still squashed into a flat patch on the back of his head, where he had rested on his pillow the night before.

Parking on the outskirts, we entered the quiet traffic free laneways of Cortona on foot. Ricardo paused the group outside la Basilica Santa Margherita. As part of our extracurricular learning, the tour was to be all in Italian. I managed to pick up the name of Cortona's patron saint from Ricardo's commentary, but little else. The woman who had travelled in the front seat of the car chattering with Ricardo was an art teacher from New York who had been studying Italian for twenty years. Recognising the lost look on my face, she slipped over beside me, introduced herself, and quietly began to translate the key stories for me.

"Thank you," I whispered with a smile.

The child of a farmer, Santa Margherita's mother had died when she was aged seven. Following a tumultuous relationship with her stepmother, she had left town with her lover Arsenio at the age of seventeen, bearing him an illegitimate son. One day when Arsenio didn't return home, Margherita discovered he had been murdered, his body lying in a nearby forest. Leaving their home near the town of Montepulciano where Arsenio was from, she returned to Laviano, the home of her father, with her child. Rejected by the family she had left ten years earlier, she put herself and her son in the care of the friars at the Church of Saint Francis in Cortona. She faced resistance due to her past choices initially, but finally she was accepted to join the Third Order of Saint Francis.

I stared at the diminutive, preserved body in a windowed silver casket on the altar. "That's her!" my new friend whispered, as we began walking down the centre aisle inside the church.

The patron saint of the falsely accused, hoboes, homeless, insane, orphaned, mentally ill, midwives, penitents, single mothers, reformed prostitutes, step-children and tramps—despite dying in 1297—was lying preserved in front of me. I had heard of relics in Catholicism before, but this? I stared aghast. This was a whole person.

The group moved closer. I approached hesitantly, taken aback by the extent of the preservation. She was obviously deeply venerated to have been preserved and canonized, but to see what was left of her lying on display more than seven-hundred years after her death I found disquieting.

"Do you think she shrunk?" I whispered to my interpreter. She shrugged with a smile. This tiny, ancient woman, left resting in state for hundreds of years, seemed not much taller than a twelve-year-old child.

Studying her from a respectful distance, I liked this woman who had run away from home, made the mistake of pairing up with a man who had let her down, taken on the task of raising a child on her own, and like all good prodigals, eventually came home. Despite facing additional rejection from her birthplace and family, she had turned around and through her own experiences of hardship, found a new purpose for her life. And a new identity. A woman who had no doubt experienced the depths of disappointment of hopes and dreams never realised, had taken lessons learnt, and committed herself to helping those who had also suffered from human failure, both their own and at the hands of others.

Leaving the musty silence of the church, we made our way up to the town square at the top of the hill. The group dispersed to wander around the Saturday morning markets. As everyone wandered away, I looked for familiar settings from the film. Unable to pick out any distinguishing features, I shook off my romantic notions and began trawling through clothes in the markets and made a few selections from the fresh produce.

I wandered past quaint art galleries before stopping in front of a Toscana Immobiliare—*Tuscan Real Estate*—window. I wondered if this was where Frances had first seen the 'For Sale' sign for her villa. I peered in and examined the properties on the market this month and considered the Vendesi—*for sale*—prices. I surreptitiously took a selfie in front of the listings to send back to the urban family at home asking,

'Anyone have a spare one point three million euro?'

No cavalier spontaneity was going to be sufficient to afford me the chance to pick up a rundown villa today.

I scuttled away before risking eye contact with anyone watching and found several of my group gathering under the lush foliage of giant trees shading a small park with sweeping views over bright fields, laden with the sturdy sunflowers we had driven past on our way here. Helene from Belgium, Chantelle from France, Andrea from Northern Italy and Benvinda from Portugal, were on their way to find lunch. With no plans to start negotiating a real estate deal, I joined them in Trattoria La Grotta. Tucked away in a shaded courtyard off the main square behind an art gallery, I plunged eagerly into fresh spaghetti with a simple tomato and chilli sauce, followed by a warm chocolate and ricotta cheesecake. A lively conversation over lunch in a combination of Italian and English with a sprinkling of French, revealed the same coy confession from each of us. It was no surprise that all at the table had been drawn here because they had seen the American film. The small town was a vibrant tourist hub thanks to its Hollywood exposure. The annual Tuscan Sun Festival had attracted Robert Redford the year before to do poetry readings and Sir Anthony Hopkins would soon be in town to exhibit some of his artwork at this year's festival.

Returning home by late afternoon I found twenty-year-old Fabian from Germany home alone. He had taken over Franco's room a week earlier. Miriam and Katharina had finished their short holiday tenure in the school, and left town this morning. It would be a quiet household tonight, with our new flatmates not due until tomorrow afternoon. Tall and gangly with silver rimmed glasses, Fabian looked like a lost cast mate of Harry Potter. Despite the age difference, we had taken a shine to each other straight away. It was his first time away from home and he seemed glad of some company on my return. As we sat on the balcony nibbling at some of the food left behind by the girls, in his lilting accent and stunted but sufficient English, he told me about his attempt to study engineering. Realising it wasn't really his thing, he planned to return to university in the fall, instead to study veterinary science. I was envious of the post high school stage in life where switching paths was not necessarily easy, but less complicated than at my age.

I had planned that evening to attend a concert at the Accademia Musicale Chigiana, a school which attracts students from around the world and contributes to Siena's outdoor musical program in the summer. The operatic tones of a student drifting from a window into the street below, had led me to the entrance of the Accademia earlier in the week. Exploring the building, I had found a poster for a free concert to be held in their courtyard this evening.

Not expecting Fabian would be interested in a classical concert, I invited him anyway. He leapt up in excitement and rushed to change for the evening. As we made our way through the city streets, my unexpected classical music aficionado chattered excitedly about what pieces they might perform.

We took our seats in the beautiful courtyard under the rooms that had reverberated with the talents of the students during the day. A hush fell over the small audience as a group of performers entered carrying flutes.

A gentle nod to the audience as they took their spots drew a round of applause, then a polite pause ensued while they settled into their seats. A filigree of musical poetry wove around us as the ancient courtyard was infused with the elegant timbre of their instruments in the hour-long concert.

Elated by the beauty of the music, we were in no mood to go straight home after the performance. I suggested to Fabian that we take a walk to the Duomo to see it by night before heading home.

"Not yet I have seen," he beamed with excitement.

"Not at all Fabian?" I asked, incredulous that the beautiful monument lying less than fifteen-minutes-walk from our home was yet to be discovered by my young friend after a whole week in the city. Shaking his head, he stepped back through the entrance archway of the Accademia and bounded enthusiastically in the wrong direction for the nearby cathedral. I grabbed his arm to turn him around. He bounced enthusiastically along beside me as we turned into the street leading us to the stripy church. I was enjoying having a little brother to hang out with. His fascination and enthusiasm for all things beautiful was endearing. Together we gazed at the beauty of the Duomo, lit up against the night sky. "I must come back tomorrow now I know she is so close," he murmured reverently.

Fabian left the apartment on Sunday morning with plans for the day with some classmates. I slept in despite the increasing heat, waiting until I heard the door close behind him before I got up. Taking some books and a cup of tea with me, I sat in the morning sun on the main balcony, making the most of having the place to myself for the first time. A call to mass echoed from the bell tower of the 800-year-old Basilica next door, and then reverberated around me as the resonant sound poured over and through the villa.

I flicked open *Dare to Journey* a small book of reflections that my sister Patricia had given me. Compiled by Dr Charles Ringma (an alumni of the School of History, Philosophy, and Religion at The University of Queensland) they focused on the writings of renowned Dutch Catholic priest, professor, theologian and writer, Henri Nouwen.

> *Change can come because we are dreaming new dreams, making new plans and pursuing new options. For such change to be productive 'the first thing we need is an open receptive place where something can happen to us' says Henri Nouwen... Change arising out of reactions will hardly be helpful and change to fill the empty places in our lives quickly will hardly be satisfying... The powerful possibilities of change first require the quiet reality of solitude. Change first needs stillness, not further activity...*

Replacing what had been taken away, not stillness, had been my response to the changes in my life. Reactive. Desperate not to feel the depths of my loss, work had replaced home, padded out by a busy social life.

Listening to the rhythm of footsteps going up and down via di Sinitraia down below, I knew solitude was more than simply being away from people. Stepping away from work, away from possessions, away from securities was perhaps the ultimate way to create isolation from the myriad of influences binding us to our past and resultant present, to create space for fresh perspective.

I had spotted a poster through the window of an art shop on one of my morning walks a few days earlier by local artist Alvalenti. His character Filo—who looks a little like Michael Leunig's Vasco Pyjama character—was perched on a building amidst the unique rooftops of Siena. He was looking up into the same velvet blue sky that had captured me with the profusion of stars glowing above.

"Infinite starry sky I look at you and ask,
'Who am I other than that which I already know myself to be?" Filo asked.

I had purposefully chosen to take the reins to force change in my life, seeking that open receptive place Nouwen spoke of. Somehow, I needed to find out what shaped me beyond marriage. Beyond career. And beyond loss.

The space for thankful reflection on what has been or the space for forgiveness for what should have been needs to be created...

Space for forgiveness for what should have been needs to be created... I closed my eyes. Had I forgiven my husband for leaving? I wanted to. I really did. I had had to convert my love for him to a version of hate to help me let go. I wasn't sure if I had yet managed to unravel the complexity of interchanging those emotions. I suspected I would always love the man I married, but not the one who left. The two emotions remained in conflict. Outside of the person

I had lost, a deep emptiness remained, as I continued to wrestle with the absence of a physical home, hope of family, emotional and physical connection, and a future direction, that had been cocooned by our relationship for so long.

> *The empty place harbouring fears of loss of significance, position and power needs to be embraced as the hopeful place, the place of new beginnings. For the empty place can bring forth new dreams, and out of seeing new possibilities purposeful change can come.*

The loss of significance had first struck home when I lost my marriage and the shared identity we had as a couple. That had been replaced by the validation gained in my work for a large high-profile organisation. While I had made the choice to leave work, as the weeks away from home passed, the disconnect from the sense of significance gained through my career intensified. When I resigned my manager Pete had suggested I might consider going for just three months; that way they might be able to hold the job open for me. In my gut I knew I needed to let go of that safety net completely and see where I landed.

> *It is this inner certainty of the rightness of the new direction that will sustain us, not whether or not the familiar place was difficult and the new is going to be wonderful…*

While some days I was haunted by the fact that I had walked away from a good job and a relatively comfortable life in Sydney, the call to change direction and gain new vision for my future had been clear.

If life is subject to our control then it becomes predictable. If life is so much greater than we can understand then it becomes open to the reality of mystery. This may at times frustrate us...

I laughed to myself as I stood up to go inside. *Frustrate huh?! Just a little...*

Contemplating the things I needed to continue to actively let go of to allow new dreams and plans to take shape, I began to make lunch.

The doorbell clanged loudly through the apartment, not long after Fabian's return mid-afternoon. With great excitement, we ran downstairs to see who our new housemates would be for the coming weeks.

Sporting a white shirt and beige chinos, Aiden, an archaeologist from Aberdeen in his early fifties, had sweated up a storm getting his luggage up the hill from the bus station. I poured him a glass of water, while he put his bags in his room and freshened up.

Studying Italian in Bologna a few years' prior, Aiden would be here for a month to brush up his Italian language skills, before commencing a two-month dig at an Etruscan site south of Siena. I wasn't sure who the Etruscans were having never studied any ancient history. Nor was I remotely au fait with anything to do with archaeology either. Images from Tomb Raider, the Mummy and Bond films flashed through my mind.

Fascinated by his profession, and still contemplating what was next for me after language school in Siena, I stood there wondering if I could perhaps use the next four weeks to impress on him what a fabulous addition I might be on the dig as an assistant of some sort. With my major events experience I had plenty of experience lugging gear around. Perhaps I could at least carry the tools?

The doorbell rang with the arrival of Olivera and Ana. From Montenegro, both worked in the task force of an Italian environmental agency in the capital of Podgorica. English was the primary business language due to the international nature of their organisation, but they had decided to spend two weeks improving their Italian so they could better connect with the Italian staff they worked with.

Olivera was a strong character with a deep throaty voice and raspy laugh who worked as a lawyer. We could often find her on the balcony with a cigarette in one hand and bottle of beer in the other. Ana—a scientist—had big, beautiful brown eyes and a soft laugh. After initial introductions, we all stood smiling at each other awkwardly in the lounge room, unsure of what to do next.

Realising we had a responsibility to orientate everyone to the apartment in the absence of Signor Pagetti who was running late, Fabian and I leapt into action. Digging out the collection of maps of the city we began sharing our limited local knowledge with the new arrivals.

Having nodded confidently when the girls had told me where they were from, I wracked my brain, trying to work out where Montenegro was, wishing there was internet access at the villa so I could do a quick check. Over a sumptuous dinner of melanzane prepared by Olivera a few hours later, I owned up to my geographical incompetence. Ana politely explained the position of the newly independent Slavic state, a former member of Yugoslavia, lying across the Adriatic Sea from Italy, sharing borders with Croatia, Bosnia and Herzegovina, Serbia and Albania. She quietly distanced her homeland and people from the wars seen in neighbouring countries as the region known as Yugoslavia broke-up during the 1990s.

She instead spoke of Nicholas I of Montenegro who had become known as the 'Father-in-law of Europe'. With his wife Queen Milena, they had had twelve children, nine of them daughters. Reports of their great beauty had seen them court suitors from royal courts across Europe in the latter part of the nineteenth century with the fifth daughter becoming Queen Elena of Italy after marrying then Crown Prince Victor Emmanuel III. Their son, Umberto II, was the last King of Italy. He was in the role for only thirty-four days in 1946 after his father abdicated. The monarchy had crumbled in the wake of World War II, and on the back of a referendum, Italy had become a republic, sending the royals into exile.

As we moved on to their work with the Italian environmental agency, Olivera told us how she had begun her legal studies after spending time working for UNICEF when she first arrived in Montenegro.

"Where had you come from?" I asked as I passed the bread.

"Kosovo," she told us. She had been displaced from her home after the Kosovan war in 1999—one of the last of the Yugoslav wars. I remembered watching news of the Kosovo war on breakfast television. It seemed so far away but tonight my dinner had been served by one of those displaced. A refugee. That once distant news story suddenly had a very human face. The table fell silent as we all took in the magnitude of her lived experience.

"More?" Oliviera filled the serving spoon and dropped some of the remaining melanzane on my plate, as the table burst back into chatter.

"Graziiiie!" I threw in the Italian shaking prayer hands gesture for emphasis.

"Prego!" she sang back over her shoulder as she continued around the table to serve the others. I watched her bustling cheerfully around the room. I had chosen to leave my country and could go back. She had not been able to. It was an acute reminder of the grace of choice and how lucky I was to be here but also—when I was ready—to be able to go home.

6

The tourists had begun to swarm into town as the August Palio della Madonna Assunta approached. My early morning walks still provided daily sanctuary from the crowds. The rumour among other students was that many local Sienese had moved outside the historic centre. The festivities around Palio go on for so long throughout the summer, the constant noise had become too much.

The Sienese place their loyalty to their contrada above church or state with fierce rivalries existing between the neighbouring districts. It was State of Origin medieval style. Arriving in Siena, I had wondered which magnificent creature would represent the contrada we lived in. Were we part of la Contrada del Leocorno—*contrada of the unicorn?* Or del Drago—*the Dragon?* That would suit the romanticism of medieval city living perfectly.

I started to notice plaques with a handsome green caterpillar with a crown perched on a rose branch on a gold background with the Cross of Savoy in silver and red, mounted on the walls of homes and premises around the streets leading into our piazza. It would seem I was living in the Nobil Contrada del Bruco—*Contrada of the Noble Caterpillar*.

The historical names of each of the contradas had evolved through various influences. Some are connected to the crests of wealthy families from the earliest established districts. Others held their identity in correlation to the primary trade of that local area in generations past. The locals from our area had traditionally worked in the silk trade. The coat of arms with the little caterpillar was a reminder of the silk and wool-makers of the district going back eight hundred years. Known for being one of the most generous districts, Bruco was also the first contrada to introduce financial aid to those in poverty. The combination of benevolence and artisanship being the legacy features of my contrada, provided me with some recompense for not having landed myself in an area with an icon suggesting speed like la contrada della Pantera—*the Panther*.

Bruco had won in August the year prior. Their thirty-seventh ever victory. With seventeen contrade in total however, only ten ever competed in one race – the selection subject to a draw. The seven that miss out on participating, are automatically selected the next year, with three more drawn from the remaining ten who had competed the year before. As il Bruco hadn't been drawn from the ten this year, I was disappointed to find out they wouldn't be competing at all this August.

Preparing a late breakfast on Sunday morning, the now familiar repetition of il Palio drums commenced their thud. Not just one or two drums this time, but several. Drawing closer, they demanded attention.

"What is it!?" Ana exclaimed as she and Olivera rushed in from the balcony.

Bracing my foot against the kitchen bench, I leant out the window as far as I could stretch, trying to see between the villa and wall of the Basilica into the Piazza. "I... can't... quite... see..." I strained further, ignoring the long drop below me as I hung precariously over the windowsill.

"I'm going out," Olivera rushed out the front door as the drumbeats grew louder. Ana and I ran to grab our cameras before hightailing down the stairs after her. In tunics with red, white and gold trim and deep blue tights, twelve men stood drumming and flag throwing in the piazza. They were from the Contrada del Nicchio—the conch shell.

Our neighbours looked nonplussed by the display, while we 'oohed' and 'aahed' at the height they catapulted the material laden sticks into the air, catching them perfectly on the descent without flinching. A backdrop of advertising posters for concerts and shows, plastered across a wall near our communal bins, made the medieval posse seem only briefly out of place in contemporary Siena.

The noise of the drums seemed to be increasing as they passed back out under the arch. As we followed them out into via dei Rossi we pulled up short at the spectacle approaching. Drummers and flag bearers were pouring down the street one by one in their tunics and tailored hats. Hundreds of men in tights. We watched the steady procession pass, our cameras clicking steadily. There was a nobility in their disposition, the serious business of the contrada clear. A civic pride in where they had come from, the families and community that they represented.

Small groups of teenage girls skirting the edges of the parade, dressed in shorts and t-shirts, sported the blue *fazzolotti* (a scarf) of the contrada around their necks. The fabric was decorated with the same crowned conch shell, and red coral emblems of the flags. With the beat of the drums pounding incessantly between the city walls, the last drummer came past, two final flag bearers sweeping their banners to either side behind him. And at the tail end, the rest of the population of the Contrada del Niccio trailed behind in contemporary civilian clothes, but for the *fazzolotti* around each neck.

We wandered back inside buzzing with excitement as the city entered the week leading up to the big race.

Powering through the deserted passageways of the city in the early hours of Thursday morning, I slipped down a steep street behind the Palazzo Publicco, the seat of the town council. Dawn light was filtering through the humid morning mist rising from nearby hilltops and swirling in and around the back entrances to the stately building. Voices and a repetitive clattering sound drew me to peer over a low wall at the top of some stairs leading down to a carpark at the rear.

The sound I had heard from a distance, was the clip-clopping of hooves. Today horse floats filled the space. A ramp was being lowered as I looked down. A mare's eager hooves found the ground as she was backed down out of the vehicle. Shaking her mane vigorously, she let out a whinny of delight as she took in the fresh morning air. Trainers slowly guided the sleek beasts in concentric circles between vehicles. The Barbary were arriving in town ahead of today's draw. Barbary was a traditional breed of horse used for the race. Bred in an area located between Morocco, Algeria and Tunisia the breed is now nearly extinct, but the term for the competitors remains.

A lottery conducted three days prior to the race allocates each horse to a contrada. Only then can the jockey, who has been elected to race for the contrada, bond with the animal that will carry him bareback around the hazardous track. A steady line of horses began ascending the path vanishing between the buildings, as they approached a side entrance to Piazza il Campo. I turned back up the slope and quickly slipped into the Piazza.

I had little interest in horse racing. Despite having lived close to the Royal Randwick Racecourse for several years, I only entered the gates once and that was for an evening work function rather than a horse race.

When I hadn't been headed towards Coogee on my morning walks, my alternate escape was to do a lap around the outside of the racecourse which afforded me another escape into a different world away from the hustle and bustle of the city. From my passage along the outer perimeter fence, I would watch the trainers finishing their early morning track work with their charges as the morning mist lifted from the racecourse; the pungent smells of horse and hay strong as I passed the stables.

The candidates that were up for selection this year for the Palio were circling in the shadow of the Torre del Mangia. A heavy police presence watched over the area, ensuring no interference. The usual stone slate path surrounding the brickwork of the piazza was now covered in truckloads of fine gravel brought in to create the track for Sunday's race. The tufo was like clay once firmed down with water. My white joggers quickly clogged up with mud as I made my way into the piazza.

Joining a small crowd of locals lining a makeshift fence, we stood within a metre of the racehorses admiring their beauty. They would be kept under guard in designated quarters under the Palazzo Publicco today, ahead of the allocation process of each horse to each contrada later that afternoon.

At midday I returned, pushing through the crowded streets to reach the busy piazza and join the masses who had come out to watch the ceremony as each of the horses were allocated. Large congregations of men in their community's colours entered the piazza under the midday sun. Singing anthems, the booming resonance of their collective voice reverberated around the space. Jostling through the crowd I pushed my way as close as possible to the stage. In the shadow of il Torre del Mangia, austere dignitaries awaited the proceedings to commence. The call of the clarions, at the lips of regal men in traditional tunics, leggings and hats, announced the beginning of the selection. As the call of the horns ended, a hush of anticipation fell over the crowd.

The first lot was drawn and members of the Contrada della Chiocciola rushed forward in excitement, clearly pleased with the horse assigned to the *Contrada of the Snail*. The horse was led away, surrounded by hundreds of adoring collaborators. The same reaction followed with la Pantera, and then la Civetta—*the Contrada of the Owl*. And so, it continued—cheers and elation for the most part—until all contrade had been allocated their steed.

The public trials—or practice runs—held in the days before the race, allow the horses to become accustomed to the track. I met my housemates in the piazza to watch the first practice run in the early evening the next day. Makeshift stands erected around il Campo, were filled with excited children from the districts. Decked out in contrada colours with their *fazzolotti* knotted uniformly around their necks they wriggled restlessly in their seats with anticipation. Male voices again boomed resonantly from the back of the stands, as the groups competed in song.

Jockeys in bright racing suits and helmets, entered the arena from the Palazzo Publicco. A deafening cheer reverberated off the buildings. The official race was still two days away, but the atmosphere was electric for the preview alone.

What was it about sport and competition that had driven such fervour in arenas since the days of the Colosseum, I wondered. I felt a pang for home, thinking of all the stadiums I had worked in. Back in Australia, season five of the A-League was kicking off. Two new clubs were entering the league this year as the code continued to grow. But I was no longer a part of it.

Some gentle laps were taken around the track one by one, before the Barbary were lined up. A starter gun reverberated off the buildings with an enormous boom. The horses leapt forward and quickly vanished from sight. Elevated on the natural rise of the amphitheatre amidst the crowd, Anna, Olivera, Aiden, Fabian and I watched them race along the lower part of the course before vanishing out of our line of sight beyond the melee of people in the top half of the piazza. The resounding cheers of the crowd rose and fell like a wave. Three times they raced the lap. From group to group the cheers rose and diminished as different Barbary pulled into the lead. In those brief electrifying moments, as the horses found their stride in their practice run, we felt the increasing pulse of il Palio.

On Saturday night, I joined a group from the school to eat, drink and savour the atmosphere of a community feast at a table hosted by a teacher from our school in her own district of the Contrada dell'Aquila—*the Eagle*. Long banquet tables ran along the street leading to the Duomo covered in paper tablecloths and set with plastic plates, cups and crockery. Socialising under the warm glow of ornate lamp fittings, embedded in the ancient walls of buildings lining the street, I found myself sitting next to Ludovic from Switzerland. A regular visitor to Siena and il Palio, Ludovic was a self-appointed expert on how to maximise one's Palio experience.

After sharing his stories of novice Nordic tourists collapsing after underestimating the impact of such a long wait in the sun, I re-evaluated my original plan of big hat, bottles of water and lots of gelato to see me through my planned sit-in to ensure a good view the following day. I was still haunted by the memory of a bout of heat stroke experienced as a child following a long, glorious day playing in the sun on the beach of Coochee Mudloe Island in Moreton Bay off Brisbane. Quizzing Ludovic further, he declared it completely unnecessary to wait in il Campo for five hours to ensure a decent spot to watch the race. Confidently he told us we could turn up "… like, uhhhh, an hour beforehand. Yes. It is okay."

Skeptical about this advice, our conversation had been interrupted as the crowd broke into song. *L'Aquila's* jockey was brought to the front to be extolled by his supporters. The jockeys would sleep beside their horses tonight. He and his horse would go to the contrada's chapel tomorrow, watched on by members of the community, to receive the padre's pre-race blessing and commission to 'go and return victorious'.

Ignoring Ludovic's advice, Aiden and I decided to walk down to the Piazza two hours ahead of the time proceedings were due to commence, just to be sure we found a spot. Ana and Olivera, playing it safer, left half an hour before us.

As Aiden and I approached the temporary gate into the piazza that we had chosen as our best access point, it was pulled closed. Looking at each other in alarm, we broke into a run to try and get around to another entrance in time. We were too late. Like Bennelong Point on New Year's Eve in Sydney, the numbers permitted on the Piazza on race day were limited. We had left our home just a five-minute walk away and missed our chance.

Aiden began making his way along the thoroughfare, peering through gaps to try and work out which entrances were still open. Frustrated, I perched on the steps of the Loggia della Mercanzia—the Merchants Lodge built in the fifteenth century—trying to think through our options.

The sound of drumming in the distance moved closer. I lost sight of Aiden who vanished into the crowds as he sought his own solution to find a view. Sighing despondently, I wandered back to the second gate we had tried—the main entrance to the arena. A small crowd hovered there, trying to see into the piazza.

The pre-race parade, known as Corteo Storico was starting. I was able to wriggle unobtrusively deeper into the gathered group. Peering between the shoulders of two towering German teenagers, I could see men in armour passing by on horseback. From this vantage point, I could see more from here, than where I had stood in the centre of the piazza for the trial race. Balanced precariously on tippy-toes for the best part of two hours, I caught sight of the almost seven-hundred participants—knights and horses, drummers and flag bearers from each district—make their way past.

As the tail end of the parade vanished from view, the rumble of the crowd increased above the fading beat of the drums. Anticipation flooded the city, though some of those around me, flagging from the heat and the constant jostling for a view dispersed. I slowly won a clearer view of the track. Shadows from the buildings began to fall over those of us that had pushed forward into the gaps, the approach of evening bringing relief from the heat of the day.

Now at the front of the crowd, I crouched down to give my legs a rest while we waited for the race to commence. A suave looking police officer in aviator sunglasses, bantered enthusiastically with the public while busy capturing small children escaping towards the gates and lifting them back into the crowd to their parents.

A loud cheer erupted. I leapt up as the crowd behind me strained forward. A taught rope had been pulled across the track in front of us. The horses and their riders appeared.

The start line? I was looking at the start line!? The horses jostled each other as the jockeys were given their positions in the line-up.

A lotto system was again used for the positioning. If there was a false start, the lottery was conducted up to three times, and if the false starts continued, they continued to repeat the three orders.

Three false starts and an hour later, the crowd was beginning to get restless as we waited for the horses to be lined up yet again. They had to run before sunset or in following with tradition, the race would be postponed until tomorrow.

My feet were sore and my back was aching from standing so long, on tippy toes during the parade, and now alternating from foot-to-foot on the hard paving.

The horses leapt past the rope one more time as it dropped simultaneously with the blast from the starter gun. It was on!

The crowd erupted as we waited for them to make their first lap.

Pounding past once, then twice, before passing the final finish line, the race I had waited four weeks and three hours for, was over in ninety seconds. A dangerous ride for both rider and barbary, the winner was the horse that reaches the finish line first; regardless if the rider was still astride.

For the first time in 30 years the *Contrada della Civetta* reached the finish line first and fortuitously, the rider also still intact on the horse's saddle-free back. The companions of the district leapt over barriers and the racetrack flooded with supporters. I braced against the crowd, trying not to get swept down the slope towards the gate.

As makeshift fencing was pulled wide open, I was carried on the tide of people into the arena. I sailed the wave for a few minutes before managing to extract myself from the flow. I turned back up the hill and pushing against the current I carefully edged my way back out.

Picking my way around the horse dung I headed towards the Duomo. Swept up the stairs and into the cathedral along with the growing crowd, I pushed towards the front. Members of the contrada flooded in to thank the Madonna for their win. The triumphant jockey was brought through the crowd, with the Palio prize itself—a decorative banner made by a local artist each year—waving ahead of him on a long pole.

The tears flowed from men as they stood with arms around each other's shoulders. Women clung to each other calling out to the jockey as he passed. I felt people squeeze my shoulders in congratulation, and laughing, I accepted the occasional passing hug.

I hadn't experienced so much elation around me since the Socceroos won against Japan in our first game at the 2006 FIFA World

Cup. Those staff who hadn't been called up to travel to Germany had met up at the Shelbourne Hotel in inner Sydney to watch the historic match. Australia had rapidly and unexpectedly scored three goals in the last six minutes of the game, downing Japan 3-1. As the final whistle blew confirming that the Socceroos had just won Australia's first ever match at a World Cup, the pub had erupted. I had never hugged so many strangers in my life. As we headed out into the streets at four in the morning, the national elation was pouring out of every venue in town. At the scramble crossing on the intersection of Park and George Street near Sydney Town Hall, the crowds were rushing to the middle of the intersection dancing, singing, yelling and waving all the green and gold they had on them every time the light was green. Then they would rush back to the sidewalk to let the early morning traffic through. Taxis beeped out celebratory noise and bus drivers honked their own mismatched harmony. Caught up in this sort of sporting passion was a new experience for me having, until then, skirted the periphery of big sporting moments in Australia. I was generally interested if we did well but I rarely watched sport. I had been out to some of the live sites during the 2000 Olympics in Sydney, but I had never experienced the level of sporting fever that the World Game seemed to drive. It had been incredible to experience the passion and joy of the collective as we celebrated the win as a community.

Like Australia achieving our first win at a FIFA World Cup, this felt like a distinctly historic moment too. Perhaps those celebrating in the crowd around me now had never experienced a win during il Palio before, or perhaps for the older generations, the last time their contrada had taken the prize was a distant memory from their childhood or young adult years.

Crammed between a rather large hairy man and his loud mate, I found myself showering in their sweat as their every move flicked perspiration over me. It seemed timely to begin to make my exit. As I reached the main doors, the Palio banner appeared overhead. I was swept up in the flow of the next part of the parade, ensconced among the winning contrada members. It was easier to keep moving by staying with them, than to retreat into the surrounding crowds. Locals and tourists that lined the streets waved as we passed. I ducked the swing of the flag of a dishevelled knight as he swept it back and forth. Teenage girls used my shoulders to propel themselves up into the air as they leapt past in excitement. I smiled back at the waving crowds, walking alone in the sea of maroon, black and white—the colours of la Civetta—an unassuming imposter.

The numbers slowly swelled in the small courtyard outside the headquarters and museum of la Civetta as I entered, having escaped the parade to take a shortcut through the side streets. I climbed up on to the steps of a closed doorway, clinging to the wall to gain a bird's-eye view of what might come next in the celebrations.

Men began pushing the crowd back, allowing others to line a small area with metal fencing. With an almighty cheer, the uncannily calm winning horse was led into the courtyard.

The horse was hosed down in front of the crowd, then brought around to greet the adoring fans. Across the courtyard, I spied the knight who had nearly taken out my eye with his flag. Gone was his elaborate tunic, tights and plumed hat. Looking overwhelmed with emotion, he now stood shirtless in black shorts with the white band of his underpants peering over the top. A thin, black hairband pushed his unruly curls off his sweaty forehead. His moment of reflective repose was verbosely interrupted when a fellow knight, now in jeans, slapped him on the back, spinning him around in a tearful embrace.

Meandering home through the busy streets, I wondered where Aiden had ended up. I hoped he had found a decent spot to see the race from. Finding myself alone though, I had enjoyed the freedom to slip into key locations, experience bespoke moments in the community swirling around me and gather my own memories to quietly take away.

Falling into bed well after midnight there was no noise or activity coming from the contrada gardens down below. Palio was over for another year.

7

Ana and Olivera's time in Siena came to an end the day after the race. As well as sharing meals prepared at home together, we had often met up throughout the week for coffee and lunches in town, making the most of the festive atmosphere. The warmth of their brief friendship had given me a much-needed emotional boost.

Katsumi from Japan arrived and took over Fabian's room. Recently made redundant in the wave of job losses caused by the global financial crisis, she had left Tokyo to head to Berlin to learn German for three months. Listening to my new housemate speaking fluent English, she told Aiden and I about her adventures in Germany before coming here with plans to also master Italian. I felt my own sense of inadequacy rising back to the surface. Here she was embarking on a fourth language as I continued my struggle to learn my second. Studies have found that once you have learnt a second language it does become easier to learn others. Like exercising any muscle, the skills and cognitive abilities develop to adopt new languages and their structures come more easily. But it had been a long time since I had triggered those cognitive abilities while learning high school Japanese with a younger, more malleable brain.

Despite spending hours battling through my homework, on arrival in class the following day, it quickly became apparent that everything I had attempted was yet again completely wrong. I felt hot tears prick the back of my eyes from the frustration. I sulked in my corner, trying to blend into the wall as the motivation to participate in class drained out of me. Julia came over to examine my work as we commenced our morning grammar exercises.

Pausing, she looked me in the eye, "Non é una problema Jacqueleenee!" she gave me a bright smile, "Non é importante."

She subtly checked I was on the right track with my exercises. I did think my inability to get my homework right was, in fact, 'una problema', but her nonplussed reassurance pulled me out of my grump for long enough to get through the day's lessons.

I went to the mid-week markets the next day instead of class. With my time at the school running out, I needed to find a way to better connect with my new language outside the classroom. To make my way around Italy in coming months, confident that I could communicate when English wasn't an option, things had to improve. Quickly.

As I browsed the market stalls, I tentatively began to interact with the marketeers.

"Quanto costa?" I asked about anything that took my fancy. I concentrated on my ability to more quickly hear numbers as stall-holders rapidly rattled off prices. I settled on a tablecloth embroidered with poppies, as a gift for mum. Proudly conducting the complete three sentence exchange in Italian—complemented by some useful hand waves and head tilts to communicate between the gaps in my vocabulary—I walked away with a marginal increase in confidence that my Italian was progressing.

Padre Rick, along with Ban, still remained my two consistent classmates. With English in common, the Padre and I had gravitated to each other as regular desk buddies, often working in a pair during group exercises.

"Ti piace andare in discoteca?"—*do you like to go to the disco?* I had one day found myself reading out loud from the exercise in the textbook. I suppressed a laugh while waiting for him to formulate the correct grammar to answer.

"Non mi piace andata alla discoteca," he bashfully confirmed his lack of interest in going to nightclubs.

During another class, Julia was handing out lists of questions for us to use as conversation starters. Pausing before placing the sheet of paper in front of the Padre and I, she gave me a sheepish grin before moving on.

"Quando hai baciato qualcuno l'ultima volta?" the Padre asked.

"When did I last kiss someone!" I had repeated loudly in English as I burst out laughing. Julia looked across quickly with a warning look to remind me that Italian was all I should be uttering; but the light of mischief sparkled in her eyes. I quietly queried of the Padre if this question was part of an impromptu confessional.

"No no, not all," he protested with a laugh.

I confessed that the last person I had kissed was, "la mia amica Alexis sulla... ummm... the cheek", I pointed to my face, thinking fondly of my friend in London who I had stayed with when I first landed.

Having the Padre to clarify things in English for me wasn't aiding the development of my comprehension. With only a fortnight left at the school, I started to move around the classroom, purposely sitting next to non-native English speakers to force me to try harder.

I hoped that removing the temptation to use English would force my brain to kick into gear.

Sitting at the kitchen table one afternoon doing some *compiti*, I had the television on quietly in the corner. Glancing up from my books, President Obama was on the screen, discussing 'il crisi economica globale'. His voice was dubbed over in Italian. All of a sudden, I heard it clearly. A full sentence.

"Una luce alla fine del tunnel."—*A light at the end of the tunnel.*

Whether there was a light at the end of the tunnel in the global financial crisis, I wasn't sure. There was, however, a sudden light in my own dark tunnel of language frustrations. Without my usual struggle to work through the sentence I had heard the words and the grammatical make-up and understood. It wasn't a complex sentence, but I nearly cried with relief.

While it only took half an hour to head directly across town on foot, it was the end of my fifth week before I found myself back at Porta San Marco, the hilltop outside the city gates where the idea to return to Italy had first been planted. I would soon be leaving Siena once again.

My September departure would coincide with the annual grape harvest. I had registered with WWOOF—Worldwide Opportunities on Organic Farms—a volunteer organisation where you work on farms in exchange for food and accommodation.

I harboured romantic visions of myself amongst the vines in a pristine, white, flowing dress. After working in the fields all day, I would be hoisted onto the shoulders of handsome farm boys (dress still pristine of course), who would deposit me into a vat of grapes that needed stomping on. Oh, there would be laughter and tears and romance and grape stains on that dress. And at the end of it all I would be swept up in the arms of the unexpected love of my life, bound practically and emotionally together by the sweet stickiness of the grapes.

After contacting a selection of large and small farms to see if they had space for me during September, only one replied to confirm they had an opening. Orti di Mare—garden by the sea—on the island of Elba, off the Tuscan coast. Katharina, the German student who had been staying at the house when I first arrived, had told me about holidays to the island she had been on with her family as a child and recommended I take the chance to visit. Not much English was spoken at the farm apparently. Daunting as that was, I hoped it would inevitably force me to boldly adopt my new language out of necessity. I would see how this first attempt at farm life went, but I hoped going farm to farm could enable me to take my time to move down the coast of Italy as I developed my language skills.

As the sun slipped toward the horizon, I turned back into Porta San Marco, and returned to the streets to head home.

"Jacqueleenee!!" a young girl screeched my name as she leapt towards me from the doorway of a tiny bookshop as I passed. I had met Daphne—who was also studying at the school—at the dinner for Contrada dell'Aquila the week before.

"Where are you going?" she grabbed my hand as we walked together along Via di Città towards the city centre. At just seventeen-years-old, my new Cypriot friend exuded confidence. She rattled off the names of the Spaniards from her class that she was on her way to meet up with.

"Come with us Jacqueleenee," she beseeched me, "They are so nice. And Miguel. He's soooo cute."

We found Miguel and Valeria at a street-side bar near the university. We perched on stools in the doorway of the hole in the wall establishment, as bottles of Moretti beer were poured into plastic cups and passed around. As neither Spaniard spoke English, Daphne enthusiastically attempted to translate across our three native, and shared but adopted language of Italian, as we found things in common, laughed and told stories. I understood little of the words but followed the facial cues and moments of laughter and joined in as best I could, feigning understanding at times, not wanting to wear Daphne's interpreting skills out.

"We're going to a bar near the Duomo that Miguel heard about," Daphne instructed me as we finished the beer.

Slipping through a nondescript doorway, we found a DJ playing nineties' music in the corner of the dark bar. It was still early, and the place was yet to fill up.

I hadn't really let my hair down since leaving Sydney. "Do you like dancing?" I asked Daphne as Slave to the Music by Twenty 4 Seven began pumping through the speakers.

"Yesssssseee!" she grabbed my hand and pulled me to the centre of the room. Cajoling the Spaniards to join us we made the most of having the space to ourselves.

I stepped away from the group briefly as the dance floor began to fill to grab a water. I felt a hand at my elbow. I turned to find myself looking up into the earnest face of a man, with green eyes and fair hair set back against a receding hairline.

"Buonasera," he said softly despite the rampant noise around us, "Tu sei bella. Come ti chiami?"

"Io sono Jacqueline," I smiled back at him nervously. "Come ti chiama?" I asked in return. I couldn't understand the name he gave me but nodded anyway.

He looked about thirty-years-old and told me he worked at the university of Siena, teaching linguistics.

He spoke no English but to my astonishment, we managed a stilted introductory conversation in Italian over the pounding music. Relaxed after a drink or two, my fears of inadequacy with comprehension were briefly forgotten. As we passed the basics though, I ran out of words. Keen to re-join my friends, I began to excuse myself.

"Posso avere… il tuo numero di telefonino?" he asked tentatively for my phone number. I paused.

"Domani," he implored, "c'incontriamo nella piazza per uno gelato no?"

An invitation to meet for gelato tomorrow wasn't too daunting. Perhaps talking further with an Italian linguistics lecturer would be good practice for me. I put my number in his phone.

"Ci vediamo domani,"—*see you tomorrow*—he smiled happily at me.

Returning to my group I rolled my eyes at them all as Daphne led the barrage asking what had happened.

"Niente! Niente!" I denied with a laugh. I still wasn't sure I would go.

I looked over my shoulder to check our bags were still where we had left them under a chair. There was a man perched on the seat with a group of rough looking mates around him. Doing my best to ignore the postulating as I broke into their midst, I ducked down to grab our belongings.

As I backed away from the group, one of the men wearing a t-shirt, long shorts and sporting a scruffy dark ponytail flecked with grey, beckoned me over.

One gelato date out of tonight was enough. I shook my head before pulling back to my group. I implored my new friends to take to the other side of the dance floor to give me some space from the eyes I still felt boring into the back of my head.

We chatted with locals between forays back onto the dance floor. A group of tattooed young men from the south kept asking me about il canguro. It was only when they brought their muscled paws up and bounced up and down on the spot, sending me into peals of laughter that I understood their heavily vowel inflected name for Kangaroo.

Abel, another Spaniard, joined the group. Cutting up the dance floor, I found myself feeding off his vivacity and unassuming joie de vivre as he spun me around with his one arm. He had lost his right arm in a work accident. He was now studying Italian at the university. I had been so absorbed with language learning and participating in all the tourist activities I could while in town, it felt good to let my hair down.

I felt someone grab my hand and try and pull me from the group. I turned to see the man with the ponytail. Reducing the slack in my arm I hung back, shaking my head at him. He tilted his head imploring me to come and talk to him next to the dance floor. Sighing, I gave in. I didn't want to be rude but I wasn't comfortable with this guy.

"Ahhh, Jacqueline," he nodded with a sly smile as I hesitantly responded to his request for my name. He swept a piece of stray hair off my face and leant in to kiss me.

Seriously??? I recoiled. Laughing at my reaction, he pulled me into an embrace to dance. I furtively tried to catch Daphne's eye over my shoulder. *What was a seventeen-year-old going to do to help me anyway*, I realised.

Clearly nothing. At the sight of me awkwardly caught up in the arms of the scruffy bloke, and oblivious to my resistance to the situation, she turned back to her companions on the dance floor.

Abel. Where was Abel? I looked around for my dance floor companion. He had his back to me at the bar.

"Io sono Nek," the man told me as he pulled me onto a seat in a lounge around a corner. Drawing me down he planted me on his knee. Exasperated I pushed myself onto the seat beside him, enduring the arm that remained around me as I worked on a plan to get away from him.

We stuttered through the basics of introductions. He used charades to demonstrate his work as a tradie. From the district of the Porcupine, we were the same age. He was a *mammone* —mummy's boy—as men who still live with their mothers are called.

I managed to lean around the corner and catch Daphne's eye. I implored her with my eyes and mouthed *COME HERE* to her in the half-light. She ducked over. Seeing Nek still trying to wrap himself around me, she burst out laughing and ran back to the dance floor. I rolled my eyes in frustration as she vanished back into the crowd.

"Perche no,"—*why not*—he implored, catching me off-guard as he tried to kiss me again. I put my hand on his mouth, becoming increasingly annoyed by his physical advances. I broke away from his hold, courtesy abandoned as I wrenched my waist from his grip. The Spaniards were picking up their bags to leave as I quickly made my way back to them.

Miguel and Abel looked at Nek warily as he came up beside me. Walking out with us, he indicated he was going to walk me home. My heart sank as I struggled to work out how to get rid of him. The streets were busy even though it was after midnight, but I didn't want to be alone with him. Daphne was busy flirting with Miguel and left without saying goodbye. I implored Abel with my eyes as he turned to leave. He returned a confused look, as he left with an "Arrivederci."

Ending the evening with amiable Abel walking me home would have been a much nicer way to finish what had been a fun night. Until now.

Triumphant as my companions dispersed, Nek took my hand. There was nothing for it but to turn for Piazza San Francesco. There would be people in the piazza in front of the church —there always was until the very early hours—and all I had to do was get safely through the front door of the villa. I reasoned that he didn't seem dangerous. Just pushy.

He chattered to me, not caring that I had no idea what he was saying. My mind busily ticked over how to safely get out of the situation.

I didn't want him to know where I lived. I began to try and take my leave from him as we entered the piazza. Instead, he firmly drew me over to the park benches under the trees outside the villa, again planting me on his knee and wrapping his arms around me. I slid onto the seat beside him. Others out enjoying the night air, sat chattering quietly on nearby benches oblivious to my angst. He cajoled me to come closer, pulling at my clothes. I was tired and had no words in Italian to respond as I tried to pull away.

He firmly planted his lips on mine catching me by surprise. "No!" I snapped. I pushed him away as hard as I could, "Sono arrabbiata! BASTA!"—*I'm angry! ENOUGH!*—Surprised by my sudden rise in tempo he pulled back a little but didn't let go.

With that firm grip again around my waist, he began to pull me toward a quiet corner of the piazza behind some cars parked there. The fire in me rose. Furious, and now more than a little afraid of what he was trying to do, I lashed out. With the best push I could muster I launched myself away from him hissing, "NO! Sono ARRABBIATA! Capisce? Vai Via!"

With a surge in my fear and fury, I untangled myself from his grip. In the midst of a war of English and Italian words and gestures, I leapt away.

His voice followed me, "Jacqueleenee... Mi dispiace..."—*I'm sorry*. I fled past the dispassionate onlookers on the piazza, bursting through the front door, slamming it unceremoniously behind me despite the late hour.

I leant back on the wood after checking the lock, I dropped my chin to my chest and regained my breath. I had hoped for a little flirtation from the locals but not to be terrorised.

Why had I felt the need to be polite when a guy was making unwanted physical advances? A swift slap was what I would have preferred to use. But I had wanted to get out of the situation safely. Guilt conflicted me as I went over in my mind how I had ended up in a situation like that and what I could have done to prevent it. But why was it my fault? I had wanted to walk away. I fell into bed angry.

My phone beeped at nine the next morning. His name was Landi apparently – the man I was to meet for gelato this afternoon. After how last night had ended, I didn't want to go. I had nothing else planned until the evening though and daylight hours did seem safer. And unlike Nek, who had made me feel uncomfortable from the moment I laid eyes on him, gentle Landi had been kind and confident, without making me feel wary.

Hesitantly I entered il Campo and texted to let him know I had arrived. My phone promptly beeped back.

'Venga e mi incontri nell'ombra del palazzo.'

I knew incontri meant meet. Somewhere near the palazzo then? I began walking across the piazza. Ombra had something to do with umbrellas, which made me think of shade. I looked down and spotted him in the shade of the one-hundred-and-two step high Torre del Mangia.

We greeted each other with a kiss to each cheek. I looked at him curiously. He seemed younger in daylight than I had perceived in the multicoloured lights of the discoteca.

He guided me to his favourite gelato store, larger than the hole in the wall gelataria I had taken to frequenting. With a large cup each of the sweet, creamy gelato in hand we found a spot on a low wall on Via Pantaneto. Mopeds were parked all the way up the street near the monument of Logge del Papa, built in the fifteenth century. A popular haunt for students, the wall was peppered with young people chattering and laughing in the shade cast by surrounding buildings.

We began to pick our way through conversation. Landi revealed he was from Albania. I raised my eyebrows quizzically.

"Allora, do you teach Italian or...", I paused in my stilted Italian for him to tell me how he would say his language in Italian...

"Albanese," he nodded.

"Si, Albanese"? I asked.

I wondered what language faux par I had made that amused him as he broke into a grin. "No no! Non sono un'insegnante,"—*I'm not a teacher*—he exclaimed. "I am studying linguistics in Siena." I gasped as I slowly interpreted what he had told me as he laughed at my misinterpretation.

"E... ok... Quanti anni hai?"—*How old are you?* I asked.

"Ho ventitré anni," he smiled. *Twenty-three!* Outrageous. He wasn't even within the ten-year-rule that I often joked about with my friends.

"E tu?" he asked cheekily. "How many years do you have?"

Frowning at him in mock admonishment for asking such a thing, I squeaked out, "Trentaquattro,"—*thirty-four.*

"Ma tu non si comporta quell'età," he smiled charmingly as I stared at him blankly wondering what he had said. Pulling out the dictionary I asked him to *'per favore ripeta'*. It seemed his observations of me in the bar the night before suggested to him I was much younger than I said. Flashbacks to my antics on the dance floor with my seventeen-year-old friend earlier in the evening made me laugh.

As the conversation continued, I sank deeper into shock at the mire of my linguistic confusion. Not only was he not Italian, nor a professor of linguistics, nor over the age of thirty, it also turned out he was funding this date with earnings from his job at the local supermercato. Not my supermercato. A much bigger one outside the city walls. Perhaps the wine hadn't been helping my comprehension as much as I had thought last night.

Chatting slowly but comfortably for more than an hour, Landi excused himself as he needed to leave as he had a shift at work. He offered to walk me home. Taking my hand as he flashed me a nervous smile, we began the ten-minute walk across town.

As we rounded the bend in via dei Rossi, I stiffened at the sight of Nek coming from the piazza. I dropped my head down, allowing my hair to fall as far across my face as it would go. Had he come looking for me? Suddenly living in such a small town seemed hazardous. We passed safely without eye contact.

"Posso vederti dopo la partita?"—*Can I see you after the game?*—Landi asked as he delivered me to my front door. I was off to see Siena take to the field again in the evening. We agreed to meet outside the stadium post-match.

"Prenderemo una una pizza!"—*we'll get a pizza*—he called out as he walked away. It would be late, but I had enjoyed his company. And using Italian in general conversation had finally begun to increase my confidence in trying to use the language.

I walked into an Irish pub across the road from the stadium an hour before gates opened. I had met Josephine Josephson—an artist from Australia—also at the Contrada dell'Aquila dinner the week before. She was the first Aussie I had met through the school and a regular student in Siena. After this visit, she and her husband were off to join a group of painters to capture the countryside for a few weeks.

I sighed wistfully. She told me she had previously had a career in interior design but had always wanted to paint. She told me about her vocational path over our tall glasses of Irish beer served with a local aperitif of olives, caper berries and an assortment of roasted vegetables.

"I wish I could draw," I told her, "I've never really tried since primary school, but it seems such a beautiful gift."

"You can draw!" she said. "Put a sketch book and some pencils in your bag. Draw what you see while you travel."

I looked at her sceptically.

"You won't know unless you try," she insisted.

"I like writing," I murmured absentmindedly.

"Then write like you are drawing a picture," Jo encouraged, "describe what you see, feel, smell, and experience."

Yoko from Japan and Esma from Turkey—both from Jo's class—joined us at the stadium. I felt stunned by the proximity of the powerhouse Italian team in front of us as Ronaldinho took to the field for warm up mere metres away. AC Milan took the victory 2 - 1, but solid play by Siena in the face of such hefty opposition made for an exciting match in the cosy stadium.

Taking my leave of the other women as we exited the grounds, I found Landi waiting across the road. I tried to explain the key moments of the game to him but found myself frustrated by my lack of vocabulary to express myself as I would in English. He smiled kindly at my attempts before taking my hand to lead me through the streets to a pizzeria next to the internet cafe I frequented. It was empty when we took a seat around 11.00pm.

"Ti piace le sopresse?"—*Do you like surprises?*—he asked while we waited for our pizzas.

"Forse…"—*maybe*—I wondered what was coming.

The wait staff emerged from the kitchen with a twinkle in their eyes, proudly presenting me with my pizza, in the shape of a love heart. I smiled sweetly at Landi and the waitress—both looking quite proud of the surprise dinner delivery—while swallowing a laugh.

I couldn't see a great romance developing with a man more than ten years my junior in the remaining week I had in town, but it was not a bad effort for my first date in Italy.

Landi convinced me to meet up with him to have lunch on Sunday. We dined salubriously at his university cafeteria, before taking a walk around the nearby ruins of the Medici Fortress. After a few wearying hours trying to make conversation in my second language, he had taken his leave for another shift at the supermercato. He had a lot of shifts this week and we were unsure when we would be able to meet up again.

During my six weeks in the house, the average age of students had steadily increased. Chuck was the last flatmate to arrive in the apartment, a retired American Naval officer and sometimes Spanish translator aged sixty-nine, he was working through his bucket list. Over glasses of expensive wine that he bought to share with us, he regaled Aiden, Katsumi and I with stories of life moving from continent to continent.

"Jac-A-lyn," he told me one night over dinner, "there were two places we used to sail into, that we would say 'if you arrive there married, you'd end up divorced and if you arrive there single, you'd end up married'."

I looked at him expectantly.

"Chile," he paused, "and AhustrAYYYlia."

"And why was that?" I asked with a laugh as I passed the breadbasket to Katsumi.

"Because AhustrAYYYlian men are knouwn fir ignorin' you women folk," he guffawed.

I reluctantly joined in the laughter as I admitted to myself that he had a point. The straightforward advances of American men let alone Italian, was extremely appealing to an Australian woman for that reason. Clear intentions. But the experience with Nek had reminded me of the darker side of those intentions and I wasn't sure it was as appealing as I had thought.

A free concert series commenced across the city in my final week. A full stage was set up in our piazza. Each night the crowds sat outside our front door watching world class musical, dance and orchestral acts.

The house was strangely empty on Wednesday night when I returned home from yet another foray through the Sienese galleries. There was no point remaining inside with music from the performances pouring through the kitchen window. After eating dinner on the balcony, I went down and found a seat in the piazza to watch an emotional contemporary dance piece.

"Excuse me madam, would you care for some company?"

With a smile, I recognised Aidan's lilting Scottish accent in my ear. He stepped past to the spare seat beside me.

Chuck coming behind him leant down and with a wink added, "Wanna meet a sailor?"

These two had been pleasant company during their respective

tenure in the house. In my final week in Siena, I became increasingly aware I was about to move on from the familiarity of my home of six weeks. I found the company of my eclectic housemates one last time an indulgence. This chapter was ending. Soon I would be off to a new destination. The connections here left behind.

Taking a final early morning walk on the Friday I sat outside the Duomo listening to the bells ringing out over the city. It had remained my daily ritual to finish my walk here before turning for home. I had befriended the security guard who came out each day for his morning cigarette. He had told me he was from Napoli. With unemployment high in the south it wasn't uncommon to find security guards, coach drivers and other service staff who came from the complex southern city. My new friend made me promise to visit his bella citta as I said farewell to him for the last time.

I knew if I didn't brave this reproachable metropolis, I would not have truly seen Italy. But it was still not time to go there yet. English was not as widely spoken further south, and I wanted to ensure my language skills were more advanced before I headed south of Rome.

Landi and I managed to catch up one more time. From a little balcony above his favourite gelateria we enjoyed a triple cup of gelato each as we watched the crowds swarm in to il Campo to enjoy the last of the summer concerts.

"Hai Facebook?" he asked?

"Si," I nodded, "Ho Facebook."

Aidan, Chuck and Katsumi were up early to see me off on the Saturday. Chuck chivalrously hoisted my bulging suitcase down the stairs. Despite sending a small box of souvenirs home to Australia already, I was now encumbered by textbooks that I wanted to keep with me so I could reference as I travelled. I chased him down the stairs, apologising profusely for the weight he had offered to bear.

Sad to leave my beautiful room looking over the town and outlying hills, the road re-opened as I prepared for a short break in Nice with Alexis who was flying in from London, before I was due to head to Elba to toughen up with a few weeks working on a farm.

8

As I exited the Stazione di Milano Centrale, traffic flew in every direction as I made my way across the busy thoroughfare to my budget hotel. The serenity of Siena was quickly forgotten only a few hours after departing as I re-entered the chaos of a big city. I was on my way to meet Alexis in Nice but had stopped off for a quick visit to the country's economic and fashion capital.

Dropping my bags off, I took a late afternoon walk into the centre to get a feel for the city. I mingled in the early evening crowds on the edge of the piazza of the Duomo, before drifting back the way I had come to pause in front of il Teatro alla Scala – the city opera house inaugurated in 1778. Weary from a day of travel I headed back to find a cheap dinner near my accommodation.

The next morning, I re-entered the historic centre via the two glass-vaulted arcades intersecting in an octagon over the street connecting Piazza della Scala and Piazza del Duomo, making up Galleria Vittorio Emanuele II – a four-storey shopping arcade built late in the nineteenth century. A feeble light filtered through the sky lights, muted by grey clouds blocking the anticipation of morning sun. As elegant storefronts came to life, I paused at a cafe near the central dome of the octagon, to enjoy the elegance of the palatial arcade for a few moments while indulging in a hot cappuccino and fresh cornetto.

Il Duomo di Milano can hold forty thousand people—only slightly less than the capacity of the old Sydney Football Stadium. One of the largest churches in the world, the imposing gothic structure of the city's great cathedral took six-hundred years to build. As I entered the cavernous interior, I spotted a space sectioned off for a service with a sign at the entrance to hold tourists at bay.

Ingresso consentito esclusivamente a chi intende partecipare alle celebrazione liturgiche. Please not tourist.

No more than twenty-five worshippers sat in the small chapel participating in the liturgy, lost in the expanse of the ancient church that once hosted the city's whole population. I thought about the thousands that poured in and out of my church, housed in a warehouse in Waterloo in inner Sydney each weekend, passing between nine services. Altogether they would have been able to at least fill half of this church with people. I was struck by the lack of the faithful on a Sunday morning: though to be fair, I couldn't imagine I would choose a venue full of passing tourists as the ideal place to engage in spiritual meditation. While being Catholic may equate to being Italian culturally, I wondered how often it equated to having a personally explored faith.

Despite the elaborate exterior architecture, the interior decor of the Duomo had retained a more severe and unemotional form, with its current style taking shape taking under neo-classical influences. Bursts of colour from spectacular stained-glass windows broke through the coldness of the grey. I was particularly struck by one of angels and demons, warring between heaven and hell. An arresting vision of intense drama, the good versus evil dichotomy that framed the core plot for so many stories. Stone carvings towered so far on high that I could barely make out their theme. Marble mosaics inlaid into the floor below again provided the contrast of colour to the severity of the stone above.

I took the two-hundred and fifty stairs to the rooftop viewing the city from between the many spires. Light rain brushed over my skin as a gentle wind picked up and I made my way back down the parapets.

I had found out too late that I should have pre-booked a visit to Leonardo da Vinci's painting of 'The Last Supper' at the convent of Santa Maria delle Grazie, weeks earlier. I crossed the wide piazza to step on the 'Hop On, Hop Off' bus hoping it would reveal some of the city's other jewels.

Disembarking at Castello Sforzesco, the sun finally burst through the clouds. Crossing the bridge of the former moat, a lush stretch of green grass within the castle walls drew me to bask a while in the warmth with hundreds of other tourists. Now September, the weight of humidity had begun to lift. Further north and closer to the mountains, perfect late summer weather re-shaped the city's afternoon atmosphere.

At the castle entrance I paid three euros to enter the multiple museums. Museo degli Strumenti Musicali—*the Museum of Musical Instruments*—was home to everything from 17th century violins and baroque guitars, to 18th century mandolins, harpsicords and wind instruments. I found myself entranced looking at the evolution of the instruments through time, and taken by the exquisite craftsmanship.

As I dawdled through the Museo d'Arte Antica, examining a case full of old guns with mild interest, a toothy security guard came over to offer his expertise.

"Ah mi scusa," I apologised before he got too far, "Non parlo l'Italiano molto bene."

Bearing a huge grin that showed the gaps where he was missing teeth, he pointed at the gun, demonstrated with his arms how it was aimed, and 'fired' yelling, "BOOM BOOM!!!"

I burst out laughing as other passers-by looked over in surprise at our noisy interaction. Taking my arm, he walked me to the next door. Pointing to some stairs, he implored me with words and gestures to turn the corner at the top and ensure I saw the Pietà Rondanini. Michelangelo's final and unfinished work before his death was one of three Pietà he had created in his lifetime, including the polished masterpiece in Saint Peter's in Rome. It is believed he had continued working on it until six days before his death. I thanked the guard and continued on to find the incomplete piece by the great master.

In its unfinished state, the roughly hewn marble already bore the mournful expressions of the Madonna and adult Christ, but in contrast to the one in Rome where Christ is draped across his mother's lap, they are upright. Mary seems to be bringing Jesus's broken body down off the cross herself. His legs are weak and bending as she rests his upper body against her. His arm is oddly dismembered from his body. I frowned as I circled the sculpture, trying to understand the final direction the master craftsman had intended to take with the work, as well as captivated by the idea of being suspended in time, as I ran my gaze over the final chisels of Michaelangelo's life.

A five-hour train ride to the Italian French border brought me into Nice the next day. I checked into the apartment Alexis had booked for us, a two-minute-walk from the rocky beaches of the French Riviera. She was arriving a few hours after me on a flight from Gatwick. I walked down to the stop near the beach where the bus from the airport would deliver her, eager to lay eyes on my friend from home. As I waited, a handsome man with dark curly hair drifted past on roller blades, then circled back to my side.

"Bonsoir," I smiled tentatively back at him as he introduced himself with a name I couldn't pronounce, "Je m'appelle Jacqueline. Enchanté," I confidently switched into my few words of French.

He slipped into the seat beside me. With a mid-seat arm rest pushing us together I was wary of this stranger, but amused by the French charm he was layering on me. He spoke few words of English, just enough to match my few words of French to move through pleasantries. I heard the sound of a familiar laugh and looked up to see Alexis with her camera out, trying to get a snap of me squished into the chair, trapped by the Frenchman's seductive lean. I leapt up in delight to embrace my mate, relieved she had seen me waiting, before waving a quick farewell to the nonplussed Casanova. I felt myself relax in the warmth of familiarity as we linked arms and headed to our accommodation to get settled in for the week.

Lingering around local markets we ate baguettes with fresh ham, tomatoes and cheese for lunch every day. We checked out the handsome lads working on the water sport outlets along the beach and fled more amorous locals pursuing us along the moonlit boardwalk in the evenings. We spent a day wandering Monaco, taking dips in the sea, swanning around the palace, posing for awkward photos on top of sculptures made from cannon balls, exploring the route of the Grand Prix, and eating crepes with obscene quantities of ice-cream, cream and melted chocolate. We frocked up for a mandatory evening at the Casino Monte Carlo, where I persisted in drinking a martini so strong it could have fuelled a rocket.

We took the quintessential tourist train tour around Cannes, had one too many ciders in an Irish pub while watching the English Premier League with the rest of the expats, and dined at McDonald's on the boardwalk to soak them up. We pretended lying on beaches covered in rocks was as enjoyable as the long stretches of golden sand back home in Australia. And most importantly we spent hours floating in the azure waters of the Ligurian sea.

Struggling to remember to use my *bonjours, silvousplaits* and *merci beaucoups* while staying across the border, I regularly slipped out *buongiornos, per favores* and *grazies*. I fancied myself trilingual as I found myself in basic conversation with local shopkeepers, interacting with an obscure combination of Italian, French and, when necessary, a little English.

Taking the train down to Florence a week later, I felt refreshed. Seeing a friend from home had allowed me to relax and have some fun, before I faced the challenge of the road on my own again.

Galleria dell'Accademia in Firenze, home to Michelangelo's infamous statue of the David, had been a highlight to visit with the tour group during my trip the year before. I had, however, fallen in love not with the infamous statue—as so many women are said to do—

but with the unfinished works of the great artist lining the Hall of the Prisoners over which the David presides. In particular, the lonely unfinished Apostle San Matteo had captured my imagination.

Making a beeline back to the Galleria as my first stop on arrival at Florence, I found the Hall of the Prisoners oddly empty when I walked in. Last time I was here, tour groups had been arriving in a constant flow, filling the gallery, bumping into each other, crowding around the statues. This time I stood alone with San Matteo, the incomplete statue from a commission for the Duomo di Firenze. Work on the statue was postponed after Michelangelo was called back to Rome to build a tomb for Pope Julius II. He never returned to the project, instead moving on to a new commission – a masterpiece for the ceiling of the Sistine Chapel. Thus, San Matteo remained permanently semi-cocooned in the marble block.

'...*the contrast between matter and idea, between finite and infinite... the incarnation of the interior torment that envelops the human soul...*' was printed in the description of the work on the card below.

I stepped back and studied the unrefined detail in the face—a beard, eyes, nose, a mouth. The bulging muscles of an emerging arm on his right. The shaping of a book clutched in the still undefined arm on his left. The torso was enrobed, and a knee was pulling up and out of the block of marble. The torment of internal formation was perfectly captured in the external physicality of the statue bursting from the stone. Character. Soul. Formation beyond the exterior we present.

No matter how much I willed myself to do the right thing, my attempts to do the right thing hadn't always resulted in follow through actions after my marriage crumbled. I had put on a brave face, and to those I worked with or who had only observed me at a distance, I probably appeared to be handling things well. But I wasn't. I didn't. I had to keep up a façade for my own sanity. But deep inside my interior had been weighted down by pain, making it hard to live authentically as the loving, kind, joyful, forbearing, principled, self-controlled human I wished to be. The realities of losing some part of who I thought I was through failure were challenges I was still reconciling with. I was reminded as I studied the unfinished apostle, that like San Matteo, I was also unfinished. And it was okay. I was a work in progress and the sculptor that I believed was behind my ongoing formation wasn't about to put down their tools and move onto another project. I felt that God had given me a lifetime to be refined. I expected I would be grey and ancient like this sculpture before I would have any sense that my interior formation was ready for a final polish.

A hullabaloo erupted at the main entrance of the hall. The flash of camera bulbs was incessant as a woman with long greying black hair, wearing a floppy hat, accompanied by a tall man with a guitar slung over his shoulder strode into the gallery towards the David. Stopping in front of him, they were surrounded by reporters asking questions into recorders and microphones, holding them out to the woman for her answers.

I found myself pressed up to the podium with San Matteo straining above me as a flood of gallery guests rushed in from the first hall to see what was happening. The woman's voice as she addressed the closest of the group, was lost to me.

"... an American singer. Famous in the seventies," I heard a guard saying in English to another tourist.

The man with the guitar strummed a few familiar bars.

"Take me now baby here as I am ... Pull me close try and understand ..." the woman's soulful voice reached up to the watchful David as I saw her gaze up at the masterpiece lovingly.

Cameras—normally banned in the gallery—popped madly.

"Because the night belongs to lovers... Because the night belongs to us..." her voice singing familiar lyrics was lifted by the acoustics of the gallery to every corner.

After ploughing through three more galleries that afternoon, I paused to enquire at the reception of the three-star Hotel Byron where I had opted to stay, as to who the rock star at the Galleria might have been. The porter pulled out the daily newspaper and flicked through.

"Ecco la," he pointed to an article with a small picture of the woman. "This?" he asked pointing to her. I nodded.

"Of course. It is Patti Smith. She has a concert here tomorrow night on the Piazza di Santa Croce." The Godmother of Punk, author, performance poet and visual artist—Patti Smith was in town to perform the following night in front of the Basilica di Santa Croce; the burial place of Galileo, Michelangelo and Machiavelli. She had been at the gallery that day in honour of her late friend Robert Mapplethorpe, whose 'Perfection in Form' photographic collection of images of the human body, was being juxtaposed in an exhibition alongside the sculptural works of Michelangelo.

Taking a shower to wash off the dust from the day, I popped the TV on while I prepared to head out to find some dinner later in the evening. A popular Australian television show appeared on the small screen. I watched for a few moments, amused to hear the

Australian actors dubbed in Italian.

I knew I was testing fate. I wasn't sure which season it was he ended up on after returning from the U.S. Perhaps he wouldn't appear.

He did.

As he came on screen, I couldn't help pausing to listen, thinking he sounded kind of cool dubbed in Italian. I quickly turned it off. We had last spoken just before Christmas, nearly a year before. Things had been left amicably, but I didn't need to be reminded of the sadness. I felt tears welling and gave myself a shake. Not here. Not now. I thought. Deep breath. *Let go.*

I stepped in front of the mirror and painted on my public face, finishing with a good dusting of glitter over the eye lids to lift my spirits for an evening on my own.

I returned to the streets at dusk. Marketeers were packing down their stalls and the frenetic activity of the day had eased. A dreamlike transition was permeating the streets as the moon rose in the inky blue sky and evening fell over the city. I walked towards Piazza della Signoria, where the strains of a classical guitarist busking nearby drifted up between the Palazzo Vecchio and the Uffizi, Italy's national gallery.

Walking through the courtyard between the adjoining buildings of the Uffizi, warm streetlights began to flicker on. Street performers posing as statues all day, amusing crowds as they lined up at the entry to the gallery, were stepping down from their tiny stages: the facade broken as they slumped from classical characters into weary workers at day's end. Cupid slouched past on his way home, bow and arrows slung over his shoulder, platform in hand. I wondered how many love matches he had made today. The Phantom of the Opera slowly began to disrobe as he chatted to Midas, who sat wearily on a stair, rubbing his stiff muscles as gold body paint flaked off.

Catching my curious stare, the Phantom leapt back into character, bashfully pulling his cape around him to hide his oddly bare torso with a plump belly lifting over the edge of his pants. Sweeping into a dramatic bow, he flashed me a charming smile raised his face and proceeded to blow me kisses as I continued on my way.

Crossing the river Arno, I made the half-hour trek up to Piazzale Michelangelo where one of two replicas of the David produced by Michelangelo now resided, joining other tourists out enjoying the panoramic evening view of the city.

I felt satiated by my indulgence at the table of the artistic feast that is Florence as I prepared for a change of pace as I departed the mainland for a few weeks. In less than three days I had feasted on the works in the Galleria and the Uffizi, climbed up into Brunelleschi's Dome at the Duomo, studied the works housed in the Medici Chapel, taken pause by the graves of Michelangelo and Galileo in the Basilica di Sante Croce, and squeezed in several other smaller galleries and churches in between. But as I sat on the hillside gazing down at the flickering lights of Florence, I looked forward to reaching Elba and having time without the pressures of work and study, time without having to worry about style and appearances and time immersed in nature.

PART 2

~ *La Contadina* ~

THE PEASANT

*We should look for someone to eat and drink with
before looking for something to eat and drink,
for dining alone is leading the life of a lion or wolf.*

~ EPICURUS ~

9

When I entered the world, Dad was working on a pig, barley and wheat farm in a small rural area called Jimbour, two hundred and thirty-eight kilometres from Brisbane on the Darling Downs. Mum, Dad and my two sisters—who had been born in Nigeria—had returned to live in England following my parents' ten year stint in Africa. But a year later, escaping the English weather, they had boarded a flight to Australia to carve out the next chapter of their lives in the tropical humidity of south-east Queensland.

Dad however found the long days circling the western Queensland wheat fields on the combine harvester a rather isolating work environment. His work had been within community in Nigeria, surrounded by other people. He decided on a career change. He left the agricultural career path that he had first set out on at the age of sixteen, to sell insurance. At thirty-eight, he began building a new career in business moving the family first to Toowoomba and then to Brisbane.

My sisters considered me a city slicker. I was only two years old when we moved to Brisbane and knew nothing else but the still emerging city I grew up in. While they had grown up playing in the dust of the western reaches of the Sahara before chasing cows in the paddocks of regional Queensland, I spent my whole childhood in the serene suburbia of sleepy Brisbane in the 1980s. Dad continued to manage our large suburban garden as a serious agricultural project. I spent my childhood delighting in an enormous vegetable patch watching it produce a variety of colourful produce each season.

"I hope you rinsed the compost out of that before you put your daughter in it!" Mum's voice would ring out, as Dad bounced me joyfully across the garden in our red wheelbarrow in between loads of biodegraded waste.

Dad would dig in barrow loads of compost twice a year before preparing furrows for the new crops. He taught me to poke my chubby little fingers into the soft damp soil, making a two-centimetre hole to drop the seeds in, before gently covering them over. I would be back down there early the next day, eagerly waiting for the first seedlings to emerge from their dark cocoon in the earth. Lettuces, tomatoes, cucumbers, carrots and an invasive crop of sweet corn that rose so high, it blocked the path to the fence that I would climb over to visit my friend who lived next door. The year the beans came the whole family was on deck to manage the harvest. Sitting in front of 'Young Talent Time' we trimmed, blanched and bagged up a healthy supply of green beans to be stored in the freezer, supplying us for months to come.

The vegetable patch decreased in size as I got older. The lawn size increased. Circling the garden with the lawn mower for hours on a Saturday, I would lose myself in a myriad of abstract thoughts around the pressing challenges of adolescent life, contented by the smell of freshly mown grass that intensified as I emptied a load from the catcher.

Where I moved to in inner Sydney, Saturday lawnmowers were rarely heard, the patches of grass behind streets full of apartment blocks were barely worth the effort. I contented myself with a scattering of herb and flowerpots on the balcony to allow me the chance to get my fingers in the dirt.

Arriving at football stadiums in the early morning ready to prepare for match days, I would luxuriate in the scent of the dew as it evaporated into the air lifting the juicy fragrances of recently tended grass. Strongest in the summer months, it offered a rewarding sensory memory of my childhood, spent engaged with the cycle of life found in the natural world. As I made my way to the farm on Elba I was looking forward to reconnecting with the earth and the soil, the elements that I had grown up with in my backyard.

After trawling through the fifty pages of possible farms I could apply to from the internet café in Siena, it was a poetic advertisement for a small fattoria on Elba that had caught my eye:

> *We are... extra-sweet strawberries gathered when ripe and mulberries • cliffs and cormorants • zero stress and noise • real nature • smell of the sea • a pinewood to fall asleep in • homemade bread baked in a wood oven • succulent fruit and vegetables full of vitamins • seabeds and cork oaks • dune lilies • pollinating bumble bees • farmers and thinkers • aleatico wine and spelt • real olive oil and yellow broom • bruschetta • almond milk • hammocks and canoes • warm soil under your feet • Mediterranean breeze at sunset• pine resin • panoramic views of the Archipelago National Park •*

Luisa, an Italian national from Milano, who had spent the summer on Elba at Orti di Mare—the 'garden married to the sea'—replied to my email enquiring if I could come to work for them.

> *"The setting is very beautiful and in September it will be the perfect weather... I'm sleeping in a little caravan in the vineyard, it's quite lonely but very nice and pleasant! You must know that there is no private bathroom, and the common ones are a bit far from your bedroom/caravan (three minutes' walk...) There is a peasant working here for a few hours every day and they would be with you in the vegetable garden in the early mornings... We recommend you take your sleeping bag... Vittorio and Cinzia speak very little English and appreciate who tries to communicate in Italian."* Luisa

Part of the Archipelago Toscano National Park, Elba is the largest of seven islands and surrounded by Montecristo, Giglio, Capraia, Giannutri, Gorgona and Pianosa. Though significantly smaller—with only one-hundred-and-forty square kilometres of dry land—Elba is the third largest island off Italy after Sicily and Sardinia. Napoleon Bonaparte was exiled there in 1814 after his kingdom crumbled and the Treaty of Fontainebleau—forged by the Austrian Empire, Prussia and Russia—forced him to abdicate the French throne. He was however given sovereignty over his new island home—perhaps to keep him occupied—and for his somewhat smaller kingdom of twelve-thousand inhabitants, he was allowed to retain the title of Emperor. In the three-hundred days he was on Elba, he drove significant infrastructure improvements on the island including building of roads, draining of marshes, boosting agriculture and developing mines, as well as overhauling the island's schools and legal system. The empire builder however made his escape from the island less than a year later, landing in southern France with plans to re-take power.

The port of Piombino was quiet when I arrived after lunchtime on Friday. The three-and-a-half-hour train ride from Florence brought me right to the waterfront. Stevedores lined the coastline to the south, mining and industry sharing the port on the busy tourist route. Today the ticket office was nearly empty of travellers. The peak summer holiday season was at an end.

Clutching my ticket and dragging my bags behind me I wandered down to the dock. The ferry in port was slowly swallowing cars into its hull. My luggage weighted down by textbooks was now also awkwardly balancing the new camouflage sleeping bag I had picked up from an army disposal store near my hotel in Florence that morning.

When I first registered to become a voluntary farmworker, I had imagined myself staying in a picturesque Tuscan farmhouse like the ones I had seen dotted around Siena, but that was not to be this time. Leaving comfortable accommodation and luxuries behind, I readied myself to toughen up for farm work and caravan accommodation for the next two weeks.

As I reached the steep set of metal stairs leading to the passenger entry of the vehicle ferry, I paused to bend my knees and braced to lift my suitcase.

"Aspetta! Aspetta!" I heard a man's voice bellowing above me. I paused, unsure if he was yelling at me. A young man came racing down the stairs to me. Hoisting the suitcase out of my arms, he ran up to the boarding deck with it as if it was as light as a feather. I clambered the rest of the way up with my small backpack alone slowing me down.

"Grazie," I smiled as he put the handle back in my hand. I turned to the elderly bursar beside him who had sent help, "Grazie mille anche a tu."—*Thank you to you also.*

As the island grew on the horizon, amidst the drone of the engines and the smell of the sea, I was flooded with memories of Queensland summers in my late teens. I would catch the car ferry across Moreton Bay to North Stradbroke Island each year, heading over with friends to volunteer on a beach mission running activities for kids staying in the campsites on the island between Christmas and New Year.

As we approached Portoferraio through clear aqua waters, the engines slowed. The craggy mountains looming around the bay were swathed in mid-afternoon sun as we pulled into the dock. The thick, shadowy walls of the sixteenth century Medici fortresses loomed up to the right, stark and unfriendly in comparison to the bustle of activity around the sunny dock as we prepared to disembark.

I rushed to find the bus stop I needed as we came on shore, afraid of missing one of the few buses now travelling across the island with the peak summer season over.

"Lacona?" I asked with one foot in the door.

The bus driver waved me onto the vehicle impatiently, eager to get on his way. Flustered, I climbed aboard hoping it was the right one to take me to the bay carved into the southern coast of the island where I was to find my farm. An elderly gentleman helped me drag my luggage up the stairs of the bus, chattering away kindly as I nodded and smiled.

The bus wound around roads shaped into the mountainside.

Perched on the edge of my seat, I anxiously watched the time. I had been told it was half an hour by road and that I should get off when I arrived at the Discoteca Essenza. Focused on preventing my luggage from toppling on to other passengers, I was too far out of ear shot of the driver to ask him to alert me to the landmark on approach.

Another passenger had pressed the bell as a wooden sign with 'Orti di Mare' burnt into it, flashed into view. Relieved I had made it to the right place, I tumbled off the bus, my bags propelling my rapid descent onto the corner of a country road. Watching my fellow passengers quickly vanish in different directions, I took the advice of the sign pointing west and began walking down the narrow road I hoped would lead to my destination.

There was no sign of any 'Discoteca Essenza'. Instead, a caravan on raised blocks next to a field came into view. I scanned the area, wondering if that was the accommodation Luisa had referred to. I couldn't see the vineyard she had mentioned, and continued walking. Ten minutes later, desperately reciting the phrase in Italian to ask for directions under my breath, I came over a rise and spotted a roadside negozio—shop. Built out of rich ochre stained wood, the building was recently built, but breathed a time-honoured charm in its design. Huge wicker baskets lined the front ledges, full of bright red tomatoes, yellow, green and orange capsicums, deep purple eggplants, fragrant bundles of basil and rosemary, and a variety of fruits. Shelves under an awning in front of the main store displayed bottles of wine and olive oil. The leaves of a grape vine wound decoratively around the awning. Clutching a bag of fresh produce and a bottle of olive oil, a customer climbed back into their car as

I approached, waving to the providore behind the counter as they pulled away.

Vittorio, with sparkling blue eyes and a warm handshake greeted me first. With silver hair, he looked to be in his mid-forties. Cinzia, with shoulder length brown hair and a bright but determined smile, emerged from inside the shop to meet me.

"Io... sono... Jacqueline," I gasped out to the owner of Orti di Mare, breathless from the last hill I had staggered up. The warmth in their faces briefly eased my fears about communication. Vittorio with a musical northern accent, asked me some questions I couldn't quite follow.

"Si, si. Tutto bene"—*everything good*—I nodded with as much confidence as I could muster, assuming he was asking about my trip over.

"NIIIIICOL-EH!!! Vieni qui!" Cinzia hollered over her shoulder.

From behind the wooden building, a fellow English-speaking farm volunteer emerged.

"Hiya," Nicole smiled as she grabbed my smaller bag, "I'll show you where you can stay". Despite my intention to embrace my new language through necessity, I was relieved to find another English speaker.

"So... there are two options," the young Nicaraguan American with dark curly hair and deep brown skin drawled in her light Californian accent. "Luisa who left last week, was living in the roulotte beside the vineyard. And you can stay there. But... Well... it's kind of far from the bathroom."

"*Roulotte?*" I asked, "Is caravan?"

"Yep," she confirmed with a nod. "And the other option is... this way..." she nudged me to cross to the other side of the road, "you can stay in the bigger roulotte with me."

Vineyards, olive groves and vegetable fields sprawled out on both sides of the road. We stepped on to the verge as a car drove past, before we turned down an unsealed driveway running past some garden sheds. A small wood cabin sat on a rise to the right looking over fruit trees lining the dirt path as we approached the large old roulotte. Resting under a tin shed with low hanging pine trees wrapped around it, there was a tarpaulin annex erected to the left of the van which sheltered a sink plumbed into a rustic wooden bench. Faded plastic tables and chairs sat under the pine trees outside the door. I climbed into the roulotte behind Nicole. Yellowing lace curtains hung at the windows, covering ragged net fly screens. There were two single beds at one end, scattered with Nicole's belongings including a small guitar. At the other end was a small cupboard and a long curtain partially covering bunk beds.

"You can sleep there if you want," she casually offered.

It was old but comfortable. I nodded gratefully, but my focus remained on the serenity of the caravan in the vineyard that Luisa had spoken of. We walked back outside.

"The toilets are over here." Twin green sheds—male and female—were partially secluded behind a green mesh screen tautly strapped between two pine trees. I cringed at the thought of having a call of nature in the middle of the night. I had become accustomed to four and five-star hotels and guest passes into the Qantas Club when travelling for work. Staying in a caravan had sounded fun. But an outhouse? I felt slight heart palpitations as I considered what I had signed up for. Behind the roulotte, she showed me where there was a basin and mirror attached to a tree stump, with a tap plumbed in somewhere nearby for running water.

"You have to see the shower," Nicole said as she walked towards a small building behind the roulotte, "It's really cool". We didn't enter the building, instead stopping beside it. On a loosely hinged entrance to a cubicle made of thin strips of bamboo, was a simple sign:

Doccia

I tried not to look aghast as she pulled the bamboo gate open. Up against the small peach coloured building, fragrant with fronds of rosemary peeping through the cracks and the silvery elegance of an overhanging olive tree, the exterior bamboo screen was lined with blue tarpaulin surrounding la doccia—*the shower*. Hints of well-established luscious green moss brought life to the interior tarpaulin and plastic drainage board under the shower head. A dirty mirror with bright flowers painted around the edge of the glass was attached to the wall of the building, which provided the one stable wall. There were some simple bamboo shelves—home to a dried-up cake of soap—providing a place for toiletries. An unfixed pavement of cracked terracotta tiles gave a spot to stand on while drying off. A small metal rack surrounded by a few tall weeds offered a dry space to hang towels or clothes on.

And far above, the bright blue sky. Apprehensions about my rustic accommodation options peaked. "Wow," was all I could say as I started to laugh.

Nicole smiled. "You get used to it."

We returned past the fruit trees and crossed the road again, entering a large vegetable field. Nicole pointed out the large yellow-washed house on the left of the field where Vittorio and Cinzia lived. Crossing through long rows of tomato plants, we skirted the edge of a vineyard and past a dry creek bed before reaching the roulotte Luisa had spoken of. It sat overlooking a field covered in tall weeds, the vineyard just beyond, was barely visible.

The idyllic image I had in my head of Luisa *'sleeping in a little caravan in the vineyard, lonely but very nice and pleasant'* vanished. Overwhelmed by the adequate but rudimentary facilities and feeling increasingly nervous about my inability to verbally express any needs or questions I may have to Vittorio and Cinzia, I decided to bunk in with Nicole. A brief look of disappointment crossed her face at the thought of a roomie, but she nodded in understanding when I suggested that walking five minutes across the fields and then a road to get to the bathroom wasn't so appealing at night.

I began unpacking into the small cupboard beside the bunk beds, as the strains of The Fugees singing Bob Marley classic *No Woman No Cry* drifted through the window over the gentle hum of nearby conversations. I peered out of the back window to see who was around. I couldn't see anyone through the broken fly screens. The voices must have been coming from the other side.

I stepped outside. Nicole, standing with a book in one hand and a hose in the other, was completely absorbed in what she was reading as she watered the fruit trees. A small arbour with a robust grape vine draping over it lay across the path from the shower. A washing line ran along the front, where several towels and swim wear hung haphazardly under the overhanging leaves.

"Hola!" a woman in her mid-thirties emerged from the bamboo shower cubicle, a big pink towel wrapped around her body, another twirling her wet hair up onto her head.

"You are from Austraaaalia!" she crooned, clasping her towel with her left hand, reaching out her right to greet me. "I would love to go to Australia!" she exclaimed in a musical accent. "I am from Brazil. I have many friends in Australia."

She was leaving the farm tomorrow along with most of the remaining summer team who had been helping both with the farm work and running activities like yoga classes for guests staying in the area. The last one remaining to do further work for Vittorio was Alessandro. He emerged at the sound of voices from the quaint wood cabin on a rise behind the fruit trees. With shaggy grey hair and salt and pepper stubble on his chin, his soft brown eyes were hidden behind silver, oval shaped glasses. He had a serious yet kind demeanour. With his few words of English, he quickly made me feel welcome.

"Andiamooooh!" Cinzia's voice bellowed across the fields alerting us for dinner. Nicole and I made our way across the road and fields to a small building housing a kitchen behind the main house. Cinzia was serving out bowls of pasta with a fresh tomato sauce as we arrived. Vittorio was putting out baskets of bread on two long trestle tables sitting under a shade cloth in front of the yellow washed farmhouse.

"You can help yourself from this kitchen," Nicole explained. "We tell Cinzia if we need any other ingredients."

The chatter was fast over dinner. Nicole, a native Spanish speaker, had studied Italian at university. She told me that she didn't get everything that was said, but she got by.

I could tell Cinzia was a tough lady, but fun and friendly. Someone I might create a great rapport with quite quickly... if we were speaking in the same language. She spoke so rapidly she didn't appear to take a breath. I concentrated as hard as I could, trying to pick up on anything I could from the conversation.

After two weeks using my basic French in Nice, speaking English with Alexis and then having the obliging Florentines speak my native tongue with me again, my hard work in Siena seemed wasted.

A few questions were thrown my way but along with tiredness from the day of travel, my comprehension seemed to be at its lowest ebb in weeks. Nicole jumped in and translated as best she could. Vittorio periodically looked up from under his long eyelashes, throwing reassuring smiles and nods my way, I fought the now familiar sense of panic and frustration when I couldn't follow a conversation.

Usually religious with my morning shower, followed by a rigorous hair and make-up routine that was part of everyday corporate life, I started the next day with a simple splash of water on my face, applied sunscreen, and platted my slightly greasy hair to one side before pulling a hat on. I paused to look in the mirror. I almost didn't recognise the woman staring back at me. It had been so long since I had looked at myself without a trace of make-up. I paused for a moment suddenly feeling exposed. Standing barefaced in front of the mirror, I tried to accept what I saw—bags under my eyes and blotchy, uneven skin. This was me. *There is no one here to impress. What does it matter?* I thought. Pushing my Prada sunglasses on to hide my bare face, I joined Nicole in the kitchen for breakfast.

"You'll meet Marco today," Nicole waved her cereal spoon towards the fields. "He works here. He's kind of fifty or something and super cool. He'll be here soon."

The image I had in my mind of the peasant Luisa had mentioned I would be working with in the vegetable garden, was that of an elderly woman from eastern Europe with crinkly eyes and craggy skin. She would be wearing a long skirt with a dirty hem that had been dragged through the fields, an apron, an old blouse and colourful head scarf knotted at her neck. I envisioned joining her in the fields with our baskets, labouring together in the Mediterranean sun. I had been keeping an eye out for a suitable headscarf to buy and wear for the task so-as-to look the part.

On mention of Marco, my expectation changed to a wizened, older Italian man, in baggy brown pants with braces over his collared work shirt, a còppola on his head, and many a story to regale me with of life on the land as we worked.

A silver van pulled up with the farm's logo on the side at nine o'clock. A six foot-something, deeply tanned, broad-shouldered man, sporting wavy brown hair to his collar bone stepped out of the van.

"Ciao, Marco!" Nicole waved as we walked over to meet him. With a warm greeting, Marco commenced with an onslaught of questions—translated by Nicole—about how and why an Australian had ended up here. He had deep brown eyes that crinkled amidst deep laugh lines as he chatted jovially with us while busy pulling equipment out of the shed for the day's projects.

Nicole handed me two huge baskets from the small shed next

to the roadway lying between our abode and the vegetable field. Marco vanished with Vittorio, while we set to work picking salad tomatoes, roma tomatoes, cherry tomatoes, capsicum, eggplant and basil. Nicole went to fetch a few bunches of grapes from the small vineyard near the house. Chilli peppers and lettuces were also coming along nicely, but she instructed me to leave them because they had harvested enough for the store yesterday.

"Put the imperfect ones in here," Nicole pointed to one of the baskets on the ground nearby. The vegetables that weren't flawless enough for selling, we took to the kitchen for use in our own dinners.

At Vittorio's instruction we grabbed two buckets each for our next job. We were to fill them up from a tap near the kitchen and water the fruit trees that bordered the vegetable fields. They hadn't had rain for a while, and this was the only other way they could be watered. Twenty-six trips later when my wrists were nearly touching the ground from lugging my two water laden buckets to the trees the furthest away, I felt myself wilting. The thought of doing manual labour this intense everyday was dire. Years of going to the gym and boot camps hadn't even prepared me for this level of physical work.

Next, we were armed with wheelbarrows and shovels from the shed. Vittorio walked with us ten minutes up and over the rise near the negozio and down through some olive groves. He stopped at an old horse manure heap. They had kept a rare breed of Spanish horses previously at the farm and though the horses were now gone, the last of their stockpile of manure remained, ready to be distributed. Loading our wheelbarrows, we began carting the decomposing poo back through the grove of olive trees, scattering the contents across a field of asparagus shoots to enrich the soil.

Initial enthusiasm again saw us speeding up and down the slight hill, but by the third and fourth wheelbarrow loads, our energy and enthusiasm waned as our weary arms began to give out.

Cinzia stayed up in the negozio and there was no sign of Vittorio at lunchtime. Rummaging through the fridge, Nicole and I made a pasta sauce with tomatoes, zucchini, onion and garlic.

In the afternoon, it was my turn to water the hose-accessible fruit trees, rosemary bushes and caper berry plants growing out of terraced brick walls around the campsite. I tried to copy Nicole's aesthetic of reading a book at the same time but resigned myself to one task at a time as the gentle breeze blew the water towards my pages.

With our work done for the day, I slipped into my swimmers. I wandered down the side of the yellow house, down a dirt road taking me past the overrun vineyard, and onto a sandy path down to a clean sandy beach. Barely five-hundred-metres from the farm, two lush green headlands curved around either side of the bay of Lacona. The odd building or roulotte appeared between the covering of dark green trees. In the western corner of the bay, the beautiful outline of mountains swept down from the centre of the island into a valley leading down to the beach.

As I drifted out into the azure water and gazed at the stunning scenery encircling me in the hazy late afternoon light, despite the beauty of my surrounds, my thoughts again turned to home. Since leaving Nice on Tuesday, powering through the two and a half days in Florence, and then reaching Elba by Friday, it had been an intense week of travel and change. I had committed to two weeks living in a *roulotte*, with an outdoor toilet without a light that worked and the corners full of spiders. Despite my expectation of swanning around in a peasant-like headscarf, demurely collecting vegetables in a basket, it seemed we faced some hefty farm work, and my brain was already hurting from trying to comprehend and communicate directly with my hosts. As well as the independence that comes with being able to ask for information when you need something, my inability to chat with the people I was meeting to get to know them and hear their stories, was sending me mad with frustration.

My mind buzzed furiously as I wondered how I could have thought this would be a good idea, wondering what I was really going to achieve and whether I really had the motivation to work my way across the country this way. Floating in the stillness of the Tyrrhenian sea, unfettered by the tug and pull of tides and currents inherent with the vigour of the Pacific Ocean I had grown up with, I gave in instead to the push and pull of my emotions.

Heading back to the campsite, I knew I would have to brave the *doccia*. Carefully hooking the slim rope over the corner pole to hold the gate closed, I tried not to drop my clean clothes on the wet ground. I closed my eyes to the green slimy walls and let the warm water run over me, inhaling the fragrance of the rosemary fronds waving above.

Pushing the water out of my eyes I suppressed a scream as I looked down. A toad was lolloping out from under the draining board, journeying over to a corner, a safe distance away from me. I remained frozen to the spot, watching as he angled himself around with amphibious ease, then sat down and looked me right in the eye. It seemed we both had our doubts about sharing the space. With poisonous Queensland cane toads on my mind, I decided after studying him that he might actually be a frog and might not be so bad. I quickly finished my shower, trying not to feel self-conscious under the gaze of my bathroom buddy. Dressing quickly, I fled back to the *roulotte* to find out if Nicole was aware of his presence.

Alessandro joined us for dinner that night. He and Marco had spent the day working in a separate part of the farm and we had seen little of them except when Marco had passed by briefly, checking to see how we were going with the manure distribution. He had a young boy with him who he introduced as his twelve-year-old son, Simone.

With a fifth person at dinner, Nicole was quieter. Vittorio and Alessandro both spoke more slowly than Cinzia, making it easier for me to follow the parts of the conversation they shared. I felt myself relax slightly. There were some laughs, which are always good for the soul, even if you aren't certain what you are all laughing about. A raucous conversation about relationships erupted at one point. Alessandro seemed to be questioning Vittorio and Cinzia about when they were going to get married.

They were a curious couple. They seemed like great mates, but I wasn't sensing a great deal of affection or intimacy between them. I couldn't see how the relationship worked with two quite strong personalities—Cinzia verbose and confident, Vittorio with a gentle demeanour, yet a strong determination about him.

Alessandro and I finished the washing up, while Nicole went to grab the little guitar she was travelling with. The five of us wandered down to the beach together. A light breeze swept around the group as we sat on the sand under a starry, yet moonless sky. Nicole opened a book of Italian songs she was learning. I didn't recognise the first few bars she strummed but the others immediately began humming along, then broke into an enthusiastic rendition of the 1958 Italian Eurovision hit 'Volare'.

The music and camaraderie broke through my travel weariness. On an empty beach on a small Mediterranean island floating between Italy and Corsica, I was saturated with a fresh sense of joy as I sat ensconced between sand and stars.

10

Sundays were a day of rest from farm work. Nicole took off after breakfast, pedalling away on a bike borrowed from someone she met at the last beach festa of the summer held a few nights earlier.

Writing my original enquiry to the farm with the help of a translation website, I had explained that I had been at a language school. As we prepared for bed on Saturday night Nicole had told me that as a result, Vittorio and Cinzia had expected I would be more fluent in Italian.

Determined to resolve my linguistic challenges rather than be swallowed by them, I started my day of rest with dictionaries and textbooks piled beside me on the plastic table in the grove of pine trees. With my increased knowledge of grammar, I had become more aware of the flaws in everything I was saying. And with that my confidence to speak had decreased.

"Start with simple sentences," Nicole suggested to me from her own language learning experiences, "A subject and a verb. Add in an object when you are ready."

Verbs and conjugating them, was my key challenge. I began my study with a focus on verbs.

The serenity of the pine grove became a distraction. I abandoned study to explore the local area. A small market selling cheap trinkets was set up on a quiet side road, which led down to a beachfront gelato bar. In the small gift shop beside the gelataria, I browsed the overpriced sunscreen, snorkelling gear and postcards with images that looked like they may have been taken in the 1970's. I selected a few and grabbed a tube of sunscreen.

Cinzia remained in the negozio during the day. I hadn't seen Vittorio or Alessandro all morning. Luisa had mentioned in her email that it was quite lonely. I reminded myself that this was a non-workday and things would pick up again tomorrow. I made a quick lunch then with the roulotte to myself, I made the most of the opportunity to take an extended siesta to ensure I had energy reserves for the week of labour ahead.

I slipped back down to the beach at sunset, gliding into the tepid water of the tranquil bay. As the sun set over the mountains in the west, it cast soft light on to the clear emerald sea that glistened around me. Two young brothers played in the shallows further along the sand but otherwise the bay was mine.

I was floating on my back watching the hazy light cascade over the mountains when Nicole splashed out to join me. She had ridden her bike across the island to Portoferraio to go to the shops, then spent the afternoon at another nearby bay she found on the way back. I was glad of company after a day on my own.

At twenty-three, Nicole was taking time out after finishing a degree in cinematography and film production. She was the same age as I had been when I was newly married and preparing to settle down to a future driven by my husband's aspirations. I wondered how different my life might have been had I stayed longer in England when I visited my extended family at twenty-one—what sort of path might my life have taken had I followed the itch of curiosity that travel had awoken in me, or even returned to university to study journalism instead of placing my vocational interests on hold for love.

The next morning, we were set to work weeding the children's playground up behind the negozio. I wondered when it had last rained. The ground was hard and dry, determined to retain its hold on the roots of the unwanted giant weeds. I forced the spade into the ground to loosen up the tall intruders by their roots, while Nicole clenched the thin branches of the tall, invasive plants with both hands. Throwing our body weight into it we vigorously pushed and pulled with all our might until the determined plants were released from the restraints of the earth.

Nicole headed to the kitchen to create a vegetable sauce to stir through the black beans she had left simmering for the morning. I followed with a barrowload of weeds to deposit in the nearby chicken and rabbit pe, I was pausing to dust the dirt off my arms and legs as Vittorio and Alessandro joined us in the kitchen.

We set out the food on the tables and sat down for lunch. Alessandro's attempts to engage with me by intercepting the conversation with English gave me courage to attempt to respond in Italian where I could.

Remembering my few phrases from Siena about working in calcio, I told them about my work in Australia. To my amusement, Vittorio and Alessandro confessed to not being proper Italians, with little personal interest in football.

Nicole was telling a story about a farm she had been working on in northern Italy in the Piedmont region and the local boys who had been chasing her.

"Le ragazze Australiane e Inglese," I started slowly as I tried to find the words to contribute something to the conversation, "sono vogliono un marito Italiano." *The Australian and English girls want an Italian husband.*

Raising their eyebrows at my candour, Vittorio and Alessandro burst out laughing.

I blushed, quickly denying, "Ma non io!" I knew my all too quick denial had inevitably revealed my own movie and memoir inspired hope of finding a life-lasting romance from this trip and gave in to the truth.

"Okay—maybe me also," I laughed.

Stepping into the doccia under the branches of the olive tree after another swim that evening, the frog-toad again emerged from under the drainage board as water poured through the gaps and disturbed his hiding place. I kept an eye on him as I rinsed my hair. He kept an eye on me in return from his safe spot across the cubicle.

A strong breeze had built up during the afternoon. The risqué bamboo door waved gently on its hinges. I kept my other eye on its erratic movement. A huge gust of wind pulled the light gate open. With a loud laugh and a deft hand, Alessandro pushed the door firmly closed as he passed from the back of the campsite. The angle he had approached from and his quick response seemed to have saved me from a naked reveal, but I couldn't be sure. Mortified, I quickly dried off and threw my towel around the top pole of the gate to support the hinge holding it closed while I raced to get dressed.

Cinzia had headed out with some girlfriends for the evening, so

Nicole and I offered to start dinner. I followed her lead as we prepared a tomato salad and some sautéed zucchini and rice. Vittorio broke apart a roasted chicken Cinzia had left for us in the fridge, then pulled out a new round loaf of homemade bread and opened a bottle of wine. Weary from the work of the day, I struggled to contribute as much to tonight's conversations. I sat quietly putting my effort into following the threads of some of the discussion. With words used in context, I was getting better at distinguishing meanings and following grammatical construction of the sentences.

I had avoided eye contact with Alessandro throughout dinner. We stood up at the same time to clear the plates. He gave me a cheeky grin as we walked to the kitchen to begin washing up.

"You ahh... you have to be careful with that shower door."

I started to laugh, grateful that he had broken the ice.

We woke with a start just after five the following morning as a deafening thunderclap cracked through the air outside. Dark clouds had begun to loom as the sun set the night before, but the anticipated temporale had done little but threaten. Until now.

Another role of thunder shook the roulotte. As the heavens opened, and the water cascaded down on the roof it felt like we were parked under a waterfall. I sat up in my bunk to peer through the small window at the darkened world outside.

More than two hours passed as we waited for it to pass. As the light began to increase, Nicole and I squeezed into the doorway together to peer out and see what the effect had been. The earth was forged with mini mud gullies from the rush of water, with rivulets still running through as the rain began to let up. The ground had been so dry it was struggling to absorb the torrent that had come down. I paddled over to the tin sheds to the toilet, storm clouds continuing to circle above. Retrieving my soaked and only towel from the clothesline under the grape vines on the way back, it proved of little use except as a giant washcloth to wipe off the twigs and mud. I climbed back into my sleeping bag in the unusual darkness contemplating what work we would be able to do after a downpour like that.

Nicole had fallen back to sleep and I finally decided to slip out to get breakfast. There was no sign of Vittorio, Alessandro or Marco preparing to start the day's activities. The negozio was closed. I returned to the dim light of the roulotte. There was no longer any power running to the van. The farm WIFI wasn't connecting into my laptop so I couldn't use the time to check emails.

The only book in English with me was Thomas More's 'Utopia'. I had owned the small book since my seventeenth birthday after ambitiously asking mum to buy the classic for me along with 'War and Peace'. I had never actually read it, but it was light enough to carry while travelling, so I had brought it with me. Ensconced on a Utopian island of my own, I was enveloped in the ideas and concepts of Moore's seminal work but somewhat overwhelmed as I struggled to absorb them, re-reading the same page for the fourth… fifth … sixth time.

Nicole and I read and chatted through the morning, before braving a walk down to the beach early afternoon during a break in the ongoing light rainfall. Windsurfers were out in force. The serene, smooth bay of the day before was choppy, generating one and two-foot waves that crashed quietly onto the shoreline. Making the most of the uneven seas, the board riders leapt the swells with glee.

Another threatening storm was brewing by night fall. We prepared ourselves an early dinner in the absence of Vittorio or Cinzia, keen to get back to the roulotte before more rain came.

As we washed up, I asked Nicole about some of the details of the conversations I had attempted to follow since my arrival, to see whether my comprehension was improving.

"On Saturday night, the conversation was about relationships, right?" I asked.

"Correct," she agreed.

"And Alessandro was hassling Vittorio and Cinzia about when they would get married?"

"Vittorio and Cinzia?" Nicole burst out laughing, "They're business partners. Cinzia has a husband on the mainland who visited last week. She only works here in the peak months."

My eyes widened as Nicole continued. "Vittorio might have a girlfriend. Luisa told me that but I'm not really sure. Maybe in Germany. I've never seen her since I've been here."

Vittorio. Wait! What? Single? HAS a girlfriend! I chided myself. *Maybe. Only maybe. And no-one has seen her recently...*

I grabbed another pan to scrub, trying not to give away where my mind had drifted to… *Vittorio's lilting chatter in his musical accent, that deep solid laugh, the long lashes that framed eyes that sparkled when he lifted his mouth into a gentle smile…*

"We thought maybe she was just a friend…" Nicole looked at me oddly her voice trailing off. I began scrubbing the pan more furiously, feeling my ears go hot as I remembered revealing the day before that I was one of those Australian women in town looking for an Italian husband. Assuming he was married I hadn't considered him a romantic prospect. But now…

The second storm rumbled away quietly through the night, the clouds again holding their bounty until dawn the following morning. As fierce as the day before, branches smacked against the roof and walls of the roulotte as we cowered nervously in our sleeping bags. We pulled the door of the roulotte open again at 7.30am. Torrents were pouring under the van and over to the toilet sheds. The earth soaked from the day before refused to absorb any more water.

"I hope this van has the capacity to become an ark," I murmured as we watched the rain continuing to come down.

When the rain began to ease mid-morning, I convinced Nicole that we should start work after slipping our way across the muddy fields to find breakfast. There was no sign of Vittorio or Marco again, but I needed to move. I couldn't face another day cooped up in the roulotte with the profundity of Thomas More.

We made our way into a small vegetable field which we had been tasked with weeding before the storms had stopped activity. In comparison to the fight on our hands in the children's playground three days earlier, the giant weeds now slid out of the soaked ground as Nicole and I slid with them. We abandoned ourselves to the joy of bathing in mud as it crept up our arms and legs.

We were nearly done when the rain started again. Initially ignoring the light drizzle, within minutes it became a downpour. Sprinting back to the van, we stood on the steps and wiped the mud off with our soaked towels.

The rain stopped as quickly as it started. I left Nicole reading a book of short stories in Italian that I had picked up in Siena, and returned to try and clear the last furrow of weeds. The rain returned. I ignored it momentarily then gave in, running back across the field to shelter. Watching it coming down through the small window of the roulotte, rivers of fresh mud began to rush past.

We dashed to the kitchen at lunchtime. Bursting through the doors, drenched despite the protection of our umbrellas, we found Vittorio inside. The space was intimate with three people squeezed around the bench in the middle of the small room with the doors closed.

I prepared a tomato salad and sliced up some fresh bread, Nicole warmed up some leftover beans and Vittorio set to work sautéeing up some zucchinis with garlic and olive oil.

Squeezed around the kitchen bench on camp chairs, we ate shoulder-to-shoulder. I tried to forget that I hadn't showered for two days. No make-up, greasy, unwashed hair, spattered in mud and feeling a little smelly, I tried to relax as I felt a crush on the possibly single Vittorio take hold. A sudden shyness came over me as I glanced up at him over the table. He caught my eye and his face broke into a gentle smile, before we both dropped out eyes back to our plates.

"Il temporale è normale per Settembre?" I hesitantly assembled a question about how normal these sorts of storms were for this time of year. Vittorio looked at me, seemingly impressed I had used a whole question, but responding with a despairing shake of his head. A little rain was expected but the storms had been extreme, he told us. Late summer crops across the island farms would be affected by the excessive downpour.

The clouds started to clear as we ate. As we cleaned up, we threw open the doors relieved to see the sunshine beaming strongly over the mountains again.

Nicole and I trekked down the sandy path to the beach. Para surfers and kite surfers were making the most of the storm surge providing tumultuous swells for them to play in. The water was full of seaweed and dirt, churned up by the storms. The crystal-clear sea I had floated in on the weekend gone. We leapt out into the waves of the murky surge to soak the mud and dirt off, racing each other as we body surfed the small waves into shore.

I picked seaweed out of my hair as we sat on the beach drying out in the sun. I had rinsed out my sodden, muddy towel and left it drying in the increasingly strong afternoon sun before we had left. After two and a half days of sloshing through mud having little way of getting or staying clean, a shower in the slimy green doccia, with a dry towel on hand would be a welcome luxury on return to the campsite.

After roughing it through the days of storms, I gave myself leave to add a little foundation around the eyes, a touch of lip gloss and hint of eyeliner and mascara after my swim that afternoon.

I took a late afternoon walk up to the Chiesa della Madonna della Neve—Church of the Madonna of the Snow. It was a tiny little building up on the hill behind the farm. The whitewashed building was the sole significant landmark visible amidst the rolling woods and fields.

I walked back past Alessandro and Marco as they packed up their tools. They had been working near the negozio in the afternoon. Alessandro paused to ask me if I would be at dinner. Vittorio apparently had some guests staying who would be there.

Marco threw a curious glance in our direction while he continued what he was doing. As I pushed my sunglasses back and on to the top of my head, he glanced over again with a look of recognition. I suppressed a laugh at the startled look on his face. With fresh clothes and a touch of make-up it seemed I was almost unrecognisable in comparison to my first few days.

As I continued walking up the road towards the far end of the beach, Marco came past in the van.

"Vuoi un passaggio da qualche parte?" he stopped to ask if I needed a lift.

"Grazie ma no," I smiled. "Prendo una passegiata."—*I'll walk*. His face broke into a warm smile as he nodded, before driving away for the evening.

At dinner, we were introduced to the friends of Vittorio. A woman who he had met at University, her sister and their husbands. The woman he had studied with was a biologist, as was her husband, a Peruvian American. They chattered to me in English about their work in immunology in their home of Denver, Colorado. They were here on holidays following a work conference in Siena. I told them about my time there and il Palio. The chatter continued in a mixture of Italian and English, with the communal conversation turning to me as the English speakers asked more about my trip so far, and how I came to be on Elba.

Vittorio nodded and smiled as I spoke in English, in the same way I often did when I was pretending I could follow the conversation. He seemed glad I was being drawn into the group and threw the occasional question to his friends when he needed something translated.

As the conversation returned to Italian and my concentration levels flagged, I sat quietly contemplating Vittorio. I wondered if the developing emotions I felt towards him, were mainly accentuated by the fine aspect of his beautiful farm, five-hundred-metres from the sea on a small Mediterranean island off Italy. This was the happy ending I was after, right? Colin Firth had managed to fall in love with the Portuguese girl in 'Love Actually' without sharing a language. I was sure we could make it work. It would make a marvellous email back to the urban family.

'... *No, I didn't buy a Tuscan Villa, or fall for a fellow traveller... I found myself a vegetable farmer... on an island in the Mediterranean... We don't speak the same language... But, it's love... Do come and visit...*"

"Hai dormire bene?"—*did you sleep well?* I asked Vittorio the next morning when he joined me in the kitchen for breakfast. I dropped my eyes back to my cereal bowl, pleased with myself for again articulating a whole sentence.

"Si, si. E tu?" he asked.

I looked up into his eyes, "Bene... Grazie..."

He threw me a gentle smile as he left. My heart beat a little faster.

Nicole chased me back across the field when I went to start the morning vegetable harvest. The fields were too wet to walk in. She told me we were to do something over by the kitchen instead.

Vittorio presented us with piles of baskets and clean tea towels, oil, jugs of water, and packets of organic flour. He placed a giant wooden board on the top of the outdoor table to work on and brought out the natural yeast he had prepared the night before.

We tipped the packets of flour in a circle on the board as instructed. He spread a little of the flour in the middle, poured the yeast into the centre of the well, then began to methodically gather the flour into the yeast. Nicole and I were tasked with pouring a little water into the large well of flour as he continued to draw everything together into a giant ball of dough.

Vittorio divided it into ten small sections, handing us each a smaller ball to begin kneading. New to bread making, I struggled to get the technique right. Vittorio regularly paused work on his own loaves to lean over and assist me. I felt myself flush at his proximity, as well as a little embarrassment that I seemed to be unable to knead bread effectively. We set the kneaded balls of dough into round baskets and wrapped a clean tea towel around each. Then we placed them in the warmth of the sun on a bench with a blanket draped over them to contain the heat, and left the loaves to rise.

Heading to the campsite for tourists, that was also part of the farm, Vittorio handed us a can of sky-blue paint and paint brush each. The fading bright yellow paint of the railings of the sun deck above the bathrooms needed a refresh.

Nicole and I chatted idly as we worked, sinking into comfortable stretches of silence. I paused mid brush stroke half an hour in. I gazed across the island landscape. The campsite for guests was perfectly positioned with views across two different bays. Vineyards rolled down the hillside away from the farm and towards the beach which arced gently around to the tree covered headland that separated the bays of Norsi and Lacona. Monte Christo, forty kilometres to the south was a mere outline on the hazy horizon today.

FFA had moved into new offices on the twenty-second floor of a building on the corner of Oxford Street, six months before I left Sydney. It had been quite the upgrade. Views of Hyde Park running down to the Harbour lay outside the windows on the north side of our floor. A swathe of sailboats and other water craft could often be seen moving about in the distance. To the south, and from the windows near my desk, we had views across Central station, out toward Sydney airport and Botany Bay.

Up on the sundeck—in the fresh air, away from a computer, technology, fluorescent lights, and time constraints—I was more than content with this new workspace. I inhaled deeply as I gazed out to sea. My head began to spin. The fumes from the paint tin had broken into my reverie.

Amid the bread baking exercise, Nicole had quietly whipped up a pear pie. She headed off to check if it was time to put it in the wood-fired oven that Vittorio had gone to fire up in preparation for the bread.

I continued painting on my own. I had survived one week in the old roulotte, three days of torrential rain, minimal showering and rudimentary toilets. And to my delight, I was now covered in dabs of blue paint. I was looking forward to some indoor facilities in Napoli where I was planning to go next, but for now the simplicity of life on the farm was suiting me well.

11

Waking up to the sound of more rain on Saturday morning filled me with dismay. But it wasn't storms that covered the skies this time and the rain eased by mid-morning. I wandered to the campground to find Vittorio and Alessandro. It was the first time I had attempted to get instructions from Vittorio without Nicole on-hand to assist with translation. She had embraced the chance to have another sleep-in on hearing the rain and was yet to surface. I seized the opportunity to attempt a conversation with Vittorio one-on-one. Between my stuttered Italian and Vittorio's few words of English, we came up with a plan for the morning.

    I made my way down to the negozio to continue the weeding we had started in the children's playground. The roots slid out of the ground this time. I quickly created piles of fodder for the rabbits and chickens. Cinzia opened the negozio in time for late morning trade. Classical music gently filtered through small speakers attached to the awning. Locals and tourists began pulling in to make their purchases, sitting down for a cool drink, chattering in Italian and German. Children ran past to play on the climbing gym in the garden as I worked. I was getting quite nifty with the hoe, and despite the effort I was throwing into the task, I relished being part of the fabric of the atmospheric morning which unfolded out of the morning clouds.

Loading up the wheelbarrows, I took the feed down the hill to the rabbit and chicken pen. Marco and Alessandro leant on the fence watching as I threw the weeds over to the rambunctious rabbits who bounded past the chickens to get first dibs on morning tea. They quickly chewed their fill, before using the remainder as cushioning to nestle up in. The chickens then quietly took their turn, pecking around the edges as the rabbits dozed off into a contented post meal slumber. It was so relaxing watching the animals eat, interact and sleep in the midday sun.

Leaning on the fence next to me, Marco asked, "Piace mangiarli?"

I smiled and nodded briefly thinking he had asked if I liked the rabbits. Then quickly recoiled.

"No no! Sono troppo carini!" *they are too cute!* I exclaimed laughing. He had asked if I liked to eat rabbit.

With a laugh he smacked his lips together declaring them, "Buona".

He wandered over to some prickly pear bushes, pulling some fruit off. Breaking it open he offered us half of one each. I had never tried to eat a prickly pear. I followed the lead of the others as we spat seeds out for the chickens to finish off.

Nicole had left the farm to run some errands and I was standing at the fridge trying to decide on options for my lunch when Vittorio wandered in. Together we put together a lunch of tomato salad, a loaf of the fresh bread, and some of Nicole's delicious pear pie left over from the day before. We sat in comfortable silence, as I mulled over all the conversation topics I would have started if we spoke the same language. We broke the silence with some basic exchanges about weather and comments about the food, before we sank back into quiet companionship.

That afternoon Nicole and I sat at the outdoor table, tasked with cleaning bunches of grapes Vittorio had collected from the small run of vines in front of his house. We picked off the dead grapes and dry leaves to prepare them for presentation and sale in the negozio. Poking small sticks gently between the gaps in the fruit, we encouraged small spiders who had made their homes in the middle of the sweet bunches, to evacuate. Some were quite plain garden variety spiders, while others were distinctly beautiful, their golden backs shining in the setting sun.

We moved on to tackle a compost heap near the rabbit and chicken enclosure to finish the day. Loading up the wheelbarrow, we scattered it at the base of the fruit trees near the house.

On my way back down from the shed where I had dropped off our tools, a car pulled up on the roadway and started to reverse back towards me. Cars regularly stopped along this stretch. Sometimes locals looking for Vittorio, or tourists asking for directions. It was the first time someone had stopped while I was on my own.

Concentrating as hard as possible on what the man was asking, I thought he was after some directions, but I couldn't work out if he was looking for Orti di Mare or trying to work out how to get to the bay.

"Non parlo Italiano molto bene," I apologised as fast as I could. "Il negozio di Orti di Mare e qui,"—I pointed back up the hill towards the shop, "o la spiaggia di Lacona, vai avanti e poi sinistra," I indicated he go straight and turn left to get down to the beach. I did my best to advise him on both possible options, employing my increasing skill of emphatic hand gestures to indicate the directions in case I had the words wrong.

He nodded slowly. Another car was coming down the road and he prepared to move his vehicle forward. It turned into the drive of a nearby farm before reaching us. He reversed back slightly again.

"Sei Spagnola?" he asked.

"No, no. Sono Australiana," I responded, flattered and more than a little surprised that my accent could be mistaken for Spanish.

"Oh, so you speak English?" he asked.

"Si," I looked back at him quizzically.

In a combination of Italian and English he asked me if I had a boyfriend and how long I would be on the island for. He was from the Lacona Pizza Bar.

Well done me, I congratulated myself realising he hadn't been asking for directions at all.

"You are very beautiful. You should come and eat there," he told me.

"Grazie," I laughed taken aback and unsure how to respond.

I wasn't feeling particularly beautiful at that moment. Perhaps my *profumo di composto* had wafted over him, creating the magic that had drawn him in. Or was he just trying to drum up business? Another car came up behind him, this time wanting to get through. Providing directions to the pizzeria in English over his shoulder, he implored me to visit before he drove on.

I stared after his car before a movement nearby drew my eyes down to Vittorio, working in the vegetable garden below and hidden from view of the road, who had been quietly watching over the interaction. With a reassuring smile he said nothing, then dropped his head and went back to what he was doing. *We had just one week to fall madly in love or I would be off to the south and the opportunity would be lost.*

"Tu e Nicol-Eeh, dovreste venire alla casa per cena OK?" Cinzia appeared at the kitchen door early evening and invited Nicole and I to join them at the house for dinner. We slipped around the side of the house half an hour later to find Vittorio, Cinzia and the couple who had been renting part of the house from Vittorio and their young son, sitting at a table under a beautiful awning draped in a wisteria vine in full bloom. The fragrance drifted gently around us, mixing with the delicious smells coming from the kitchen as bowls of food were brought out. Nicole took a seat in the middle of the table. I took the spare seat next to Vittorio.

Spaghetti with pesto and a side of bread was served, followed by freshly barbecued meat with salad. I eyed the meat warily as it was served up, wondering if it was rabbit. It didn't seem too gamey on first taste, so I convinced myself it was more likely beef and unlikely from any animal I had recently looked in the eye.

The couple—who I had never really spoken to, except to share a greeting in passing—asked me a few questions. Answering their questions carefully, I managed to raise a smile and a laugh as I tried to sum up my communication difficulties, "Non ho sempre abbastanza parole,"—*I never have enough words*. I retreated quietly into my thoughts as the conversation continued in Italian.

Vittorio's hand rested on the table beside me. I glanced to the side to study it briefly. Tanned and smooth, it was a nice hand. I liked this hand. I could hold that hand. But what did I really know of this man. Very little. But I allowed myself again to indulge in the idea of falling in love with a nice Italian farmer on a Mediterranean island.

The table erupted into laughter. Emerging from my daydream, I wasn't sure what the conversation had been about, but broke into a big smile again pretending that I had understood the conversation.

Gelato and biscotti came out for dessert and the night wrapped up close to midnight with a shot of limoncello. New company had been enjoyable, but I was relieved to be freed from the exertion of focused listening and maintaining a mask of engagement in conversations I simply could not follow.

I raced off after lunch on Monday to catch the bus to Portoferraio. Now in the off-season, the buses only came by once an hour and I was relieved to see it running on time.

I found a Ristorante near the Medici fortress that had an internet cafe tucked down the side. My onward journey in a week's time was still unplanned other than my intention to head south. It had been more than seven days since I had been online. I was relishing the complete disconnect from the rest of the world without access to television, radio or internet, but I did need to confirm my accommodation in Napoli and check emails in case there was any important news from home.

A short man in his mid-forties with emerald green rimmed glasses pushed back into black spiky hair welcomed me enthusiastically, before taking me through the exorbitant charges.

He grasped my hand firmly and looked me directly in the eye as he introduced himself as Giovanni. Seeing the blue paint still spattered on my arms from our work in the campsite a few days earlier, he asked if I was working on the island. I explained I was volunteering on a farm.

"Bene, bene," he said distractedly. "Mi faccia sapere se Lei ha bisogno qualcosa,"—he told me to let him know if I needed anything.

I smiled weakly, trying to diplomatically withdraw my hand from his determined grip, uncomfortable with the way he held on to it longer than necessary.

Setting me up on a computer in a room beside the bar, he chattered away with pace in Italian despite my protest that, 'Non parlo Italiano molto bene' to try and slow him down.

I emailed a hostel in Naples to make a booking, before contacting a few farms further south in the Amalfi coast area to see if they would welcome me in late October. After uploading some photos to Facebook, I responded to emails from home. Two hours and twenty minutes later, I approached the counter to let Giovanni know I was finished. He pushed his glasses back into his hair and came out from behind the rear counter. He took my hand again and locked eyes firmly with me. Even though I had gone over the two hours booked, he told me, he would give me the extra time for free. Given the exorbitant price I had already paid for the two hours, I didn't feel anything had been free. But, I would have preferred to pay extra than have him think he was doing me any favours. I thanked him as I tried to gently withdraw my hand from his. Flashbacks to Nek in Siena flooded back.

He retained his grip and insisted on kissing me goodbye on both cheeks. Then in an instant tried to shift to my lips. A waiters' station blocked us from view of the customers out the front. Torn between outrage and amusement at his brazen behaviour, I again tried to excuse myself politely. My ire rose as he tried to pull me around a corner, "Lei capisce quello che io voglio? Hai capisco?"

There is no doubt that I understand what you want, I thought as I desperately tried to pull away. Italian men are known for their charm, but like the circumstance of Nek, this was not charm. With one hand he pulled at my hip, then with the other hand in his grasp he tried to press it against the front of his pants to ensure I understood what he wanted. Blind fury kicked in as I pulled my hand away in disgust.

A customer called for attention out front.

"UN MOMENTO," Giovanni yelled out in irritation as he kept a tight grip on the wrist he hadn't let go off. He tried to kiss me again. The customer provided enough distraction for me to wrestle out of his grip and take a step away.

"Aspetti qui," he told me to wait, as he headed to the counter.

WAIT! I thought. *Wait for what???* Furious to find myself again in a situation where I felt put upon, I pushed past the waiter's station and burst out under the front awning of the restaurant. Some of the local men sitting in the front cafe since I arrived sat there laughing. They clearly knew his form. The fact I seemed to be part of a spectator sport only inflamed my anger further.

Tripping over the single step onto the footpath as I fled the scene, the laughter of the onlookers rang in my angry ears.

"Un aperitivo?" I heard his voice call after me.

"NO!!!" I yelled back pausing to turn around and look back in his direction. *"BASTA!"* —*ENOUGH!*

I had missed the last bus of the day to take me back to Lacona. The tourist office recommended I hitchhike back. Shaken by the incident, I wasn't keen to get into a car with a stranger. I stepped into a taxi, accepting the cost to get back to the farm. As I sat in the back of the vehicle, I felt my skin burn with fury at his behaviour.

In the early evening a few beach fishermen were busy further down the shoreline but no-one else was swimming. Despite some cloud cover, the early evening was perfect. The bay was clear and still again after the storms, tiny waves lapping gently at the shore. Gliding through the cool waters, I felt the heat of my anger over the incident slide away as I dived under the surface and allowed it to float away.

Watching the friendly frog-toad in the corner of the doccia as I rinsed the shampoo out of my hair, I wondered if there was a prince inside the little guy. He wasn't a beautiful green tree frog making him a lot less appealing to kiss, but I felt like I needed a hero this evening. A flash of lightening suddenly lit up the darkening sky above the pine trees. A roll of thunder followed close behind. I dried off and dressed quickly, hiding back in the roulotte as the rain poured down.

A friend of Cinzia and Vittorio's was cooking up her own storm in the kitchen later that evening. Standing at a height of perhaps four-and-a-half foot, she barely came up to my shoulder. Unable to understand how to pronounce her name, I dubbed her Thumbelina in my head. She chattered away to me as she bustled around the kitchen preparing the dinner. Handing me a spoon of pasta sauce she indicated I should blow on it to cool it down, then taste.

She looked at me expectantly. "C'è abbastanza sale? o troppo?"

"Il gusto è perfetto," I assured her the seasoning was fine.

Vittorio had moved back into the main section of the farmhouse. The family renting it who we had had dinner with, had left that morning. While the initial stormy downpour had eased, with more rain coming Vittorio decided we should eat inside. As we all dashed back and forth from the outside kitchen to the house with food items, I nearly ran into him in the dark. Laughing as we passed, I was glad of the dark to mask my blush.

Vittorio, Cinzia, Alessandro, Thumbelina, Nicole and I sat down at the table for spaghetti with tomatoes, garlic and chilli, followed by a fried zucchini salad and fresh bread. The simplest ingredients always tasted good here.

Feeling tired, I found it hard to follow the conversation at all tonight. I hoped my comprehension wasn't going backwards. The mood seemed light-hearted. Vittorio was generally quiet but when he got going, he seemed to raise quite a laugh.

Alessandro and I stood up to do the washing up as the others headed outside for their post dinner cigarette. He spoke very slowly and intently to me about a little house in the forest near the Austrian border where he was going to move to for the winter.

Sitting outside under the beautiful awning chatting for a while longer in the semi darkness, I studied Vittorio. He was sitting on a step in the corner in dim light, languidly waving a cigarette in one hand as he spoke. I was sure I saw him glance my way but I was almost also certain I was imagining what I wanted to see.

A wave of sadness swept over me. Tears pricked the back of my eyes as I felt a melancholy kick in. I had missed having someone to walk through life with. Instead, here I was, harbouring an irrational—albeit sometimes enjoyable—crush on someone I couldn't even communicate with. I didn't want to have to hunt down a new great love and the sense of connection I dreamed of. But I hoped there was still a chance, that one day it would find me.

12

Marco swung past in the van after breakfast on Tuesday to take us across the island to begin the grape harvest. Nicole explained to me on the trip across the island that we would be spending the day at his place today. Each year a small vintage of Aleatico wine was prepared for sale in the negozio of Orti di Mare. A common grape variety grown on the island for generations, it is believed that even Napoleon had once enjoyed the produce of the Aleatico vine during his exile on the island. We were set to harvest from the main vineyard today, which lay on the other side of the island where Marco lived.

As we stepped out of the vehicle, Nicole and I froze in terror. A wolf-like beast barrelled towards us. Grabbing each other, we put our heads down and braced for impact.

"RUUUUBIIIOOO!!!" Marco bellowed at the large German Shepherd careening towards us. "Vieni qui!" Rubio hit the brakes within metres of us. Obediently returning to his master's side in brief acknowledgement of his master's instruction, he then returned to greet us at a politer trot. An enthusiastic but gentle giant, Rubio quickly claimed our affections. Having taken his fill of pats and fussing, he wandered over to sniff two cats sedately watching our arrival from a safe distance. He bumped heads gently with each of them as they tolerated his affections with feline indifference.

Lush green leaves on sturdy branches wrapped their tendrils around the building we stood beside. Green shutters were pushed open amidst the foliage to reveal a darkened room. A terracotta tiled roof capped the corners of the whitewashed walls protruding from between the vines. The slim dirt road we had arrived on continued past a disorderly selection of two or three small sheds and crumbling rooms that were linked to the side of the small house, beyond the front door.

Alessandro was busy loading up his silver ute with dark red crates. Marco handed us each a pair of secateurs, with a stern warning not to lose them. With Rubio trotting happily at his master's side we set off on foot back up the dirt road, past the neighbour's large stone house surrounded by olive trees and entered the vineyard.

Tall weeds, briars and spider webs hindered our passage between the trellises as Marco directed us off the road and into the vines. Taking giant steps, he squashed a path through the undergrowth ahead of us. Nicole and I followed as closely as possible, some of the taller weeds flicking back aggressively into our faces as Marco's feet released them. Lengths of an untamed rose bush reached through the undergrowth and painfully embraced the bare skin of my lower legs. Delicately disentangling myself, I wished I had worn full length jeans rather than the pair I had cut off just below the knee to work in. These were not the carefully manicured vineyards I had expected to find myself harvesting.

Marco pulled out a spray can and threw it over to Nicole to use. "Ci sono molte zanzare," he advised.

I looked blankly at Nicole. "Mosquito spray. Lots of mosquitos in the vineyards," she explained.

A car drove past barking out some short toots that drew a wave in return from Marco. My eyes followed the vehicle as it travelled on the road. As it vanished around a bend, my gaze drifted higher up the steep, craggy mountain rising behind the fields. At the very top, precariously built into the rock, a crumbling fortress loomed. I could see no possible approach to the steep barren cliff faces leading up to the castle walls.

"Eleventh century," Nicole advised after asking Marco. Still functioning until the eighteenth century, Fortezza del Volterraio was now abandoned, remaining in the care of the trustees of the national park.

Gently taking a bunch of burgundy-coloured grapes in his hand, Marco showed us the violet hue in the fruit that we were looking for to determine whether the fruit was ready for harvest. If the grapes were still red or a little transparent, we were to leave them behind. He demonstrated where we needed to make the cut in the stem.

"Ok?" he finished his explanation with a pointed look at me for confirmation I had understood.

I smiled back confidently this time "Si! Va bene."

Leaving a red crate between Nicole and I, Marco moved around to the other side of the vine to work opposite us. Alessandro joined Marco as we started to work in tandem.

Together our small group wove through the vines, releasing the ripe fruit from the scratchy claws of the vines. Sticky trails of grape juice began dripping down our hands and wrists to our elbows. We cleaned the bunches as we went—removing any obviously bad grapes and chasing out a few spiders, before dropping the bunches into the big red crate. Nicole and I moved the crate along with us, until the steadily increasing weight was too much for us to lift alone. As the layers of fruit reached the top, one of the men would hoist the full crate to their shoulder and take it to a collection point at the end of the row, leaving us with a fresh one to fill.

By lunchtime an older man joined them who I hadn't met before. Nicole explained that he was a partner on the wine making side of the business. I nodded in greeting to him over the vines. The rhythm of the work and peace of the vineyard in the shadow of the Fortezza was only interrupted by Rubio periodically pushing past our legs to settle in spots of shade on the tangled path for a rest. And Marco's gentle chatter. His voice was deep and raspy. He plied me with questions about Australia, patiently waiting for me to formulate my short answers. We wove our way up and down the vines—sometimes chattering, sometimes in silence. There was already an intimacy in the work. Peeping through the vines, making regular eye contact as we worked, occasionally brushing hands in passing. I could see why vineyards and grape harvesting had always seemed so romantic.

The church bells chimed midday—the call to farm workers all around that it was time to start packing up and head home for lunch. Alessandro had taken one load of grapes back down to the sheds already. We loaded up the ute with the rest of the morning's harvest. Nicole and I leapt onto the running board, clinging to the sides for the short drive back. Sweeping views down to Portoferraio rolled in front of us, the resonance of the bells still echoing around the hilltop as we bumped gently down the track.

Beside silver vats, a rectangular receptacle with a large mechanical corkscrew whirled through a jumble of grapes. We started pouring the crate loads of fruit slowly into the small machine under Alessandro's instruction. It pulled the grapes into its maelstrom, as the spinning corkscrew pushed the grapes and their juices into a long tube leading to a giant red bucket. The twigs flew out an opening at the front and piled up on the ground. We peered over the edge of the bucket at the sloppy mess of juice and skin. There would be no grape stomping required today. I had arrived on the island without the romantic floaty dress to wear for the task as seen in movies. Instead, my cut-off jeans—that I had worn to work in every day since arriving—were so caked with dirt, they could almost stand up on their own. It was probably for the best that my foot service wasn't required.

"Un momento," Alessandro jogged over to the house and brought a couple of glasses back from the kitchen. We pushed the bottom of the glasses down into the thick fruity mush, letting the juice seep over the edges. The sweet, refreshing first taste of succo dell'uve—*grape juice*—was rewarding after a morning in the sun.

On Elba, school days are Monday through Saturday from eight in the morning until one in the afternoon. Leaving us to get cleaned up, Marco left to collect his son Simone to bring him back for lunch.

We took turns to slip inside his home to freshen up in the bathroom. As I stepped through the door, I found myself in a combined kitchen, dining and lounge area five or six metres square. A small square table sat in the centre of the room, with a hard-looking old sofa pushed to the left, a tiny television on a small table at the end, a rabbit ear aerial resting on a shelf beside it. Dishes and plates were piled up by the sink on the right. The floor was concrete with some simple mats scattered around. Dusty, empty wine bottles assembled like bowling pins sat at the base of a small chimney.

The bathroom was across from Marco's son's room. As I passed a dresser in the hall, my eyes fell on a single photo frame with a formal image, perhaps done through the school, of Marco and his son.

I carefully ran cool, soapy water over my scratched arms as I washed my hands. The rose trellises used for companion planting in the vineyards had torn at my skin several times, leaving red welts interspersed between the blue paint from a few days earlier.

Alessandro beckoned us over to the natural arbour of an enormous tree when we re-emerged. We lifted a sheet of wood lying on the ground nearby, balancing it on two work blocks to make a long trestle table. Dusting off as much dirt as possible, Alessandro draped a large tablecloth on top, while I gathered some white plastic seats scattered nearby. Our outdoor dining room decor included a bright orange fungus more than fifty centimetres in diameter and shaped like a rosette, growing at the base of the trunk of the tree.

The man who had partnered with Alessandro in the fields brought out a magnum of white wine and jugs of water. No one had introduced us. I placed my hand on his arm and asked his name.

"Cirilo," he told me.

I nodded and smiled, "Io sono Jacqueline".

"Separated from his wife recently," Alessandro whispered to me as the man walked away. I glanced at him. He raised his eyebrows a little. I smiled and nodded understanding the alert. I would keep my distance.

Returning with Simone, Marco brought out a large baking dish filled with a rich lasagne while Simone carried out a garden salad and crusty bread. As we started on the lasagne, Marco began cooking the second course on a portable grill he had set-up beside the table. Rich pork and fennel sausages. My glass—or plastic cup as it was that day—was never empty. The wine vanished quickly between us.

The branches of the luminous leafy tree draped down like a curtain around our group. The cats emerged from their morning sleeping spots—ever hopeful of scraps from the table. Rubio inspected the group before opting to settle at my side. Spotting the beautiful dog staring up at me with his big brown eyes as I stroked his head, Marco laughed, "Lui é innamorato con te!"

And I might just be in love with him, I thought as I smiled down at the gentle furry giant panting beside me in the midday heat.

Marco asked me something else. I looked back at him, unsure whether he had asked if I would like another sausage—which he was holding up with a pair of tongs—or something else. I paused. I got the feeling yes or no was an adequate answer, but I didn't really know what I was answering. I slowly answered, "Si...?"

Laughing, he shook his head and beckoned for Nicole's attention to ask her to ask me what we ate in Australia. Having translated the question, she continued in English, "Never say yes if you don't know what they are asking you, as they are probably asking you to sleep with them. They're Italian, remember!"

Alessandro burst into laughter, before translating. Marco raised his eyebrows in surprise at her statement, gave me a cheeky look, and roared with laughter before turning back to tend his grill.

The newly single Cirillo, aged in his fifties, had sat down next to Nicole. I cringed as I watched him leaning right into the personal space of the twenty-three-year-old, suggestively trailing the frond of a fern across her knee. She defended her space well and with good humor, but Alessandro and I exchanged glances periodically, knowing if necessary one of us would leap to her defence.

Marco went to make coffees inside just as a car pulled up. Simone, who had been sitting quietly beside me, went to speak to the woman in the car. Looking over, a sad expression passed over Alessandro's face, "La mama," he said looking me in the eye with resignation.

Marco spoke briefly to the woman as he came out with the coffee, before leaving Simone to continue speaking with her, continuing to keep a wary eye on the interaction. Simone's mother did not live with them but came past each day to see him. I wondered what had happened.

Alessandro pulled the attention away from the boy and his mother, to take a poll on who might like gelato. As he vanished in his car to go purchase a supply from a local store, Marco seemed lost in thought as he waited for Simone to return to the group. He kept busy as he served up a nip of straight vodka, followed by strong espressos for each of us. With a hand resting on Rubio's head beside my knee, and a cat resting under my chair, I relaxed back. I hoped we wouldn't be expected to return to work in the vineyard anytime soon. When we dragged our full bellies back up to the rows of tangled vines an hour later, the pace was notably slower. My ability to identify the readiness of the grapes I picked seemed significantly reduced by the combined impact of food, wine, vodka and the sunshine beating down on my head. We hadn't been working long when we hit a spot in the vineyard where a lot of the grapes had been ruined by mould stimulated by the recent storms. Despondent at the small yield from the crop, Marco called it a day.

On our return to Lacona, Nicole and I rushed down to jump into the dusk waters, eager to rinse away the stickiness of the grapes, the dirt and the scratches from the briars born across our legs and arms, and bites from the zanzare which had persisted despite the spray. The setting sun danced across the waters as the last of the tourists packed up and headed back to their accommodation, leaving us to enjoy our daily ritual of watching the sun slipping behind the headland. We floated on our backs in the stillness, tired but content.

The next morning Vittorio armed us with baskets ready to collect tomatoes for the store. After dropping the produce off to Cinzia, we collected shovels and forks from the shed and headed to a compost heap, bound by a wooden crate-like-fence, sitting in the olive grove behind the store. A pile of dried grass had been left nearby, which we had to fork over the top of the refuse to help the decomposing process.

With more horse manure to be distributed, we returned to the pile in the lower olive grove. After all the rain, the firm asparagus heads that had begun to poke through the soil last week were steadily gaining height. Enthusiastically I tore up and down the hill with my wheelbarrow, determined we would have the job done by lunchtime. With sweat pouring down my back as I powered around the property this morning, I realised I was feeling fitter and healthier with every day of increasing activity on the farm. I was so happy away from a desk and computer, instead active and busy out in the mild Autumn sunshine.

I didn't feel ready to leave the tranquillity of the island to take on the intensity of Napoli. With my next destination confirmed on a farm in the Cilento National Park near Salerno, south of the Amalfi Coast towards the end of October, I was starting to wonder whether I really needed the full ten nights I had planned in Napoli first.

My fascination with Penelope Green's book *See Naples and Die* had led me to read the seminal work, *Gomorrah*, by Napolitano journalist Roberto Saviano. Saviano now lived under police protection following his 2007 exposé of the illegal activities of organised crime syndicate—the Camorra—in his hometown. He had alleged drugs, high fashion, construction, and toxic waste were at the core of Camorra business activities in Campania with their tentacles reaching throughout Italy and beyond.

All my reading stimulated fascination, hope, fear. Napoli had at no point captured me as a romantic tourist destination – but something in my heart continued to draw me to her. The feeling was profound, inexplicable even, but every time I thought of the city, I felt her calling me. As much as I wanted to get there though, perhaps it was also the reason I was in no rush to go. I was starting to think it might be nice to stay a little longer here at Orti di Mare, ensconced in the romantic whimsy of Mediterranean island life.

I was still managing to continue my grammar study and I could listen to authentic chatter and attempt conversation with my new friends. Nicole and Alessandro were both due to leave on the weekend, so if I stayed on I would be without my translators but I was beginning to feel braver in communicating with my broken sentences. Perhaps I could get by. And there was the little crush on Vittorio that my imagination was still feeding into. As I drifted off to sleep that night, I decided to ask if I could stay another week.

I briefed Nicole up to ask Vittorio on my behalf, as we headed to the kitchen for breakfast the next morning.

"Jacqueline stava chiedendosi se lei potesse stare per un'altra settimana?" Nicole asked as we walked into the kitchen the following morning. Vittorio's face lit up.

"Si, Certo!"—*certainly*—he beamed at me. I desperately tried to push out of my mind that the bright smile might indicate that he was thrilled I was staying on because he fancied me too. That big smile and immediate positive response. We might not speak the same language, but I was taken by his enthusiasm for me to stay on.

I nodded happily, "Va bene."

We got to work weeding the same asparagus field we had spread manure across the day before. Sturdy, protective gloves were a gift from God as we picked past the manure, wrenching determined weeds out of the ground. I wondered why we hadn't done the two tasks the other way around. Working hard all morning, we ploughed up and down the lines of asparagus, taking turns hoeing, raking and collecting the weeds so neither of us were bent over for too long at any one time.

Vittorio and Cinzia, who were sitting together behind the computer on the counter in the negozio, called us over as we walked past on our way back for lunch.

"They want to know how long you can stay for?" Nicole told me. "For them the longer the better as they start the olive harvest next week and no other volunteers have applied to come during October," she explained.

I had planned to cut my stay in Napoli shorter and still aim to reach the farm near Sapri in mid-October, but perhaps I could change my date of arrival there. I agreed to stay two more weeks.

"They are really happy you are staying," Nicole told me as we walked away.

With the beach, a handsome farmer, a charming peasant and fresh produce and manual work ahead, I was more than happy to be staying too.

After our evening swim, with no-one else around for dinner, Nicole and I cooked up some pasta with a fresh pesto. Having placed our bundles of fresh basil from the enormous bush behind the kitchen in the blender on the bench that had sat dormant so far during our stay, we peeled some cloves of garlic, adding them with a liberal pour of olive oil before discovering the device didn't work. Dusting off a large mortar and pestle from a bottom shelf, I transferred the ingredients. Taking turns at grinding the ingredients, we created an authentic, rustic pesto to be proud of. We finished off a bottle of wine, before deciding to head to the nearby beach café for a gelato to end the evening. We sat on the steps leading from the cafe down to the sand, watching the light of a full moon sparkling across the ripples of inky water. My gaze went out past the curve of the headland to our left and to the mysterious outline of Monte Cristo, lying in darkness on the horizon.

"I think that Vittorio really likes us," Nicole said.

"What makes you think that?" I asked casually.

"Well, I interviewed him on my handycam yesterday about the history of the farm. I heard him telling some friends about it later and he seemed quite chuffed," she told me. "And then when I asked if you could stay longer this morning, did you see that big smile?"

She had seen it too.

"And how quickly he said yes?"

She heard it too.

My fantasies ran out of control about what his enthusiasm could mean.

"Oh?" I said calmly. "Perhaps it's just because we're good workers?" Nicole shrugged.

"I don't know. I think he just likes us."

Likes me, perhaps?

We returned to finish the remnants of the grape harvest at Marco's on Saturday morning. After further inspection, Marco had found another section that had been unspoilt by the rains.

"Sai delle temporale di sabbia in Australia," Marco peered over the leaves as we worked along the vines opposite each other. Sandstorms had been sweeping across Australian East coast cities in the past week. Alessandro had leant me his laptop to get online the day before, so I could change my accommodation plans for Napoli and dates for arrival at the next farm. I had received a link from a news website from my friend Tom back home. The images of haunting red skies over Sydney and Brisbane were eerie as the east coast began to look like a landscape from Mars. Under the clear blue skies of Elba, it was hard to imagine the apocalyptic atmosphere my friends and family were experiencing on the other side of the world. I confirmed I had heard about le temporale di sabbia as Marco shook his head in wonder at the weather phenomenon caused by an intense low-pressure system bringing thick clouds of dry dust from the red centre into the coastal cities.

We sat down for another large lunch back under the trees. A huge tray of cannelloni was brought out this time with shots of limoncello again to finish.

With only a small section that remained and worth salvaging, there was no need for us all to return to the fields after lunch.

Nicole and I decided to eat out for her last Saturday night on the island. She had found a pizza bar poised on the eastern headland, located within a large campervan site. As we walked the half hour along the beach, I could smell the local eucalypts filling the landscape of the campsite before I saw them. I savoured the smell from home.

The chef himself brought the pizzas to our table. I looked up to thank him as he placed the pizza in front of me. "You found it," the man who I had drawn in with my *profumo di composto* on the roadside the week before smiled down at me.

"Oh... yes..." I stammered out not realising we were in his pizzeria.

He entered into a conversation with Nicole, all the while keeping an eye on me. I tried to understand what was being said given it seemed to centre around me.

"Buon Appetito," he gave me a wink as they finished chatting and he returned to the kitchen.

I looked at her expectantly. "He wanted to know where we were working and how long we would be here for," she said as she started hacking into her pizza.

"And? What did you tell him?"

"That we had been working at Orti di Mare and staying in the campsite. That I was leaving tomorrow but you would be here for two more weeks." I rolled my eyes. "Did you have to tell him that I would be alone in the caravan?!" I groaned.

"He's from Naples," she continued as she bit into her first slice oblivious to my angst, "so he reckons his pizza is the best on the island."

I stared down at the inky bay. Naples. It wasn't unusual to come across pizza chefs from Napoli all over Italy; all over the world in fact. But it felt like the random connection I had made with this one was to serve as a gentle nudge, reminding me that my time on the island was still limited. Napoli was still calling me on.

13

"Hmmmm... Sei sola," Marco frowned, as he paused above the carciofi field on Monday afternoon. He was working on a water pump at the lower end of the field, passing back and forth, to retrieve things from his van parked on the nearby rise.

We embarked on our first conversation together—without an English speaker on-hand to assist—with words heavily supplemented by hand movements and facial expression.

He was already missing Alessandro who had left the day before. He didn't enjoy working alone. As I had walked into the carciofi field that morning, I had also needed to dig deep to summon the energy to commit wholeheartedly to the field of weeding that I now faced alone. After some last photos and a quick hug at lunchtime, Nicole had dropped her small backpack with her six-string guitar strapped to the side into the boot of Vittorio's car, before they vanished around the bend in the road and off to the ferry terminal in Portoferraio. The silence at the campsite had been deafening as I realised just how alone I would be without Nicole and Alessandro around.

My fears about not being able to communicate without their help eased as I interacted one-on-one with Marco. I revealed to him how little of the island I had seen. With the lack of public transport and my resistance to hitchhiking, I had seen very little of either inland Elba or other parts of the coastline. And with my energy sapped by the extent of physical activity involved in the daily farm work, I had lacked motivation to hike to nearby bays less than five kilometres away. Marco offered to take me around one afternoon when he was free.

I eyed him cautiously—Nicole's light-hearted warning about not saying, "Si," unless you were sure of what is being suggested rang in my ears.

"Ma... sempre ho mio figlio con me,"—I *always have my son with me*—he told me apologetically. I nodded gratefully in acceptance of the offer. A young chaperone was a good safeguard.

"Sono STANCA!"—*I'm TIRED*—I moaned at the travel clock beeping loudly beside me the next day. In the dim morning light, I stretched my legs to the bottom of my sleeping bag, the sinew of my muscles pulling apart to allow blood to flow through the fibres. My hamstring muscles, along with my back and arms, had supported hoe swinging activities for three days now. Pushing a little harder into my cat stretch, I knew my muscles hadn't felt this taut since my last boot camp, now more than twelve months earlier. I had loved sunrise on Coogee Beach, while doing sand runs, push-ups on the shoreline, and staggering up and down the steep hill and stair challenges. The steady rhythm of two weeks working on the farm had however, proven a far more pleasurable way of increasing my fitness and sense of well-being. This was not my everyday life. If it was, I'm sure my appreciation for it would soon fade. But for now, I would make the most of my increasing physical health and the sense of peaceful mental and spiritual balance.

Cooler air greeted me as I opened the door. A shiver ran through me. I pulled on a jumper for my trip to the loo. As I slipped my rubber thongs on, I wished I had a pair of Ugg boots on hand to keep my feet warm instead. I walked through a light mist that was drifting down over the mountains and across the fields as I made my way to the kitchen to find breakfast. The change in season scented the air.

Lopping my hoe and rake over my shoulder, I headed up the road, to return to the *carciofi* field for another day of weeding. I quietly sang cheerfully to myself, 'Hi ho, hi ho, it's off to work I go.'

"This afternoon... hmmm... we will... mmmh... dropping the olives," Vittorio came past to tell me mid-morning. He had tried to tell me in Italian. I was still slowly deconstructing his words with my usual lack of comprehensive velocity, when he had tried again—this time incorporating a few key words of his stilted English to fast track our interaction. I smiled and nodded that I understood. He paused, with a look like he wanted to say something else. I waited. With a nod and a *va bene*, he seemed to decide it would be too hard to attempt further conversation. With a quick wave he continued on.

"Questo pomeriggio raccoglieremo le olive," Marco came past later to tell me the same information. Perhaps it was because I had heard the information once already, but I comprehended what he was telling me immediately. I found Marco easy to communicate with. He always spoke very slowly and carefully and threw in plenty of elaborate hand gestures. Sporadically he would try and use some of the words in English he had learnt through music on the radio, or through English speaking workers and visitors to the island.

Bent over in the field mid-morning, I was rhythmically throwing my body behind the hoe, ploughing down a long furrow, when an increasing drone of rowdy voices moved closer from down the hill. Raising my head, I saw a group of almost a hundred people come into view as they walked along the road coming from the direction of a beach front hotel. Dressed for a hike, their conversations in German drifted towards me. I heard references in Italian to la signorina and il suo lavoro—her work—filter down from the ridge above me as they passed by. Peeping out from under my hat, I saw the group studying my efforts as they made their way past.

I was the vision of Italian farm life they would take away from their own trip to the island. I took it on myself to add value to their holiday.

"...Giorrrr...nooh," I responded to their eager greetings with the cheery yet languid abbreviated greeting I had heard the locals use, throwing in a casual wave for effect.

I tried to ignore the click of the cameras, knowing the tourists were busy capturing photos of *la signorina* at work, butt firmly planted in the air as I reached down to pull out the more stubborn of the trespassers gathered around the sturdy young vegetable plants. A man broke from the group to ask what was growing in the field.

"Carciofi," I proudly pronounced perfectly after days of repeating the word around in my head, "E qui... abbiamo l'asparagi," I pointed to the asparagus field below.

Nodding in interest he asked me another question I didn't understand.

"Non parlo Italiano molto bene," I apologised that I didn't speak much Italian.

Nodding kindly, he asked me, "Sei Spagnola?"

Pleased that for a second time on the island my accent had been mistaken for something remotely Latino, I shook my head with a smile. "Sono Australiana."

Marco tailed them up the hill as the last of the group moved by, laughing and applauding my performance as he walked by. He was headed to his van to collect more bags of concrete for the shed he was constructing to shelter the water pump near the vineyard. Crouching down on the ridge above he told me, "Tu lavori molto duramente,"—*you work very hard*.

By his assessment, the women who came to the farm always worked harder than the men. Apart from the burn in my hamstrings and the potential reward of less cellulite thanks to my labours, I enjoyed the methodical work of weeding the field. I liked the reward of seeing the progress made and looked forward to the end result.

"Buon lavoro Jacqueline"—*good job*—he gave me a nod as he stood up to continue on.

Coming past again half an hour later, he sat down this time on the grassy knoll above the carciofi field, his arms loosely wrapped around his knees. I stopped my work mid swing and casually leant on my hoe, smiling up at the brawny—today shirtless—man, with long scruffy brown curls, as we took a break to chat.

He told me how he travelled a lot when he was young. All over Europe. He had worked in Norway for a while. Once he was married and had a child, it was no longer possible. He was forty-eight years old now, his son twelve.

I told him about my trip to Monte Carlo with Alexis where we had glammed up for the casino.

I broke into laughter as he in turn told me about the time, he burned around the streets of Monaco on a rickety moped, weaving between the luxury cars of the rich and powerful.

I told him that I had two sisters and how they had ten children between them—his eyes nearly popped out of his head—and that I and my sister were divorced also.

He nodded sympathetically.

He went back down the hill to keep working for a while, but half an hour later he was back. His day was not going well as he battled with his task alone. I was in a rhythm with the weeding now, but appreciated the half hourly visits so I could take a rest and have chat.

He had been working for Vittorio for four years, he told me. He preferred work in the vineyard and the wine making process. The vegetables he found, were a lot of work, repetitive and boring.

Before noon he beckoned me out of the field, "Okay... Hai fatto abbastanza,"—*you have done enough*—he told me. With olive harvest scheduled for the afternoon I didn't like leaving the field not quite finished, but I knew I had done a cracking job so far with the amount of ground I had covered.

Driving me back to the house, I slipped in a subtle query as to Vittorio's relationship status. Marco suggested there was a serious girlfriend from Germany as Luisa and Nicole had suspected—my heart sank a little—but Marco had only seen her twice.

Whipping up a quick tomato, mozzarella, tuna and basil salad, with a healthy drizzle of olive oil and some slices of fresh bread, I ate lunch alone before a quick siesta.

Unable to find Vittorio, I wasn't sure where I was supposed to be for the olive harvest. I spotted Marco driving back down to the shed he was constructing and followed him down the hill to offer my assistance.

Looking around to work out what he could give me to do, he finally passed me a hose and sent me up the ladder to rinse the concrete on the roof of the shed, while he stood below giving directions. Leaning on a post on the edge of the vines we started to talk about travel again. He was surprised I did so much travelling on my own. Thinking about it made me feel tired. I had grown to love the independence of travelling alone, but standing in the warmth of the sun, listening to Marco, I realised there was an overwhelming feeling of loneliness in the adventures I had embarked upon solo. The experiences were mine and mine alone. Shared with people who were merely ships—albeit friendly ones—passing through my life.

He had finished what he needed to do so we packed everything back into the van and drove back to the sheds. We found Vittorio pulling out crates, small rakes on very long poles, and enormous green and black tarpaulins.

Taking everything up to the olive grove running behind the shop, we ran into Thumbelina who had just arrived. She was eager to be involved. Marco and I carefully spread the tarpaulins under the first tree, ensuring they covered all the ground under the spread of the branches of the tree. Each of us claimed a spot under the leaves and reached up into the branches to begin raking the olives down. With no customers in the shop Cinzia also came out to join us for a while.

It was the first time I had worked with Vittorio and Marco together. My eyes flicked between the two men. Something had shifted. There was of course the reality that—while somewhat in denial—I now had confirmation that Vittorio was likely attached. But the ability to communicate at length with Marco, despite the language barrier, had heightened my sense of connection to him. Despite my recent illusions of love for Vittorio, I suspected that Marco's efforts to get to know me had seen him catch a deeper sort of affection in a corner of my heart.

The strains of Cinzia's classical music swelled from the speakers in the shop behind us as I reached up with my rake to pull more olives off the tree. The green oval fruit cascaded down on our heads and on to the tarpaulins. Thumbelina kept to the lower branches, using her hands to rake the olives off their stems. As evening fell, we left everything there, including the olives we had dropped, ready to continue in the morning.

Filthy from the weeding earlier in the day and with happily aching muscles, I sank into the soothing waters of the bay in the setting sun. Swimming a few stretches up and down in the shallows, my taut back muscles lengthened out again. The evening air had an increasingly cool nip to it. I wished I had a larger towel to wrap up in, as I shivered my way back from the beach.

With no-one else around the kitchen at dinner time, I rummaged through the fridge to see what food was in there. I settled on making a potato, onion, garlic, rosemary, pancetta and tomato frittata. It seemed a good idea, until I burnt the vegetables and seared the egg in my too hot pan. Possibly the worst frittata in history, I ate the sections that survived as quickly as possible, fearing someone might enter the kitchen and witness my culinary failure.

Eating alone for the third time today I felt a little woeful. Dinner had brought me no joy. I washed up quickly, getting rid of the remaining evidence by feeding it to the rabbits before retreating back to the caravan with a cup of tea. Using the last remaining credit on my mobile, I sent a text to Debbie in Brisbane, letting her know I was thinking of her. Though we had lived in different cities for over a decade now we had always stayed in weekly, if not daily contact. She suddenly seemed very far away. I drifted off to sleep realising how much I was missing the familiarity of friends and family after talking with Marco.

The night was cold, and dawn offered little anticipation of a clear day ahead. The mountains were hidden in soft mist drifting gently down towards the sea.

Marco appeared around nine o'clock with more drop sheets and a pair of clippers for me to tame some of the tall weeds sprouting from the base of the olive trees.

"Io sono spiacente per lasciarLa lavorando da sola, ma io devo finire il lavoro sul capannone," he apologised for leaving me to work alone, but he had to continue working on his shed.

Local and island visitors popped into the shop and peered into the grove to watch me at work. Trying to portray the image of someone with extensive experience in the art of 'dropping' olives, I endeavoured to keep them entertained, nodding and waving back. I found myself again performing for the tourists. The olives towards the top branches were far out of my reach, the branches waving four or five metres above me. To give myself a little height, I clambered up amidst the branches, so I could push my rake further up to reach some of the higher hung fruit. Perched within the hold of the beautiful tree I felt at peace as the small green fruits showered over me as I worked.

A mix of Eskimo Joe (to remind me of home) and a little Eros Ramazotti (to practice my Italian) to listen to on my iPod, motivated me to stay busy through the afternoon.

Staring down the lines of trees wishing I had someone to talk to, I feared I would be the sole harvester bringing in the crop this year.

I walked up to the campsite on the headland above Laconella where the pizzeria was located in the evening. Still having problems connecting into the farm's internet connection, we had discovered when we were there for dinner that there was cheap public Wi-Fi I could access. Desperate to avoid returning to the internet cafe at Portoferraio and risking further interactions with the offensive Giovanni, I hoped by chance I would have more luck there. The office had closed before I arrived. Tired and frustrated that I didn't think to check the closing time, I brushed off my concerns about running into the pizza chef and headed into the pizzeria to buy dinner. It seemed a good opportunity to eat something not involving tomatoes or pasta.

Pouring my first glass of wine from the carafe the waitress placed on my table, I noticed a couple sitting nearby with the same size carafe—half a litre—that they were sharing between them. I was still yet to master the measurements on European menus. Ordering a glass often seemed to mean receiving something akin to half the size of an Australian serve. That night, I had gone straight to the half-litre thinking more about my value for money rather than considering the alcohol absorption rate of my robust metabolism following days of farm work.

As the wine relaxed me, the sense of isolation haunting me since Nicole's departure drifted away. I relaxed, regrouped and came around to again appreciate where I was and what I was doing.

Standing at the counter preparing to pay as I fought the effects of the half litre of wine on my delicate equilibrium, the pizza chef appeared from the kitchen. I eyed him nervously. He asked me if the pizza had been good and I felt a pang of guilt. I confessed I had chosen the (questionable) chicken schnitzel, some great chips, and a side of Greek salad. He looked less than impressed by my meal choice. I quickly sculled the complimentary shot of limoncello handed to me by the waitress while she printed out a receipt and bid them both a 'buonaserata'.

The following morning Marco intercepted me on my journey up to the olive grove. He set me to work digging up strawberry shoots coming off the older plants at their season end. He mounted a small tractor and ploughed some ground near the rabbit run in preparation. Setting a neat string marker between two pegs, he showed me how much room to leave between each shoot as I planted. With all the weeding and harvesting done in the preceding weeks, I felt refreshed by the experience of planting something new. Crouched on my haunches, I gently dug in the dirt, tucking the shoots back into the long row of soft earth. Sensory memories of childhood in my parent's garden came flooding back.

Vittorio and Marco had been loosening irrigation tubes from the ground in the main vegetable field the day before. Marco apologised for the prehistoric tool we had to use to roll up the long stretches of piping later that afternoon. The wooden A-frame was balanced at the front by a rock as Marco turned a winding arm connected to a plastic pole to draw the tubing in and around. My job was to hold it still as we cleared the fields of the soft irrigation pipes. I wasn't convinced it was a two-person job, but Marco seemed to be looking for things we could do together.

"Ti piace a andare alla discoteca?" he asked me. He himself didn't like the discoteca because the women were too confusing. I laughed, finding it hard to picture Marco in a disco or nightclub. A local bar perhaps but nothing about him equated to flashing lights and flirtatious women seeking his attention.

He told me again that I did a good job each day. I blushed, feeling proud of my ability to transition into the physical work required on the farm.

"Il mio padre, lui ha lavorato nella fattoria con... emmm," I tried to explain to him that my father worked on a pig farm in Australia. Having no idea what the word for pig was, I tested out some oinking noises. Marco looked at me blankly before roaring with laughter. He had no idea what I was talking about. Clearly 'oink' does not translate into Italian. I started grunting instead. Now nodding in recognition, Marco joined in with some exceptional pig grunts, sending me into peals of laughter. Vittorio, working nearby turning the soil in the rabbit pen, looked up quickly. Marco raised his eyebrows like a naughty schoolboy caught out.

With pig noises mastered, we moved on to a conversation about Australian animals. Of course, he knew koala and *canguro*. Without first thinking through how I might explain some of our more peculiar native animals, I started explaining emus and wombats. I couldn't remember the word for bird which wasn't a great start. I flapped my own 'wings' and tried to demonstrate the largess of the ostrich like birds. I then pointed to the chickens, to prompt the word for bird.

"I polli?" Marco looked completely confused. *Great*, I think, *I've made him think we have giant chickens in Australia.*

Shaking my head laughing, I flapped my wings again and point at the hens asking, "il nome di...?"

He frowned in confusion, "i conigli...?"

Now he thinks that emus are giant flying rabbits! I paused trying to work out how to reverse the confusion.

"Ahhhhhh gli uccelli!!!" he shouted. Clapping my hands I recognised the word for birds.

"Si si! Emu. I uccelli molti grandi!" I demonstrated my giant flapping wings again. Then stopped suddenly. I could tell he was going to ask me if they could fly. I decided to avoid trying to explain wombats.

"Tu sei andando alla festa dell'uva?" Marco asked if I was going to the festival held at the end of vendemmia—the grape harvest. There was a public party planned in the town of Capoliveri on Saturday night. I had been to the picturesque hilltop town—only a fifteen-minute drive away from the farm—for dinner one night with Cinzia, Alessandro and Nicole in my first week.

"Vittorio!" Marco called across the field, "Sei tu o Cinzia andando alla festa d'uva domani sera?" he queried whether he or Cinzia were going to the festival.

"No. Non questo anno," Vittorio shook his head—*not this year*.

Marco studied me for a moment, "La come me per prenderLa?" he had asked. Looking blankly at him, we utilised our usual routine of charades and alternative mix of Italian and English words until I understood that he was offering to take me. It was my turn to pause.

"Si... volentieri," I accepted—*Love to*.

On Saturday Vittorio and his friend Andre, a robust fellow with chubby red cheeks and mad curly black hair, joined me in the olive grove. Andre had come from the mainland with his family for a few days to help with the olive harvest. From the little I understood of Vittorio's introduction he either owned an olive farm or was involved in the production of olive oil somewhere in Tuscany. Explaining to Andre that I was Australian, he nodded with interest.

"Ci sono alcuni ottimi oli di oliva dall'Australia" he told me. *There are some excellent olive oils from Australia.*

I nodded proudly, though this was news to me. He explained that it had been winning international awards. I glowed with pride despite knowing little of the local industry back home.

Andre had brought a harvesting machine over to the island for Vittorio to trial. Powered by a portable battery pack the long arm with twisting prongs on the end, reached up, spun madly around in the branches and knocked the olives down in record time. After hand harvesting alone for most of the previous week, I couldn't believe the speed with which the olives dropped.

Despite the ease on my workload, I felt some disappointment to see the olives coming down so fast, thanks to the brusque activity of the machine. At a commercial farm, perhaps the need to work faster could be helped by the efficiency of this machine. But I much preferred the quiet sanctuary of the olive grove when the whirring stopped and we continued removing olives with our rakes and hands. The therapy of working at human pace rather than machine efficiency was far more restorative to the senses.

Folk guitar music played loudly from the shop while we worked. Mid-morning, we were joined by Andre's wife and bambini. Mini Andre was a boy of about five and his daughter Francesca, a sturdy baby girl with thick black curls like her papá, who had also inherited his rosy cheeks. Taking a break, Andre lay down on his side on the tarpaulin, surrounded by all the olives he had dropped. Franchesca raced over to him on uncertain legs. She plonked down by his side in relief that she had made enough steps to get there, before curling up in his arms.

I knelt beside the last crate of olives we had filled from the tarpaulin, sifting through the olives to pull out the stems and leaves. I glanced up smiling as I listened in on the casual banter. Under the silvery trees, it didn't matter how much I missed of the verbal interactions due to my low quota of vocabulary. After a quiet week with few interactions except those with Marco, I felt content to bask in the unexpected joy of the company of strangers.

14

"Giahhhc-ah-lyn!" I heard Marco's call. I checked my freshly blow-dried hair one last time and stepped out of the roulotte. He was rummaging in the back of the silver minivan as I walked over to meet him.

"Ecco lo!" he exclaimed as he found what he was looking for.

He turned and presented me with a plug-in mosquito-repeller he had brought from home. I had been complaining about my inability to combat le zanzare, that had plagued me night and day since the start of the olive harvest, no matter how much repellent I wore. The rains had obviously caused a breeding frenzy. I couldn't have been more touched if he had brought me flowers.

We were off to the *vendemmia* celebrations in Capoliveri. While I had showered and thrown on fresh clothes for the evening, Marco was still in his workwear. As we drove away, he explained that he would drop me at the festival, then he would leave to collect his son. They would return at 7:00pm to bring me home. With a build-up of nervous anticipation as I prepared to spend the evening with him, I realised he had actually just offered to give me a lift. Traditional celebrations are perhaps not always as exciting when you grow up attending them. I tried to quell the disappointment, realising I was going to the event alone.

The picturesque streets of the small town quickly drew me in with old stone buildings wrapped in thick bougainvillea vines covered in thick swathes of deep red, pink and white blooms.

No-one seemed to be in a rush to set up for the party. A few small stalls were operating on the edge of the piazza. Long trestle tables were gradually being brought out and set-up under long white marquees. Most of the festivities wouldn't start until after I left.

I found a hole in the wall cafe that sold un tagliato di pizza—pizza by the slice—then wandered down a side street to find a spot to take in the sweeping views across the nearby bays as the sun began to drop lower in the sky while I ate. Back in the central piazza I grabbed a cup of nocciola, cioccolato and stracciatella gelato to keep me company as the square began to fill. But my time was up.

As I awaited Marco's return at our designated meeting spot on the outskirts of the town, I watched as the sun set on one side of the ridge of Monte Calamita, while the moon rose on the other. As the last rays of sun slid from the skies, I saw the van coming up the hill with Simone waving to me from the front seat. He clambered into the back as they pulled to a stop, throwing me a quick 'ciao' over his shoulder as I climbed in.

Marco's hair was clean and brushed now. He wore a blue and white striped shirt, beige shorts and a pair of loafers. There was a mild scent of cologne in the vehicle.

"Noi La porteremo al porto Azurro. Okay?"

"Hmmm. We take you... to Porto Azurro?" Simone's hesitant voice interpreted his father from the back of the van.

"Ti parli inglese?" I turned to ask in surprise. Smiling shyly, he confirmed he spoke a little English. Marco interjected to explain they have to learn in school, "Ma Simone non fa pratica!" Gesturing madly, he encouraged us to use English to give him some practice.

We wove around the mountainside, down to the small port of Azurro further east of Capoliveri. I smiled to myself realising I was to have company for the evening after all.

Marco dropped us off by the waterfront while he went to find somewhere to park. Simone and I wandered along the forefront making small talk in English and Italian. Despite his initial confidence with his first translation—which I suspected had been well rehearsed—he became timid with his use of English, preferring to try and understand my broken Italian.

"Babbo! Babbo!" Simone called out on spotting Marco searching for us from the top of the street. This endearing term for Father was new to me. I followed Simone as he led the way to meet his Dad.

"Prendiamo gelato?" Marco asked brightly as we joined him. Feeling slightly ill from the triple gelato eaten an hour before, I nodded enthusiastically anyway. Warm lights beamed out of a few artigianale shops still open for the evening. Clutching our cones, we slowly wandered the streets of the portside town. We meandered down to the marina where we inspected the beautiful cruisers, sail boats and yachts that none of us would ever own.

"Allora..." I stopped on our way back to the van. "Insieme! Insieme!" I gestured for the two of them to stand close together so I could capture the moment.

Behind the lens of my camera, I felt a pang. I wanted to be part of the photo. Part of the intimacy of the family made up in front of me. But for every romantic notion, every endearing picture, there is another frame. I was too much of a realist not to realise that there were other pictures that I may struggle to be a part of. Minimal language skills, being on the other side of the world to family and friends, what work I would do, where I would live, the difference in the environment I was used to living in, and what Elba... and Marco... could offer me as a future. Warmth and longing filled me as they leant in on either side of me, to see the photo on the back of my camera. In the books and the movies that had drawn me to take this trip, people seemed to be able to make these grand romances work. I wasn't sure that the realist in me could.

"È stata una bella serata,"—*It was a beautiful evening*—I smiled in gratitude as I stepped down from the van near the pine grove later that evening.

As I fell asleep, I pushed the increasing sense of loneliness to one side and basked in the warmth of being part of a little family, in a beautiful place, for those few hours.

I was glad there was no need to emerge from my warm sleeping bag when I woke early on Sunday morning. Lying in the cool dim light of the early morning I reflected on the evening with Marco and Simone. I dosed a little and woke up thinking of them again.

I walked back up to the campsite at Laconella later in the morning and gained internet access. Perched at a picnic table amidst the unexpected grove of Australian eucalypts, the battery power on my rickety laptop lasted until I hit send on my final email.

A sandy path leading down the other side of the headland attracted my attention as I prepared to walk back. I wandered down to the hidden inlet of Laconella. Aqua waters even clearer than that of the main beach of Lacona lapped gently onto the sand. I stood a while in the shallows, watching small fish dart in and out between my legs, before sitting down on the sand to read. Utopia, tucked in my bag, was still unfinished. I progressed in staccato, reading one page before being distracted by swimmers, another before finding myself gazing at boats, and another before being hypnotized by the gentle shoreline lapping nearby.

Vittorio, Andrea—with the beaming Francesca in her pram—and Cirilo came by to look at the wood fired oven mid-afternoon. I had set myself up at the plastic table outside the caravan. With a cup of tea beside me and some gypsy jazz playing quietly, I sat flicking through some of the photos I had taken of Elba.

Coming over and pushing into my personal space, Cirillo complimented me on my tranquil spot under the tree. I hadn't seen him since Nicole had left. I still didn't feel comfortable with him in the way I was with Vittorio, Alessandro and Marco.

"Perché non era Lei a pranzo oggi?"—*why weren't you at lunch today*—he pressed me. I tried to explain my morning, while recoiling from his uncomfortable proximity. Tsk, tsking, me he admonished, "Essere tutta la durata da solo non è buono,"—*Being alone all the time isn't good.*

Andre and his family had departed for home on the mainland after the weekend but left the harvesting device behind. Returning to the olive grove Marco used the machine to keep dropping the olives while I continued to drag the fruit off the lower branches. He paused between branches.

"Perché non eri a pranzo con tutti ieri?" he asked me why I hadn't been at lunch with everyone yesterday. Wondering how he knew, I explained my trip to Lacona, how I had returned late for lunch and made my own meal. I wondered if I had missed a specific invitation for lunch the day before which was arousing such concern from everyone. I was disappointed now not to have been there. I sighed quietly to myself, the language barrier frustrating me again.

"We were looking for you," he told me in Italian. I looked at him questioningly as he continued. "Simone and I were out driving. We took Rubio to the beach and thought you might like to come with us." My heart sank with disappointment. It had been late in the afternoon when they had come past, and I must have been down having my daily swim.

We resumed work, but within a minute Marco stopped again.

"Vuoi avere pranzo con noi oggi? A casa mia?" he asked.

I paused to ensure I had understood the invitation to have lunch today at his house, "Si! Certo," I smiled with gratitude before reaching up for the fruit on the next branch.

We continued work on the grove until it was impossible to reach any more olives. Walking around checking the trees which had taken more than a week to harvest, Marco told me it was very important to check everything was done well as Vittorio was very particular. Certain the grove was clear of fruit, we packed up. The midday church bells rang out as we drove away from the farm for lunch.

He pulled to a stop at the side of a T-Junction on the way to his house and explained that we were waiting for the school bus. Alighting from the bus a few moments later and waving to his friends as the bus continued on its way, Simone came to the front of the car and opened the door.

"Ciao," I smiled back at him.

"Aaaahhh, ciao," he broke into a big smile in return, closed the door and climbed in the back.

Letting Rubio off his rope outside the house, Marco watched him attentively as the giant beast bounded around the corner and all but leapt into my arms with a hug of greeting. I was ready for him this time and braced for the impact of his affection.

Marco turned on a tiny television in the corner of the compact living space. "Tu hai bisogno dell'Internet?"—he offered me internet access while he started to prepare lunch. The computer was in Marco's bedroom and he apologised that the setting wasn't very pretty.

I took a curious look around his room as he left me to prepare lunch. The simple double bed had a doona cover in neutral colours pulled roughly across it, while a selection of brightly coloured and patterned shirts hung on the partially open wardrobe door.

I turned back to the computer. Emails confirmed everything for my journey south. I was sad at the thought of leaving Elba, but the pull of Napoli continued to call me onward.

There were lengthy emails from both my sisters. It was refreshing to hear about my ten nieces and nephews.

Marco set me to work chopping up some tomatoes when I returned to the living area, planting a bottle of olive oil and bowl of salt beside me. He gestured that I should apply both liberally.

Adding a pair of spectacles to his nose, Marco pulled out his dictionary to look up a word while leaving everything to cook.

"I... I am ass-hahm-med," he attempted to articulate in English.

"Ass what?" I look at him perplexed.

He leant over and pointed out the word.

"Ohhhh... 'Ashamed'!"

Laughing at himself on hearing the pronunciation he explained he was ashamed of Simone.

"Ma, perche?" I asked, wondering if the note from school anything had to do with it. It wasn't the note. He was ashamed that Simone had failed to come and assist with the lunch preparations.

"Forse lui é timido,"—perhaps he is shy—I offered.

"Hmmm," he rolled his eyes as he stood up to check something on the stove. Looking through the one window in the room, my eyes travelled out to the neighbouring vineyard rolling down toward the aqua blue waters of Portoferraio in the distance. The house was rustic and certainly not large, but the views were breathtaking.

Marco prepared a sumptuous midday feast. Pasta with tomato and pesto sauce (that he proudly told me was his own creation) was followed by a tender steak. The tomato salad then followed with bread and extra lashings of olive oil and all was washed down with wine and water.

Simone vanished to his bedroom soon after finishing his meal while Marco and I sat talking a while. I told him that Nicole and I had found Cirillo a bit creepy. Marco pushed his glasses on his nose again to look for another descriptor in his dictionary.

"He is ... sleemy," he smiled with a twinkle in his green eyes as he peered over his glasses at me. "Ma non lui é pericoloso,"—*but not dangerous*—he reassured me.

I couldn't help but notice he looked rather distinguished with glasses on.

Vittorio, he told me, had asked him to keep an eye out and make sure I was caused no trouble by any men at or around the farm.

I felt a sudden warmth flow through me as I realised they had both been looking out for me. For the first time, I spoke of the incident in the internet cafe at the Port. I had tried to tell Nicole about it, but she had shrugged her shoulders, non-plussed having experienced regular harassment while travelling as well.

A weight lifted as indignation glowered in Marco's face. Angrily shaking his head, I understood only a little of his sentences, but enough of the sentiment to know he thought Giovanni was a bad man who already had a bad reputation for being over-priced and not looking after tourists. His treatment of me, he declared, was a disgrace.

"Tu sei un spirito libero,"—*you are a free spirit*—he told me as I tried to explain why I left my job to travel. I liked the idea but told him that sometimes I thought I was crazy for taking the risk. Flicking through his dictionary to find a word he pointed out what he wanted me to read.

"Hai... audace," he told me.

Audacious. Courageous. Bold. Daring. He pointed to a phrase to provide context, 'la fortuna aiuta gli audaci'—*Fortune favours the brave*. The moments of physical and emotional exhaustion so far had been borne, because I was certain that only good could come of forcing change in my world. I hoped fortune would somehow carry me as my journey continued.

Marco excused himself to check his own emails. I began clearing the table and headed to the sink. At the sound of the tap running, an uproar erupted in the household. Simone came running out to admonish me and demand that I let him do it, while at the same time I could hear Marco calling out from the bedroom indicating

I stop what I was doing. Arguing that I wanted to help, Simone pleaded with me to let him do his allocated chore. Stepping away from the sink, I took a seat with a laugh, relishing being part of a full-blown Italian family argument.

We returned to the farm a little late. Marco headed off on a small tractor to plough up the vegetable fields after directing me to start work on the olive trees running between the fields. I started on a smaller, much bushier plant than the more established trees in the grove. The branches hung low, heavily laden with fruit. I clambered to sit in the fork under the canopy. For an hour I sat there dragging mountains of fruit off the branches, until my crate was full.

Waving Marco off as he headed for home later that afternoon, I raced down for my ritual swim. Invigorated by a day of friendship and kindness, I plunged into the emerald water floating out in the dimming dusk light, before launching into handstands and somersaults, playing happily on my own in a peaceful sea.

A heavy dew covered everything as I set up the drop cloths to work alone under the olive tree lining the vegetable field the following morning. The morning was particularly serene. The rustle of the leaves as I dragged the fruit off the branches followed by the gentle thud of olives hitting the ground below, along with the distant sound of the small waves coming ashore on Lacona Beach was all that broke the silence. The isolation of my work was tempered after having quality time with Marco and Simone the day before and I worked steadily throughout the day.

But in the evening, as I prepared a tomato sauce with onion, garlic, prosciutto and zucchini to again eat alone, I thought back to our conversation the day before, when I had confessed to Marco of my loneliness at mealtimes in recent days.

"Si Jacqueline. Perche, i gusti di cibo migliorano quando condiviso con altri," he had nodded sympathetically—*Because the taste of food improves when shared with others.*

15

Quietly dropping olives in the still of the morning mid-week, I found myself working alone with Vittorio for the first time in the new grove I was making my way through.

In his musical northern accent, he explained how the way they harvest the olives and prepared the oil in the north, was different to the techniques common in the south. Below Rome they often place nets down in advance, to collect the ripened olives as they dropped off the tree of their own accord. They harvest earlier in Tuscany due to lower temperatures as autumn approaches which puts the fruit at risk from frost. The olive oil in the south is often made from riper fruit, unlike the firm green fruit we were releasing from the branches on Elba.

All my practice speaking with Marco had helped—Vittorio and I were having a conversation. I still had so few words but taking things slowly and with the patience of whoever I was talking to, my comprehension and ability to respond had steadily improved out of necessity.

At lunchtime Vittorio sautéed some zucchini in olive oil and garlic, while I pulled out the bucket of marinated olives Andrea had left for us, diced up tomatoes and sliced the fresh bread. The conversation was not as verbose as with Marco, but I enjoyed Vittorio's gentle company as we sat down at the table in the sun with another simple feast.

I worked away quietly on my own again in the afternoon. Liberating another tree of the weight of its bounty, I finished the day watering the strawberry shoots I had planted on Friday. Marco confirmed that the olive harvest was nearly finished and the next day the priority would be to plant more strawberries together. Doing a quick check at the end of the day to ensure I hadn't left any tools out I spotted a line of olive trees on the far border of the property heavy with fruit. I groaned inside, hoping they would be forgotten until I left the island.

Cinzia was sitting outside the kitchen working on her laptop when I arrived to cook dinner. I had only seen her in passing since Nicole had left. Going over the phrase in my head ten times to make sure I had the grammar right, I leant out the door and asked, "Prendi qualcosa da mangiare?"—*do you want something to eat?*

"I'm fine, thanks," she surprised me in English before telling me in Italian that my language practice was paying off. I smiled, chuffed that someone else had noticed my progress.

My evening shower was tepid at best. As much as I didn't want to leave Elba, the changing weather had started to put me off the rudimentary facilities. A cold outdoor shower was no longer appealing as we moved further into Autumn.

With the morning light taking longer and longer to appear, I reluctantly responded to the demanding call of my alarm clock the next morning. The caravan was awash with red and orange hues as I peered around through bleary eyes. I felt despondent at the sight of the beautiful colours knowing the solitude they indicated for my day ahead. I was certain that the rain threatening in dark clouds on the horizon yesterday would deliver this morning.

I dragged myself out of bed to get ready for work anyway. As I walked over to get breakfast the clouds above me trembled with desire, ready to release their torrents. The first few drops of rain began to fall after I had eaten, and I raced back to the caravan to take shelter.

I had embraced the idea of solitude from my everyday life in Siena. Coming to Elba had taken it a step further with the lack of access to media, language barriers, and the serenity and simplicity of farm life. But peering out into the silent but steady rain—hoping to see Vittorio, Cinzia, Marco, the guy from the pizzeria, anyone—my need for solitude had waned.

The sun re-emerged mid-afternoon. I heard activity behind the caravan and saw Vittorio wander past. I pulled on my work shoes and grabbed my gloves, chasing him to ask what work I should be doing. Without pausing he pointed towards a row of olive trees I hoped he had forgotten. He laughed at my groan in response, patting my shoulder amicably, as I dragged myself off to collect my tools.

I had only been working for a few minutes when I heard Marco's voice. Wandering over with a bucket and small spade in hand he sent me off to collect strawberry shoots. Grateful for the reprieve from the olives, I embraced the task with delight.

Once we had finished gathering the shoots, we squatted side by side, spacing them out and re-planting them together.

Marco was out of sight over at the sheds when Cirillo appeared, strolling across the field toward me as I watered the new plants in.

"Che stai facendo?" he asked what I was up to, as he leant into my personal space. Holding my ground, I glanced past him to see Marco on his way back. Glaring at Cirillo's back, he picked up his pace as he strode in my direction. Vittorio appeared around the corner of the house in the other direction. I saw him make eye contact with Cirilo with a look of warning. The man promptly stepped back a metre or two away from me.

I looked back and forth between my two guardians striding towards us from different directions. Flashing a smile at each of my protectors gratefully as they arrived and moved Cirillo a few steps away, I returned to concentrate on my watering, while a conversation about the poor grape harvest swirled around me. He was more annoying than anything, but I was grateful to have the defence of two good men.

Marco and I returned to olive harvesting for the rest of the afternoon.

"Che libri che ti piace leggere?" he asked me what books I liked to read.

"Hmmm... true stories about women living very different lives to mine... and fairy-tales," I told him with a smile. "E tu?" I asked. "Che libri che ti piace leggere?"

"Mi piace leggere libri sui disastri, sulle guerre passate e sui tempi del medioevo,"—*books about disasters, past wars and medieval times*—he told me.

The storm clouds were getting darker again and the threat of impending rain was on the air. Together we reached for the last of the olives from the top branches. Marco used his height to reach his rake up to catch the branch and pull it down lower, then I used my rake to drag the olives off it while he held it down. Then it was released back to the sky to wave above us in the increasing breeze.

Finally, Marco declared "Basta,"—*enough*—and we drew in the collection of olives on the ground sheets. It was a big haul from just two trees. There were a lot of leaves and twigs to be removed. I squatted down and began to sift through to pull them out.

Clearing away the other surrounding ground covers, Marco sank down on the ground on the other side of the pile to assist with the task. Discussing the weekend, Marco grimaced as he told me he had to do the cleaning. I looked up at him and articulated as best I could, "You don't have much opportunity to rest? Being both father and mother?"

Shaking his head sadly he conceded that the half an hour rest after lunch each day was his time. His eyes dropped as he told me, "Sometimes I cannot sleep." He demonstrated the whirring of his brain with a finger going around and around beside his head. "Simone. A good future for him. Is he doing enough schoolwork? Enough money. Work..." he trailed off. I nodded understanding the essence of what was left unsaid as he dropped his eyes down again.

"Quando non posso dormire,"—*when I can't sleep*—I demonstrated a pen and paper, "Io scrivo,"—*I write*.

Juggling a new and busy job and the fall out of a marriage breakdown had given me many sleepless nights. I had learnt to keep a notebook and pen beside the bed so I could jot down whatever was worrying me, rather than lying there with the cogs turning for hours preventing sleep from coming. The things worrying me were never as bad when I reviewed my notes from the darkest hours the next morning.

We were about to continue the conversation when we were interrupted by Vittorio calling Marco as he came across the field.

As they talked beside me, I wondered if I could ask Marco if I could take he and Simone out for dinner on my last night on Elba.

He wandered away with Vittorio while I rushed to pack up before the storm. I would need to work out the words to articulate my invitation. There was no chance to ask him today. We exchanged warm smiles and bid a farewell to each other with an 'a domani'—*until tomorrow*—as he left for the day.

The storm held, despite the ominous darkness that continued to hover above while I completed my ablutions. I went to the kitchen to cook an early dinner so I could retreat back to the caravan as quickly as possible. As I walked over to the kitchen I turned around in the premature darkness and was stopped in my tracks. A vision of pure and powerful beauty loomed as deep purple clouds billowed over the western mountaintops, briefly luminescent with the glow of sheet lightening embraced in the folds of approaching rain. The fear of the potential damage a storm could bring alongside the majesty of the approaching tempest was overwhelming. I thanked God for the combined vision of beauty and power.

As I cooked and ate, the wind picked up. I closed the kitchen door against the spattering of rain as I finished cleaning up. Turning out the lights I braced myself for the journey back to the caravan as I heard the rain starting to come down hard outside. Torrents of water were pouring off the sloping roof of the kitchen as I opened the door. Quickly slipping out I slammed it behind me. A blinding flash of lightening lit the fields. I tried not to shriek into the wind with every deafening thunder roll going overhead as I raced through the dark across the rain-soaked field to the relative safety of the roulotte.

Saturday was bright and clear after the storm of the night before. Cinzia came to bid me farewell after breakfast. She was leaving the island herself today, returning to her family near Bologna for the cooler months. With a few more verbal interactions in recent days, it was odd to say goodbye when I felt we were only now getting to know each other a month after my arrival.

I was relieved to see Marco arrive wielding the harvesting machine. Despite appreciating how nice it was to do by hand, for my own satisfaction I now wanted to see the *raccolto delle olive* completed before I left and was glad of the device to help us fast track to the finish line.

As we set up, we were careful not to slip in the mud. The trees were now weighted down by both the fruit and also the drenching from the storm. Fresh droplets of rain still covering the leaves, brushed my skin as I wrestled the fruit off the branches.

"Hai sentito la notizia?"—*have you heard the news*—Marco asked me as I crouched beside a pile of olives, removing twigs, sticks and leaves before pouring them from the drop covers into the crates. I shook my head. I had barely heard any news in the past month.

"Obama ha vinto il nobile premio per la pace."—*Barrack Obama had won the Nobel Peace Prize*—he told me, looking impressed.

As we discussed my onward journey, Marco implored me with worry in his eyes, "Sono preoccupato per te. Stai attenta a Napoli. È molto pericoloso,"—*I'm worried for you. Stay attentive in Napoli*. It's very dangerous. "They are crazy in the south," he warned.

Nodding obediently at his instruction and touched by his concern, a mixture of chill and thrill went through me. My booking in the city was still set for ten days. The farm in Salerno had been happy for me to come later in October.

A visit to the Museo Archeologico in central Napoli and hopefully a climb up to the crater of Mt Vesuvius and a trip to Herculaneum were on my touristy list, but I also hoped to find a way to get to know the heart of the city. Maybe find a way to meet some locals. And importantly, I wanted to leave plenty of time to discover whether the ovens of the birthplace of pizza really produced the best in the world.

Sitting in the middle of the field sifting through the olives, the mud under the drop sheets seeped through to our shorts. Unperturbed, Marco—shirtless—stretched out on his back and soaked up the sun for a few moments. He didn't have the chiselled build of the gym junkies of Sydney's eastern suburbs but sported a healthy natural build from the farm work.

As I continued running my fingers through the olives, sifting leaves and twigs out of the mix, I summoned up the courage to stutter out the suggestion that he and Simone join me for dinner that night. Opening one eye to look at me with a cocked eyebrow, he seemed pleased. He explained Simone had plans. Every Saturday night he went for pizza in Capoliveri with his friends. It would be Marco alone if I was okay with that.

I nodded with a smile.

For the last time, the midday church bells rang across the fields to tell me it was lunchtime. Taking the olives and some crates of wine up to the store Marco bid me farewell, advising he would be back to pick me up at six o'clock.

Enjoying the buoyancy of the salty Tyrrhenian Sea for the last time, I reluctantly dragged myself out of the crystal waters to dry out on the beach. The frog-toad broke his routine and didn't make an appearance to farewell me in the outdoor doccia. Instead, my grit was tested anew. A giant grasshopper hovered on the swinging door. Keeping one eye on him as I showered, I willed it not to start jumping around.

The thought of picking up my bags and moving on again filled me with dread, but I was excited about visiting Napoli, longing for some time in galleries after a month without setting foot in a single museum.

Marco appeared at six o'clock wearing bright red chinos and his same blue and white striped shirt from our evening out the week before. Laughing at me singing along to Eros Ramazotti on the radio as we drove, he told me how so much of the English he had learnt was through music on the radio. After studying Spanish at school in Sardinia, he had also unsuccessfully tried to learn Norwegian when living and working in the northern country when he was younger.

Driving to Portoferraio he asked me if I had seen the beach. I had visited the home of the exiled Napoleon and the Medici Fort, but I hadn't realised there was a beach near the small town. Pure white rocks covered the shoreline and shallows, ensuring the colour of the water was almost phosphorescent. On the horizon the luxury sailboat of someone rich, famous, or both, was caught in the sun's setting rays. The sky was cloudy and the last of the sunlight peering through the gap fell perfectly on the boat, casting it in gold in its peculiar light. We stood silent for a moment.

With the sun fading I took photos of the boat, the sea and the sweep of Scoglietto, a tiny rocky island sitting offshore. With a lighthouse its only ornament, the slanting rock face was bathed in the pink light of dusk with the same elusive rays of sunlight elegantly reflected from the windows of the lighthouse.

We walked back to the car. To Marco's dismay I admitted that while I had managed a visit to Napoleon's residence in Portoferraio on the day I had come over in search of internet access, I hadn't had the chance to get to San Martino where another of Napoleon's residences in exile was situated. Located in a small valley planted with vines away from the heat and turmoil of Portoferraio, he drove me down to see how the French emperor survived his containment on Elba. The gates had just closed as we arrived. Disappointed he wasn't able to show me around, we pressed our faces to the bars. I took in what I could see as Marco told me what he could remember of the stories of the former Emperor's life there.

After dinner in Portoferraio we drove the winding road up to Capoliveri to meet Simone. We took a seat in a wine bar to wait. Marco spoke again of his concerns for his son, how he wanted him to work hard, stay out of trouble and find the best opportunities. Simone waved cheerfully to us as he sauntered past with all his young friends trying to project their pre-teen cool.

As I prepared to step out of the car and bid them farewell that evening, my eyes met Marco's in understanding of the connection we had formed. Simone saw it too.

"Ciao Giac-a-lyn," he burst out a friendly but insistent farewell as he leant into the front of the van.

"A domani," I whispered to Marco with a smile.

"Dorma bene," he responded with a nod.

When the van pulled up the following morning my suitcases were out the front of the roulotte ready. I bequeathed my sleeping bag to Marco for Simone to use. I couldn't carry it with me. Declaring it un regalo—*a gift*—Marco had shaken his head, "Finche tu ritorno,"—*until you return*. My heart caught in my throat. Maybe… just maybe …

Vittorio gave me a hug and kiss on both cheeks, telling me I was welcome to come back any time. As Marco and I reversed back out onto the road I fought back the tears already threatening. Neither of us spoke much during the drive to the port.

Ensuring I had the correct ticket, Marco delivered me to the bottom of the stairs of the ferry. Embracing tightly, I rested my hands on the warm skin of his shoulders as we kissed quickly on both cheeks in farewell. "Grazie per… il suo… amicizia," I stuttered out.

Looking frustrated Marco shrugged a little and sighed, "Hmmm… Amicizia uh," —*friendship*. He embraced me gently again, before pulling back to kiss me on each cheek again, our lips this time almost brushed in passing between. He released me and with a brusque "Buon viaggio," he walked back to the van.

My eyes followed the back of the vehicle before it vanished out of sight. The tears began to roll. Trying not to let the few passengers gathering around me ready to embark see, I hung my head down as I desperately tried to stop the flow.

As the Moby ferry pulled out of the port, I found a spot to stand on the deck. Finding *Fortezza il Volterraio* reflecting the morning sunlight from its pinnacle over the bay, my eye slowly ran down the green slopes sweeping toward the water. I wondered if Marco was home yet. I wondered if he was watching the boat pull out from his kitchen window. No matter what came next, I would always remember the contadino I once knew. The peasant who lived in a humble home with his son by the vineyards in the shadow of a medieval castle, and who had shared a corner of his life with me for a short time, showing me kindness and respect, protection and friendship.

Knowing there was no way I could articulate anything that I might have wanted to say in farewell, I had meticulously worked out a message using my dictionary, written it on pretty note paper that I had bought in Siena, and left it in the car for him.

Mi è piaciuta l'opportunità di conoscerti mentre ero all'Elba. Grazie per la pratica di conversazione e l'amicizia. Io spero che noi possiamo essere in contatto. Forse Lei e Simone verrete ad Australia un giorno.

I have enjoyed the opportunity to get to know you while I have been on Elba. Thanks for the conversation practice and the friendship. I hope that we can be in touch. Perhaps you and Simone will come to Australia one day.

After a month of spending my days in the sunshine, swimming in the sea, and drinking in the fresh air, I watched as Elba faded on the horizon. It was sad to say goodbye. I left feeling refreshed from a month away from the hustle and bustle of life and intrusions of media and technology. As the Moby Ferry powered across the water back to Piombino, I hoped the people at the next farm would be as kind as Marco, Vittorio, Cinzia and Alessandro.

My phone beeped.

Grazie per la Sua comunicazione, la bella società e la conversazione. Noi dobbiamo ascoltare i nostri cuori ma anche il nostro cervello. Buon viaggio... Marco xxx

Thank you for your message, beautiful company and conversation. We must listen to our hearts, but also our brains. Journey well. Marco xxx

PART 3

~ *La Pellegrina* ~

THE PILGRIM

*I pack my trunk,
embrace my friends,
embark on the sea,
and at last wake up in Naples,
and there beside me is the stern fact,
the sad self,
unrelenting,
identical,
that I fled from..."*

~ Ralph Waldo Emerson ~

16

A heavy rainstorm swept in across the gulf of Napoli as I ventured down via Toledo amid the heaving populace. The dark clouds that had gathered began releasing heavy drops. The crowd around me broke into a run, dispersing as we all sought to find cover.

I had been supposed to travel all day from Elba and arrive in Naples by early evening. On reaching the train station in the port at Piombino, the Sunday trains were not running as listed online. Three Swiss German hikers were also stranded at the provincial station, and we raced around trying to find a driver for the taxi sitting locked and empty in front of the station. We found an amicable fellow settled in at a nearby café in no rush to pick up a fare. We begged him to finish his cappuccino with haste and get us to the next station half-an-hour away, so we could meet the train travelling from Pisa to Rome.

"Napoli?" the man who had paused to assist me with translation at the ticket office in Campiglia Marritima, shook his head despairingly, "É...pericoloso,"—*it is dangerous*. "You don't want to arrive there at night," he warned. With the changes to my journey, I would be pulling into Naples closer to midnight if I continued as planned.

I decided he had a point and booked my tickets so I could stay the night in Rome before continuing my journey the next day and arrive in daylight hours.

The chaos of Rome was overwhelming after a month in the serenity of life on Elba. I found a hotel close to Stazione Termini then headed out to find dinner in a small pizzeria near the Quirinal Palace—one of three official residences of the President of Italy.

Taking my time to adjust to being surrounded by so many people again, I strolled through the streets after eating, passing through the tourist hot spot of Piazza Navona and taking some time gazing at Bernini's Fontana dei Quattro Fiumi—the Fountain of the Four Rivers. I slipped around to the Pantheon and sat on the steps for a while, watching the evening visitors moving in and out of the ancient temple. As the crowds began to dwindle I headed back to the hotel. It was nice not to be rushing through Rome on a mission to see and do everything I could in the time I had available. Instead my unexpected visit allowed me to enjoy the rich evening ambiance of a city layered in thousands of years of stories, while watching wide-eyed tourists taking it all in for the first time, just as I had the year before.

An early train from Rome had brought me into Naples by lunchtime the next day. The train station was undergoing major renovations making it challenging to find my way around. When I found a taxi to take me to my hostel, the driver spoke no English and didn't seem to understand my attempts to communicate. As soon as I walked into the piazza where he had dropped me, I knew he had left me in the wrong place. I dragged my overweight luggage up via Monteoliveto, through the weekday crowds, reaching my hostel half-a-kilometre further up the road. I was relieved I had made the decision not to come in on the night train.

Eager to get my bearings in the new city, I headed out for a walk mid-afternoon only to find myself racing to find shelter under the ornate glass roof of the city's palatial nineteenth century shopping arcade, Galleria Umberto I Plazetta not long after setting out. The sound of the water pouring over the roof was deafening as the city was enveloped in the early autumn storm.

I waited it out for a while, then dashed across the road during a small reprieve in the torrent and found protection under the entrance arch of il Teatro San Carlo, the city's Opera House. I scanned the posters on the noticeboards to see what might be playing during my stay.

After ten years living in Sydney, I had never been to an actual Opera at the Opera House until a year earlier. I had seen dramas, dance performances, even attended an A-League awards night in Bennelong Restaurant, but hadn't experienced an actual Opera. I persuaded Elise to join me one evening after work. We had meticulously dressed up in the FFA office bathrooms before settling into a bar at Circular Quay for a glass of wine and a light dinner before the performance. As Sydney Ferry's moved in and out of the Quay framed by the Sydney Harbour Bridge below our window seat, I re-checked our tickets. Curtains would be up half an hour earlier than I had thought. Our plans to arrive in a cloud of elegance and sophistication were abandoned as we cancelled our food order, finished our drinks and belted down Bennelong Point in our evening gowns and heels, desperate to get there before lockout. As we tripped up the stairs at pace on our way to the Joan Sutherland Theatre, an usher called us over and whisked us through the first entry we reached. She directed us to take two available seats nearby as quickly as possible. The urgency to be seated provided us with an exceptional upgrade from the C Reserve seats up the back that we had lashed out on. Our show was Mozart's Don Giovanni and I was immediately enamoured—the passion and emotion of the performance enveloped me.

Now, I hoped, I would have the chance to experience Italy's cultural heart and see an opera in the country of its origin, in the beauty of an old-world European theatre.

Opening in 1737, il Teatro San Carlo is arguably the oldest opera house in Italy. But it is a claim held in contention with il Teatro La Scala in Milan. A fire destroyed a large part of the San Carlo interior in 1816. While quickly restored and re-opened within a year, La Scala—which opened in 1778—promptly contested the title and made claim of seniority in the wake of the blaze.

I scanned the posters only to realise the next Opera season wasn't due to start until well after I would have left the city. A sheet of rain blew in under the archway causing me to leap further along the walkway. I would need to come back tomorrow to find out what other sorts of performances might be on during my stay.

The squalling winds pushed the rainstorm around the streets, deluging… then easing… then releasing another downpour. During the gaps, I began picking my way around the edge of Piazza Trieste e Trento.

"Belllll-aaaaah… Ahhhhh… Bell-aaaaah."

I avoided eye contact with the African hawkers holding out ten-euro umbrellas, seeking a sale from the colourful collection slung on their arms. The moisture seeped through my clothes and dampened my skin. Even if I had remembered to bring my handbag size brolly with me this afternoon, it would have offered little protection from this storm.

I hugged the wall of Palazzo Reale to escape a fresh downpour. Ruggiero il Normanno—Roger, the first of the Norman Kings to rule over the city in the twelfth century—loomed above me from the façade, grimly watching over the sweeping arc of Piazza Del Plebiscito.

Naples, founded nearly three-thousand years ago by the Greeks, has always been a busy Mediterranean port city, attracting many foreign rulers through the centuries: from the Byzantines to the Goths, Lombards and Normans, the Spanish, the Austrian Hapsburgs and the Bourbons. At the time of Roger's rule from 1130 it comprised a rich cosmopolitan society, reflective of its international trading economy with remnants of Greco-Roman society, Byzantine Greeks, Syrians, Jews, Arabs, Lombards and descendants of the Goths.

The Normans who settled in the north-west of France in the eleventh century, had gone on to conquer southern Italy. Dismantling the Lombard principalities, they removed the dominant power of the Byzantines in Calabria and Apulia, and the Arabs in Sicily. The Duchy of Napoli—independent for five centuries—was the final state in Southern Italy to fall under their rule. King Roger had unified the southern half of the peninsular along with the island of Sicily and declared the southern region the 'Kingdom of the Two Sicilies.'

The grey stonework of Basilica di San Francesco di Paolo swept around in an austere curve across the front of the piazza opposite the palace. The large piazza suggested a space committed to the celebration of power and prestige when first commissioned by Joachim-Napoléon Murat when King of Naples in the early years of the nineteenth century. But his famous brother-in-law—Napoleon who he had planned it in tribute too—was soon exiled for the second time. This time to St Helena in the South Atlantic Ocean from which—unlike Elba—he would never return. The Bourbons had resumed power and completed the project, but ultimately the name the piazza now holds was in recognition of a plebiscite taken on October 21, 1860, that brought Naples into the unified Kingdom of Italy.

In 1963, a municipal ordinance transformed the square into a public parking lot to cope with the uncontrolled increase of cars in the city. In the late eighties it had been used as a holding yard during the construction of the Rapid Tramway. Finally, in 1994 when the G7 Summit came to town, the square was restored with traditional paving stones and it was reclaimed for those venturing the city on foot.

Today though, the largest piazza in Napoli seemed dirty, unkempt and marred by characterless graffiti across ancient stone and statue. I wondered why the city, which had been one of the four largest in Europe and the envy of Paris, seemed so in want of a refresh.

The storm showed no sign of abating. Through the heavy rain, I could just make out what appeared to be a café and made a dash for it.

The maitre'D who stood by the entry frowned with disdain as I bounded toward his door. Trying not to burst in like an excitable puppy, fresh from a frolic in the rain, I paused to straighten up.

Pushing the damp hair out of my eyes, I tried to flatten the fly away strands and pull my askew attire back into place, before stepping past him as gracefully as possible into the room.

My internal princess told me that I fitted in perfectly as I slipped through the door. Vaulted ceilings and frescos, ornate cream walls trimmed with gold, furniture fashioned from dark russet wood and sparkling chandeliers. Glistening trays of sweet treats tempted passers-by in immaculately presented displays. Debonair waiters worked briskly to fulfil customer orders from behind a spotless bar. I had burst into the Gran Caffé Gambrinas.

Vincenzo Apuzzo had founded the café in 1860, dreaming his club would be an important part of newborn Italy in the wake of unification. An icon in the city with its art nouveau interiors, it was once frequented by visitors to the city like Jean-Paul Sartre, Ernest Hemingway and Oscar Wilde, and locals like philosopher Benedetto Croce and the musician Toto.

I gazed down at my jeans. Soaked hems, slightly crumpled t-shirt. I was no princess and in fact looked more like a peasant straight from the fields of Elba. Aside from fellow dishevelled tourists of all ages crowding around the pastry display, the majority of tables in the side parlour were occupied by the cafe's well-heeled, business clientele. Eyeing me impatiently, a waiter hovered close to the bar awaiting my order. The extensive list of coffee options was overwhelming.

I finally selected a Caffé Viennese which included chocolate, cream and a splash of Sambucca to warm me up. I stood awkwardly by the bar, to avoid paying the surcharge if I was to take a seat at a table in the parlour. While I watched the careful preparation of my coffee, I eavesdropped on the banter of the well-dressed bar staff, listening for words I might recognise.

A tall glass was presented to me. I lifted the chocolate stick lying across the top and dipped it into the cream and dropped a dollop into my mouth before nibbling on the wafer. The hot, sharp, yet sweet liquid was a kaleidoscope of flavours as it tumbled around in my mouth. Coffee, chocolate, traces of cream and at last the fire of the Sambucca slid down my throat. The complexity of the beverage in my elegant surrounds felt utterly luxurious after a month on the farm.

Warmed internally and drying out a little externally, I exited back into the now glistening city. Making my way down Via Console Cesario, sunshine pushed itself between the clouds and dispersed them over the city. The streets had begun to move again.

Storm clouds still darkened the bay lying in front of me as I paused in a park looking out over Rada Santa Lucia, an inlet housing the bobbing masts of leisure craft north of the busy ferry and cruise ship passenger port. Cargo ships lay brooding off the coastline, tossed by the inky swell where they were anchored waiting for conditions to improve to permit a safe entry into the port. The outline of mountains, including the haunting presence of Mount Vesuvius—the only active volcano on mainland Europe to have erupted in the past 100 years—lay all but invisible behind the veil of rain that was still falling to the south-east.

Evening approached as I walked back to the hostel. I didn't want to stand out by moving too quickly amidst the leisurely amble of the locals. A group of boys aged eleven or twelve came past me, jostling each other, pulling at each other's clothes. One crashed into me as they passed. Suspicious of everyone, I pushed him off with a warning glare. Nonchalantly they continued on. I had watched the movie Gomorrah based on Roberto Savianno's book before leaving Sydney. Kids were known to be at risk of becoming drawn into the activities of the local mafia—the Camorra, one of the oldest and largest criminal organisations in Italy—from a young age. I wondered if any from that group had yet been caught up in the sinister side of the city.

Continuing north east on Via Toledo—the central thoroughfare constructed under the city's most famous Spanish Viceroy, Don Pedro Alvarez de Toledo, in the sixteenth century—I turned into the shadowy side streets off Piazza Monteoliveto that led to my hostel. As I passed by the darkened doorways of closed workshops and shopfronts, my thoughts turned to Marco. His warning rang in my ears to "stai attenta". I wondered what he was doing in the serenity of his island home.

Tourists often pass through Napoli for only a day or two. A visit to the galleries and the archaeology museum to see the collected treasures from Pompeii before they slip out of the madness of the city with a belly full of pizza. From there they head south to explore the luxurious pleasures of the Sorrentine Pensinsula and Amalfi coastline, or to marvel through the archaeological sites of Herculaneum, Pompeii, then on to Salerno, and the Greek temples at Paestum. With a week and a half booked for my own stay in the city, I didn't feel rushed to launch straight into museums and castles the next day. In Siena I had been connected to the city through the language school. In Elba I was connected to the community through the farm. I hoped in this southern, much larger community, I would find a way to make a connection with some locals so I could know the city through their eyes.

I stepped outdoors just before midday clasping a map with the centro storico (historical centre) of the city, marked up with highlights for me by Jenny, the Australian expat owner of Six Small Rooms. Setting up the hostel I was staying in after she had moved to Italy over a decade earlier, Jenny was not only from Australia but was a Brisbane girl too. She had started out driving tour groups from Rome before taking on the friendly hostel she now ran in the historic centre. Her recommendation for my first day was to work my way towards Vomero to enjoy lunch and take in the magnificent views across the city while I ate.

The inky, tumultuous bay of the afternoon before had been replaced by sparkling blue waters flowing in from the Tyrrhenian Sea. Sunlight danced across the light ripples of an almost smooth surface. The clear sky was interrupted by an occasional soft white, wispy cloud drifting across the cobalt canvas.

The siren Parthenope is embedded in the foundation stories of Napoli and ancient Greek mythology, along with her sisters Ligeia and Leucosia. Their story dates back to the eighth century BC, when the Greeks first created a settlement on the shores of the bay. These three daughters of Melpomene the Muse of Tragedy and the River God Achelous were companions of Persephone, the daughter of Zeus and Demeter Goddess of the Harvest. When Persephone was abducted by Hades to be made Queen of the Underworld, the sirens begged Demeter to give them wings to search for her daughter and their beloved friend. Demeter granted their wishes but let them retain their female faces and human voices.

Creatures of the sea, these siren sisters had haunted the shores of Campania in the search for their friend; the calling of their voices became weapons of seduction that lured unsuspecting sailors to their deaths on the rocks of the shore. Ulysses, hero of Homer's epic poem 'The Odyssey', was the one to devise a plan to withstand their seduction. He had his crew block their ears with wax and then tie him to the mast of the ship. He wanted to be the only man to hear their enchanting song and live to tell the tale. Parthenope and her sisters were so devastated at their failure to lure his ship in, that they leapt into the sea and drowned. The legend tells that Parthenope's body had washed ashore on Megaride, an outcrop of rock now separated from the mainland, where it is said Greek sailors found her and buried her. The area rising up from the shoreline became the foundation point for the early Greek settlement that was first named after her.

I began making my way towards Castel dell'Ovo—the oldest fort in Naples—perched on the small outcrop of Megaride which is now accessed by a causeway off via Partenope. Two thousand years ago, the classical Roman poet and renowned sorcerer Virgil, is said to have placed an egg, an alchemic symbol of protection, into the foundations of the earliest building on the site. Legend tells that the magical egg was hidden in a glass jar placed inside a metal cage to preserve it. While the egg remains unbroken, it is believed that the city and its people are protected from disaster or danger. I looked over to Mount Vesuvius looming beyond the shoreline of the southern side of the bay. Living in the shadow of this sleeping but still active giant, I wasn't surprised the city needed to cling to folklore in hope of ongoing protection. With the last eruption of the dozing giant in 1944 she is closely monitored by scientists, as locals await warning of new activity.

I wandered around the ramparts and turrets of the Castel dell'Ovo peering into renovated rooms, imagining the events that could be held here as I passed conference groups using the spaces for meetings. Strolling back over the causeway from the castle to the shore, one or two swimmers clambered from the water as I passed, laying back on their towels on nearby rocks to bask in the sun on the quiet Parthenopean waterfront.

Ambling north along via Riviera di Chiaia, I turned away from the bay, passing Piazza Vittoria. I wandered side streets cluttered with clothing and bric-a-brac markets. Mopeds and cars also squeezed down the narrow passage between the marquee stalls, while pedestrians were forced to squeeze tightly to the sides.

Opportune thieves on mopeds were known to cut the straps of bags from shoulders, quickly vanishing with the target's possessions. I was determined not to fall victim. I pulled my satchel close and kept a wary ear and eye out for mopeds in the clutter of people and other marketplace obstacles. In the Spanish Quarter, the streets were darkened by tall buildings overshadowing the narrow thoroughfares. Crates and refuse from vegetables lay discarded along the edges. The smell of il pesce was overpowering as I wandered through the fish markets.

As I emerged back on to the footpath of via Toledo I turned towards the archaeological museum, home to Pompeian and Herculaneum relics and the extensive Farnese collection. I knew it wasn't open on Tuesdays but thought I would check the noticeboards for information given I was nearby. I needed to cross the wide and busy road with traffic flying in both directions to reach the Museo Archeologico Nazional. I wondered if it was worth heading up to a crossing about two hundred metres further up the road. A group of teenage girls dressed in skinny jeans, short skirts and bright tops hovered on the curb near me preparing to cross. I latched on to the back of the group instead, trusting local survival skills to get across. We dived through a brief gap in the chaotic traffic, making it safely across.

There was a small noticeboard outside the closed museum, but I couldn't find any information about opening times. I would check online back at the hostel when I returned later.

As I walked back down the stairs, I paused to pull out my map. I had been planning to continue along Piazza Cavour. Propping my backside on a cement bollard, I reviewed which way I should walk next. If I continued the way I was going, I may end up at the Duomo. But I was enjoying being out in the fresh air and wasn't sure I was quite ready for the dark interior of a church. Now well past lunchtime, my stomach was growling. If I crossed back over Via Toledo and headed up Viale Salvator Rosa, it would take me up to the suburb of Vomero where I could find somewhere for lunch and take in the view as Jenny had recommended.

I made my way up to the pedestrian crossing around the other side of the Museo which would take me back over the busy street to start my ascent.

Studying my feet in my silver Birkenstocks as I stood there waiting for the lights to change, I examined my relatively clean but chipped toenails. I made a mental note to give myself a bit of a pedicure when I returned to the hostel in an attempt to feel a little more gentrified with my return to city life.

The traffic was stopped on the right side of the road when I looked up. The walk light changed to green. I turned my head for a cursory check to the left as I took a step out. Perhaps I screamed. Or perhaps my breath was momentarily taken away.

All I knew was… I seemed to be flying.

17

"Aiuto..." my muted cry for help was in Italian. Semi-bilingual still. A good sign my brain was functioning. I wasn't dead. That was a relief.

I could see the curb a metre or two beyond my feet. I hadn't been thrown too far into the centre of the thoroughfare. But, cars continued to fly around the corner from Piazza Museo Nazionale, tooting in annoyance as they swerved to avoid the gathering crowd who had emerged from cars and buildings and begun to gather protectively around my crumpled body.

It seemed I was centre stage, the central protagonist in a story that couldn't possibly involve me. I tried to piece together what had happened as bedlam reigned around me. There had been the helmet of the rider in my line of vision as I had turned my head. I heard a yell. Then impact. No escape. Flying. Falling. Hitting the ground. Rolling once. Twice. Throwing my arm out to stop the momentum. Now lying here, gazing down Via Toledo.

I squeezed my toes and tried to move my feet. Movement. Not paralysed. I shifted my legs ever so slightly. *Definitely have feeling.*

My left hand still clung to my bag. Being robbed I had been prepared for. Run down however, was not what I expected. I released my grip on the strap and placed my left hand on the ground. I tried to raise myself up slightly.

"NO! NO! NO! Non normale! Non normale!" the crowd surged towards me gesturing frantically at me to stop.

You're telling ME 'non normale', I thought in horror as excruciating pain enveloped my upper right arm. *What can they see that I can't?* I tried to tilt my head slightly to see what was going on between the weight of my body and the road. There didn't seem to be any blood or open wounds. *Perhaps a dislocation? That wouldn't be too hard to fix would it?*

"Questi sono i Tuoi?" a man crouched beside me and handed me my sunglasses. They must have flown off my face. Still intact. Barely a new scratch.

I gazed up at the growing audience—predominantly dark, swarthy, southern Italian men —and alarm swept through me as the distinct voice of my mother echoed urgently from my childhood.

"Always make sure you are wearing good underwear when you leave the house in case you are in an accident!"

I had left two bags of washing at the hostel to be done. Undie supplies were low. I had hit the bottom of the suitcase and inherently knew I had failed—on today of all days—in following this lifelong parental instruction. I was wearing the most decrepit pair I had with me. I surreptitiously tried to push the stringy, frayed seam out of sight below my waistband.

"C'e una ambulanza venendo," the man crouching beside me confirmed an ambulance was on the way.

"Mi dispiace!" I finally spoke, "Non parlo Italiano molto bene. Sono… Australiana."

Renewed curiosity and looks of dismay crossed the faces in the crowd. I could hear them murmuring to one another, "La ragazza, lei è un tourista,"—*the girl, she is a tourist*—they shook their heads.

The man asked me something else. I tried to understand his words. He showed me the phone in his hand.

"C'è qualcuno che posso contattare per te?"—he asked who he could contact on my behalf.

"Nessuno," I sighed—*no-one*, "Sono sola."

Looks of horror this time. "Sola! Lei è sola!"—*She is alone!*

The murmuring swept through the crowd again.

The consistent draw to this city throughout my trip, left me with a feeling of calm resignation about the situation I now found myself in. As if this was exactly where I was meant to be. Or perhaps it was simply the adrenaline coursing through my body triggered by the impact, imbuing me with the sense of peace despite what I now seemed to be facing.

An elderly lady crouched down and leant forward to offer me a sip of water from a plastic bottle. She stood up and stepped over to the nearby gutter.

"Sono queste le Tue scarpe?" she asked lifting one of my silver Birkenstocks asking if they were mine. I hadn't realised my footwear, a farewell gift from the urban family, had flown off my feet on impact. I nodded gratefully as she picked the other sandal up.

With her approach a couple of other onlookers moved in a little closer to peer at me. The man who had found my sunglasses reappeared through the crowd.

"I speak only little English," he apologised. He crouched down again and handed me a business card. "This…," he pointed to the name, "she is my wife. She know more. If you need anything," he said, "call this numbers. Am sorry but I have to go now. Buona fortuna."

I awkwardly pushed the card into the back pocket of my jeans for safekeeping. The slight movement caused more pain to shoot through my arm. All movement, even breathing, had begun to inflict piercing pain.

A siren approached. "Attenzione, l'arriva dell'ambulanza!" the cry went up as the crowd prepared to make a path for its arrival. The direction of the sound changed as the ambulance took a turn off before reaching us.

I took a slow, deep, breath. The rush of adrenaline in my system that had created a sense of painlessness on first impact was decreasing.

The older woman crouched beside me again, and cupped my cheek gently, "Vuoi che venga con Te? All'ospedale?"—She offered to come to the hospital with me.

"Ok," I smiled weakly in gratitude.

The pace of the city reverberated around me as traffic continued to roar around the corner. I lay motionless, and gazed sideways down Via Toledo, as we waited for what felt like hours for the sound of another siren.

A tanned, blond haired, blue-eyed young man appeared in front of me.

Strains of romantic music played through my addled mind. A knight in shining armour? The reason I had been drawn to Napoli? Whatever happens next is meant to be…?

"Sei va bene? Va bene? Va bene?"—*Are you okay?*—his incessant demand dragged me back to reality. *Instant concern for me. So lovely!*

I smiled up at him, shrugging the functioning left shoulder, and answered without conviction, "Hmmm... cosi, cosi,"—*So, so*.

He turned back to the animated conversation of the other onlookers standing near a sorry looking moped. For the first time, I wondered which of these curious bystanders had been the driver that had brought about my downfall. *Were they injured too?*

A second siren approached. The crowd parted as the vehicle pulled up.

"Can you move your legs?" the paramedic who knelt down beside me spoke a little English. I demonstrated my ability to move slightly from my odd landing spot, as a second paramedic arrived with the stretcher. They eased me on to my back, releasing my injured arm from its position embedded in the road. The pain swept through the top of my arm, then ricocheted throughout my body. I screamed.

Placed on the spinal board, a precautionary brace was put around my neck. The English-speaking paramedic supported my agonised limb with his hands as the driver of the ambulance assisted the second paramedic to lift me into the ambulance. I gasped for breath, shuddering through the pain. The crowd evaporated into little more than a dark haze. With my pain sensors overwhelmed, I was only semi-conscious as I was carried through the crowd to the back of the waiting vehicle.

The English-speaking paramedic sat beside me still holding my limb. It felt almost like it was disconnected from my body. I tried to take more slow, deep, breaths. The haze of pain eased briefly as all movement stopped. I couldn't see any medical equipment from where I lay. Odd. It felt like I was in the back of a transit van. I peered at the logo on the paramedics uniform to check that in my delirium I wasn't being kidnapped. The warnings about crime activity in the city were still pulsing through my mind.

The tanned, blonde-haired, blue-eyed knight, re-materialised beside me through the haze of pain. He took the spare seat across from me. The romantic music pulsed louder in my mind as I watched him settling into the ambulance, looking over me with concern. *He's coming with me? What's going on? Has he stepped in to come with me instead of the elderly woman who had offered? That is so sweet!*

My eyes fell to his wrist which he was clutching with his opposite hand. My internal soundtrack went on shuffle. The dramatic strains of music forewarned the drama of deceit. I realised my assumed knight in shining armour was in fact the rider of the lethal steed that had taken me down. Not my future husband rescuing me.

The elderly woman, with her husband beside her, appeared at the door of the ambulance. With two patients and two paramedics already on-board, she was not going to be able to come with me to the hospital she apologised.

"Abitiamo a numero otto. Non tu dimentici. Numero otto."

They lived at number eight. *Number eight what?* I struggled to return their final well wishes but promised not to forget the number as the ambulance doors closed.

On the edge of consciousness, I still experienced the buzz of being in an emergency vehicle with its siren on. But the novelty of the moment vanished quickly as we began jolting over cobblestoned roads. Immense pain coursed through my body with every bump.

I stared up helplessly into the sympathetic warm brown eyes of the paramedic.

"Come si dice in Italiano 'pain'?" I gasped.

He paused momentarily.

"Dolore."

"Ho dolore," I screeched with the next bump—*I have pain!*

18

The siren petered out to silence as the driver eased around a corner and pulled to a stop. The doors were thrown open. I released an agonised scream as the thud of the wheels of the stretcher trolley hit the ground, causing another flood of pain to sweep through my nervous system. "Tranquilla," the paramedic soothed as he leant over me, gently sweeping the hair out of my eyes, "Con calma". I glared up at him. *Be tranquil!? Be calm!?*

My former husband had once tried to teach me his breathing techniques for voice projection when on stage. Today I tapped into my own my latent natural talent. I drew breath as far into my core as I could, and in a rush of sound, I released the pain from deep within my diaphragm. As the physical agony was expressed, I felt an unexpected rush of repressed emotional pain flood out at the same time. I remembered him also telling me they had learnt at drama school how we hold emotional pain deep within our body. Tapping into that muscle memory was a technique that actors sometimes used when connecting to play deep emotional roles. Back then, the only pain I seemed to hold was a few overhanging friendship rejection issues from my school years. But to my shock, in this moment of physical agony, the deep-seeded pain from the loss of my marriage and the numbing disappointment that the expectations of a life I had expected to have had crumbled into ruins also rushed to the surface. I had wept for months after the marriage ended, to a point where I thought I could weep no more. But lying on that stretcher I realised how deeply the loss still sat within me.

The paramedic wheeled me into accident and emergency, his face wincing as I evoked wordless incantations to lose myself from the present physical and long-held emotional agony. I ignored the vague concern that I may have been contributing more than my fair share of decibels to the emergency rooms. I felt at liberty to make a contribution. Until someone medicated me, screaming as loud as I could at this moment felt like a right.

The paramedics vanished from view. The source of my physical agony lay somewhere beside me. My arm was definitely still attached—that was a relief—but I couldn't sense the presence of the limb, beyond associating it with the cause of the agonising pain wracking my body. I held the rest of my body rigid, resisting the waves of pain sweeping throughout me. Grubby grey doors swung open and closed nearby. I watched as medical staff moved in and out of the emergency area.

The paramedic re-appeared above me and gently stroked some strands of hair off my face again. "Buona fortuna,"—*good luck*—he offered.

"Grazie. Grazie mille," I whispered. Another burst of pain re-ignited my banshee-like screaming. My pain echoed down the hallway after him.

The emotionless grey eyes of an orderly appeared above me. He gave me a brusque nod of acknowledgement and began to pull my trolley backwards down the hallway, weaving around until we reached a darkened room.

My body was covered with a lead apron as I tried to manage my oxygen intake with small, deliberate breathes to manage the explosive vibrations of pain with every slight movement as they bumped me around in the dim light. A song from church floated into my mind. I began to hum it quietly.

> *No weeping; no hurt or pain; no suffering you hold me now;*
> *you hold me now...*
> *No darkness; no sick or lame; no suffering... you hold me now;*
> *you hold me now.*

I felt the strength of the loving omnipresence of God alongside me as the words drifted through my mind. The irrepressible energy that was pushing out from my core abated a little. My screams were reduced to dramatic groans as I continued to take tiny gasps of air while the x-rays were taken, fearing the pain would set off on its rampant journey through me again.

Hours seemed to pass before the orderly reappeared only minutes later to wheel me back to emergency. This time he rolled me into a consultation room.

With silver flecked finger-length dark hair and serious dark eyes peering over silver rimmed spectacles, il Dottore who was waiting for me, took my right hand. Gently lifting the limp arm, he bent it slowly at the elbow. My eyes pleaded fearfully with him.

"It is okay," he reassured me in strongly accented English while holding eye contact, "we bend and rest your arm across your body, hold your right hand with your left. You will have more comfortable." The new position offered some relief as I regained a modicum of control over my agonised limb.

With the help of a male infermiere—nurse—he gently sat me up. I sobbed in misery. Tentacles of pain reached all over my body. I plunged towards a feeling of utter madness as they raised my body upright for the first time in the hour and a half since impact.

"The pain?" I pleaded, "Something for the pain?"

He shook his head, "Not yet. It is better not."

I pursed my lips and pinched my eyebrows together as I levelled my best attempt at a death stare at him in response.

"You have pain in your head or neck?" he asked calmly, ignoring my glare.

"No."

"In your back?"

"No."

"You have pain anywhere more?" he asked as the neck brace was removed. It took some concentration to work my way around the other nerve endings in my body. My left thigh, where the moped must have hit me, was throbbing.

"Il motorino. It hit my leg."

He checked I could move it.

"Not broken," he declared.

The doctor supported me on my uninjured side, while the infermiere gently removed my top and bra. I concentrated on my lower core muscles to help me stay upright, as I sat precariously on the edge of the trolley. Breathe in. Breathe out.

They began to strap my arm to my torso with rolls and rolls of padding and bandaging. I felt like a mummy being prepared for internment. The doctor left the room as the infermiere completed a final layer to my dressing with a thick snowy white tape with a satin finish. He spoke reassuringly to me as he finished his task.

"How did it happen?"—he had asked.

"Non lo so," I sighed. *I don't know*. And even if I did, I didn't have enough words in Italian to explain the little I knew of what had happened. I didn't know why a moped had come flying at me when the walk light was green. Except this was Italy, and sometimes it seemed that traffic lights were more of a suggestion than a rule.

Returning to the room, the doctor pushed the top of my jeans down at the back to find my gluteus muscle. "Anti-dolorifico," he said as I felt the sharp jab. Pain relief at last.

They assisted me from my perch on the trolley and lowered me into a wheelchair. As the pain relief started to take effect, the other muscles in my body—held in complete tension to manage every minute movement including breathing—began to relax.

"Dove sono le sue scarpe?" the infermiere asked looking at my bare feet.

My shoes? I wondered if my Birkenstocks had reached the ambulance. The last time I had seen them had been in the hands of the kind lady who was going to come with me. Perhaps they never made it out of the ambulance. I shook my head.

He wheeled me out into the hallway and parked me to one side. Left on my own, other patients with lesser complaints and family members meandering in the hallway surrounded my wheelchair. They leant into my personal space, peering down at me, chattering with each other, chattering at me, unaware that I neither understood nor cared what they were saying. Like a goldfish that has accidentally flipped out of the bowl, unable to go anywhere or do anything, I gazed up at them wondering what elements of my circumstance the discussion was covering.

Un straniere—*a foreigner*—I heard the rumour begin to spread. The alarmed expressions and head shaking began as it had done out in the street. And the icing on the cake causing a significant new angle of horror, was the fact I didn't seem to have any scarpe—*shoes*—and no one knew where they were. The conversation became more animated as the discussion about my missing scarpe caused increasing consternation amongst the gathered group.

I looked to my right and spotted the fallen knight through a doorway. He held his shirt up while a doctor examined his torso. A police officer spoke intensely to them both. I felt incapacitated by lack of language as I watched the debate going on, wondering what the conversation was about.

The fallen knight pulled his shirt down as the conversation came to an end. As he came out of the room, my crowd of onlookers scattered so he could approach me.

"Stai... Tutto bene?" he asked hesitantly.

"Tutto bene..." everything good. I smiled unconvincingly knowing it was obvious that I was clearly lying. I still didn't know what my injury was but given I had been put in a half body cast everything was clearly not good.

He gazed at me with what seemed to be genuine concern for a long moment and his tarnished armour regained a little shine.

"Hmmm... Devo andare..."—*I have to leave*. An older man had come to pick him up, and he gave me a nod of sympathy before they walked away.

My wheelchair was rolled into a consultation room.

"How long are you here for?" the doctor now sitting behind a desk asked abruptly in English.

"Ten days," I told him.

"And then where are you going?" he asked.

"Sapri," I answered wondering why he was asking, "I have work on a farm."

"No. You will stay with us in Napoli," he stated firmly.

He held up an x-ray. I could see a rib cage, but the rest of the rather cluttered image was a mystery to me.

"It is broken."

I studied the blurry white shapes on the x-ray. *What even is that?* I wondered.

The doctor kept referring to 'la tua spalla'. Spalla was shoulder. I frowned. That sounded a little more complicated.

Someone leant through the door to ask the doctor something. As I waited for his attention to return to me, my mind drifted.

Six weeks in plaster or immobilized for breaks?... Won't be able to carry my luggage with one arm... I wonder what I'll do in Naples for all that time?... I really wanted a chance to meet the locals... This is a little unorthodox but could work... I wonder how difficult it will be to get myself to Mt Vesuvius with my arm in a plaster cast. Lucky the bus gets you quite close... I guess I can't go and work on that farm near Sapri next week... That's upsetting... Really wanted to learn how to milk a goat... And to work in the vegetable garden, the vineyards, picking chestnuts and wild mushrooms... Wonder how I can contact them and let them know I won't be coming... Don't have Sebastiano's phone number... Only email... I wonder how much credit I have left on my phone... Should I tell

Marco what's happened? ... I wish I had put some more credit on my phone this morning..

"You will need the operation," the doctor looked at me gravely.

"OH!" I felt internal alarm spread visibly across my face.

"We need to mend your bone so you will need the operation."

It took more effort to process this crucial piece of new information. Sudden exhaustion washed over me. Trying to stay upright had begun to overwhelm me. My whole upper body felt so weak.

A policeman walked into the small room with three other medical staff trailing behind. They seemed to have just come in to see what was going on and perched themselves against the desk and walls to listen in.

"Passaporto per favore?" the policeman asked me. I stared at him blankly for a moment, going over my exit from the hostel only a few hours before. I had locked my passport in my locker for the day, in case I had succumbed to a bag snatcher. With only a walk around the city and lunch planned, I hadn't been too concerned about carrying it today.

I shook my head in resignation, "Non, ho il passaporto con me."

I opened my shoulder bag—resting heavy in my lap—and struggled with my free hand to extract my driver's license from my purse as an alternative.

"Permesso?" the infermiere who had helped with my dressings leant over. I nodded gratefully accepting his request for permission to assist me.

The policeman asked where I was staying.

"Il nome è Inglese,"—*the name is English*—"Six Small Rooms".

The policeman looked at me perplexed and asked for the name

again. I racked my brain for the right words in Italian, and stuttered out, "Sei … letti... piccoli," —Six... rooms... small...

It still made no sense to him. The infermiere, helped me find my diary in my bag. I showed the policemen where I had written the name and address down for my arrival the day prior.

"In vicino via Toledo," I volunteered. "Hmmmm... in vicino Piazza MontehhhOLiiiveteeOooh," I overemphasised my vowels hoping it would help.

His face remained blank. I was getting exasperated. *The full address is written down for crying out loud*, I frowned at him in annoyance pushing my diary forward again. An animated conversation erupted about where it might be.

"Ah si si! Lo so. La Piazza Monteoliveto..." the face of my assistant lit up as he recognised the location. He patted my hand and explained the location to the confused officer.

I held out my locker key to the policeman as I tried fruitlessly to explain in English where my passport was located at the hostel. The doctor tried to translate as much as he could. I was relieved I had decided to stay at a hostel run by an Australian. As the policeman headed off, I hoped Jenny would be able to help, if he ever worked out where the hostel was.

Taken to another x-ray room, I was carefully raised to my feet for another scan. The feat was almost impossible with still unchecked pain in my leg where the moped had hit. I was overwhelmed by the effort, as I coaxed the bruised limb to support my weight. Exhausted by the trauma, pain and language barriers of the past two hours, I was desperate to lie down and close my eyes.

Two nurses in deep green uniforms welcomed me as I was

wheeled into the orthopaedic ward. They gingerly assisted me up onto a bed in the hallway. Still wearing my skinny jeans, now accessorised by the soft cast wrapped thickly around my torso, they tucked my handbag in beside me.

"Stai attenta alla tua borsa," they said as one of them pulled the sheet over both me and the bag. I obediently draped my protective left arm over the sheet on top of my valuables.

The drugs had relieved the piercing pain, but a drawing agony to the injured limb remained. I lay back against the pillows hoping the pain relief would smother my agony soon. It didn't. The pain deepened with every passing minute. I closed my eyes to try and find relief through rest.

As late afternoon drifted into evening, I opened my eyes to find three women beside my bed. With kindly eyes and crinkles of age weaving a map of knowledge across her face, Nina reached out to stroke my left hand where it lay on the sheet beside me. A younger woman beside her introduced herself as Patrizia. The third young woman's name was Pina. Exhaustion hindered my ability to comprehend much of what they were saying except to understand that they had heard I was on my own and had come to check on me. They had family members in the ward behind me. Touched by their concern for me, I gazed at them thoughtfully. *Local connections. This was a dramatic but effective way to achieve that goal I guess...*

Smells of warm food drifted through the ward around six o'clock, reminding me that I never found that scenic spot for lunch. Despite the trauma I hadn't lost my appetite. Three alfoil tubs were left on the side table beside me. Unable to move into any position other than that in which I had been left propped, I looked longingly at the containers on the trolley beside me, curious to know what was served in an Italian hospital.

"Allora... Vuoi che ti aiuti a mangiare?" Pina intuitively appeared at my side. The idea of dependence on strangers overwhelmed me.

I thanked her but told her I could feed myself. I allowed her to assist and open the food containers revealing a pasta dish, vegetables, one with some meat, and of course, as with every Italian meal, bread. Making everything as accessible as possible, she graciously left me to precariously balance the containers on my torso and attempt to get the food to my mouth. Attempting ambidexterity for the first time, I raised a little of each course to my mouth with my left hand, trying not to spill anything on my pristine white dressings.

As dinner was cleared away, Patrizia appeared at my bedside with a two-litre bottle of water.

She tilted her head down the hall, "Un regalo da Rosa," she explained as she poured some into a plastic cup for me. *A gift from Rosa.*

Why would water be a gift? I wondered as I nodded in thanks. Rosa was the infermiere who had looked after me when I arrived. I thought it was odd that no staff had brought me anything to drink since arrival. It seemed water came at a cost.

The throng of activity and noise died down as visitors in the ward started to leave for the evening. I stared vacantly at the hallway wall, trying to ignore the increasing pain as the initial dose of relief began to wear off.

Jenny from the hostel rushed in just after visiting hours ended, able to bypass the rules as she arrived with a different policeman in tow. I was overwhelmed with relief to see her striding up the hallway towards me with her young daughter Alyn. "I'm so sorry I couldn't get here sooner!" she exclaimed.

As my only contact in the city, I was stunned with relief with the confirmation that someone knew of my fate.

The policeman arrived with her and to my relief handed me my passport and returned my keys. Jenny and Alyn had pulled together some essentials – pyjamas and singlet tops, my toiletries, some books, and my pocket Bible. Alyn proudly pointed out my multivitamins. "I told mum to bring them. Help you get better!" she nodded sagely at me for her eleven years.

Armed with granola biscuits, chocolate, lollies and water, Jenny tucked things around me within arm's reach. She promised that she or someone from the hostel would be happy to bring up anything else I needed tomorrow.

"One question," I asked, "Where am I? As in, what hospital is this?"

Jenny wrote down for me 'Ospedale C.T.O.' and the phone number. Pulling the tourist map from my bag, she pointed to roughly where the hospital was. I inhaled sharply. I had made it to my destination after all. Not quite as planned and not in time for lunch, but at least in time for dinner. The trauma hospital sat in the hilltop suburb of Vomero.

"Would you like me to take you to the bathroom?" Jenny offered. I hadn't thought about the bathroom for hours and still didn't sense I needed to use the facilities. I was appreciative but felt she had already gone above and beyond. Thanking her but uncomfortable at the thought of a stranger having to assist me in such an intimate situation, I declined. She looked at me with concern. "Are you sure?"

"Tutto bene," I smiled. I would be up and about tomorrow.

Hopefully I could wait until then.

I wondered what and how to tell my parents. I didn't want to disturb them in the middle of the night. I waited for dawn to arrive in Australia, then sent them a non-alarmist text to broach the matter.

> *Unexpected change in travel plans that I need to discuss.*
> *Please call me on Italian mobile urgently in the morning.*

While the doctor in emergency had reassured me that I would be taken care of, I called my travel insurance company to let them know what had happened. The girl on the emergency line took my number and called me back. Taking down all details of the accident and the little I could tell her about my condition—something is broken, and it needs to be operated on was about all I could offer—she advised she would fax paperwork through to the hospital. I wondered if the paperwork would find me.

Sending a text to Debbie in Brisbane, Elise back home in Sydney and Alexis in London, I included the important details:

> *Small drama. Knocked down by moped in Napoli. Seriously!*
> *In hospital but okay. Broken shoulder. Needs operation.*
> *Driver handsome.*

As the messages went through, my phone beeped in reply with a message from the Italian carrier. Less than E2.00 credit remaining. The phone beeped again as my friends all texted back frantically. Alarmed about using any more of my minimal credit I couldn't respond. I stared at the screen apologetically knowing they would now be worried. There was little I could do.

The noise of televisions blared from the wards on either side of where I lay in the hall. I watched the infermieri wandering past in the hallway. Just before the lights began to go out, Rosa stopped beside me and administered another injection of anti-dolorifico into my glute.

"Grazie per l'acqua," I said quietly.

She cupped my cheek gently, "Di Niente Jacqueline,"—*it's nothing.*

The bright fluorescent bulbs in the hallway were turned off. With the approach of midnight televisions gradually quietened.

Adrenaline continued to rush through my body after the impact and despite my exhaustion, I lay wide awake. I could hear an elderly lady in a nearby bed muttering to herself, sometimes quietly, sometimes quite loudly. There was a verbose passing of wind from another bed somewhere behind me. I clasped my left hand to my mouth to suppress a giggle. And with the rumble of snoring from two others in front of me, I realised I was one of several in the hallway tonight.

As the night deepened, my anxiety increased. I clutched my phone in anticipation of my parents' call for hours. I needed them to know that something had happened to me. I needed to hear their voices. The phone vibrated just after 2am. I pulled the sheet over my head to muffle my voice.

"So, what's this change in plans?" Dad asked cheerfully. He and mum hadn't had mobiles for long and were still getting used to checking them. He had pulled his phone out to check it sometime after nine in the morning.

"Ummm... Well... I'm in hospital Dad."

19

A flurry of activity erupted at dawn as the infermieri began moving through the halls, checking temperatures, taking blood samples, and giving morning medications. I lay listlessly watching everything go on around me.

"Buongiorno! Io sono Dominico," a man in a navy uniform stopped next to my bed unperturbed by the rush of the nurses around him. "Stai bene questa mattina?"—how are you this morning. He looked into my eyes with genuine concern.

"Piacere Dominico. Io sono Jacqueline," I offered with a weak smile.

"Io sono qui ogni giorno,"—*I'm here every day*—he told me. "Lei mi fa sapere se Lei ha bisogno di qualsiasi cosa,"—*Let me know if you need anything.*

"Ok," I nodded. I wondered who he was as he wandered on.

A drink in a plastic cup sealed with foil along with a biscotti in a packet was left on the trolley beside me. Infermiere Gennaro—a man in his fifties—stopped and picked up the packet. He raised an eyebrow in query as to whether I needed help. I nodded gratefully.

He showed how they crumble the biscotti into the milky drink and then he insisted on spoon feeding me. It felt awkward as he spooned the sweet mushy mix into my mouth like I was a baby. He cleared away my breakfast packaging, then rolled my bed a little further up the hallway. Jenny had told me that it was common to see beds in the hallways when the hospitals had too many patients. There seemed to be quite a few of us lying out in the open area today.

From my new spot further up the hall, I could see Dominico leaning on a counter chatting to someone just out of my view through a doorway across the hall. "Un caffe?" he held up a plastic espresso cup as he caught my eye.

"Si... Per favore," I nodded. He dispensed a coffee from the staff espresso machine beside him then came over to pop it in my hand with a wink and a smile before disappearing down the hall. A few minutes later, he returned this time pushing a bucket along with his foot, flicking his mop back and forth across the hallway floors.

"Buongiorno Jacqueline. Come stai questa mattina?"—*how are you this morning*—Dottore Russolillo, with a mop of pure white hair, introduced himself as he came alongside my bed on morning rounds. He directed a group of young registrars to gather around. He held some x-rays up to one of the fluorescent lights for them to see. The young doctors passed the x-rays around. One by one, they looked from the x-ray, then back down at me, then back to the x-ray. Their faces appeared to sink into frowns of concern as they examined the scan.

"Le ragazze Australiane sono MOLTO indipendente!" I heard Dottore Russolillo telling them—*Australian girls are VERY independent.*

For the past three months it was true—I had never felt so independent. I had been free of the constraints of everyday life, seeing where the road would take me. Until yesterday, when I ended up embedded in the road, instead of travelling it. And now here I was completely and utterly reliant on strangers... in a foreign hospital... badly injured... thousands of kilometres from friends and family... in a place where I barely spoke the language.

Gennaro came over and introduced Infermiere Antonio who had white hair and kind eyes. He indicated that they were going to take me to the toilet. I felt the broken bone shifting as they gently brought me up to a sitting position. *Breathe...2, 3, 4... and out 2, 3, 4...* The pain was still immense, but I rallied at the thought of being able to get up.

"Dove sono le tue scarpe?" they asked looking around the bottom of the bed.

"No scarpe."—*No shoes*—I shook my head.

A third Infermiera was summoned. She brought plastic bags which were tied around my feet in lieu of my missing shoes, while the two men supported me on the edge of the bed. I began to shudder from the pain that was again coursing from my injury throughout my body. *Breathe... 2, 3, 4... I really need to go to the bathroom. I can do this...*

They eased me off the bed and on to my feet.

And breath... 2, 3... Oh, sweet JESUS! TAKE ME NOW, I screamed internally. Agony engulfed me as the movement disturbed my broken bone.

"Aspetta! Aspetta!" I gasped—*Wait! Wait!*

They supported me as I found equilibrium on my feet as the hallway spun around. The agony of the day before returned, but with new depth. With my left arm across the shoulder of one, the other held me delicately around the waist from the right, carefully avoiding contact with my injury site. We staggered together a few metres towards a doorway into a ward. I wondered why no-one thought to bring a wheelchair on seeing how weak I was.

"*Piano piano Giac-a-leen...*" the voice of Signor Pagetti in Siena came back to me. *Step by step...*

My whole body raged. *I can't do this, I can't do this, I can't do this.* My bladder was desperate for release. My leg throbbed with the pain where the moped had hit me. The agony in my arm consumed me. I felt myself grow weaker with each feeble step.

Hazy figures drifted into view, as we passed through a doorway into a ward. I saw concern on the familiar face of Patrizia as we passed. Dominico had stopped work and was leaning on his mop watching on with a look of concern. We turned into the bathroom. As I laid eyes on my target, every muscle in my body released. Every muscle. I didn't care.

As I slumped in a partial faint in the arms of my escorts, chaos erupted around me. Blissed out on the rush of serotonin and endorphins with the slight loss of consciousness, I relished the release of my bladder at last, unconcerned about the public nature of my circumstances as the agony in my body was momentarily overridden. I was carried back out to a treatment room, and a female infermiera summoned to clean me up. As the endorphins faded, I was hit with despair. My fresh and only pyjama pants and dodgy underwear were now ruined. I had nothing else with me to wear.

My hallway bed was wheeled into the room and I was lifted back in. A sheet and light blanket was pulled over and tucked in over my nakedness. Wheeled back into the hallway, my soiled clothing was left in a plastic bag hanging on a nob on the trolley beside me.

I had no family to come to collect it and take it home to wash it. It was going to get stinky fast. The staff disappeared to check on other patients as the doors opened for the start of visiting hours. I was left feeling overwhelmed by vulnerability—now wearing nothing but my torso wrap under the covers—as the morning crowd of family members began rolling in.

Brendon, another Aussie working part-time at the hostel, dropped in during the morning with another bag urgently packed by Jenny with fresh underwear and tracksuit pants, my phone charger, glasses and contact lens solution. Also from Brisbane, Brendon thought I seemed familiar when I had arrived the day before. When you grow up in Brisbane it is still a small world even when you are on the other side of it to your hometown. You will nearly always find a connection. We had managed to work out that he had possibly gone to school with my best friend Debbie's brother. At some point we must have crossed paths years before. He offered to take my phone to a nearby retailer and organised credit to be added to my account. As he dropped it back to me, he promised to try and visit again soon.

Infermiere Antonio wheeled me to an alcove in the hall after lunch. He had cordoned off a spot near an unused nurses station with a partition and positioned my bed so I had a view through one of the few windows in the hall. The immediate landscape was a carpark, but I could at least see the clear blue sky. He brought two female infermieri over to wriggle me into the fresh underwear and tracksuit pants that had been delivered in the privacy of my new corner. Feeling more secure with clothing on again, I drifted off into a restless sleep for the first time in twenty-four hours.

When I opened my eyes later that afternoon three staff wandered over to check on me. Things seemed less hectic in the ward at this time of day.

"Hai bisogno di fare la pipi?" one of them asked.

I couldn't understand the question.

"La pipi? Bisogno di fare la pipi?" they all asked over the top of each.

Pipi? Pipi? Oh... PIPI! I managed a smile and nodded. I wasn't busting but knew it was best to say yes rather than have a repeat of this morning.

"Puoi camminare fin lì?—*Do you think you can walk there?*—they asked. Perché altrimenti potremmo doverti dare un catetere."—*otherwise we will have to give you a catheter.*

I was nervous after this morning. But I didn't fancy a catheter either.

"Si... posso... ma, avete un..." I hesitated, wishing I knew the words to ask for a wheelchair. Somehow my one-handed charade of a wheel going around seemed to make sense. Someone appeared five-minutes later with a wheelchair, ready to take me to the bathroom.

My phone beeped as I was settled back into my bed.

Jacq. Tutto okay?

Dear Marco. My heart beat a little faster. I was so happy to hear from him. I took a deep breath before texting back news of the past twenty-four hours. "Stai attenta," he had told me.

Nooooo... What do you need?
Would you like me to come?
I can come Jacqueline, it's no problem.

Of course I wanted him to come. But I still really had no idea what I needed. I was just trying to survive right now. I hoped that once they operated, I would be on the mend and out and about in a few days.

Non ti preoccupato Marco. Tutto bene.

Everything wasn't good, but I didn't want him to worry. He had enough to do at home on Elba. But I secretly wished he would still appear at my bedside despite declining his offer.

I managed little sleep overnight and woke before dawn. I waited for the sun to rise over the carpark and activity in the ward to begin. I wet a tissue with water in my plastic cup to dab my face and was in the middle of battling to brush knots out of my hair by the time the infermieri came to take my temperature at daybreak. My vanity had kicked back in.

"Brava!" the handsome younger man exclaimed with a bright smile of encouragement. He handed me my phone which they had charged down in the infermieri office overnight. Without being in a proper ward there had been nowhere near my bed to plug it in, leaving me anxious without it in case family called. I had no missed messages from overnight.

Gennaro and Antonio came over after breakfast had been cleared away. With my handbag still safe under the covers, they pulled the blanket up to my neck, ensuring it was firmly tucked in around the whole bed. As Gennaro wheeled me out of the ward, Antonio demonstrated that I should keep the blanket up high, as where I was going may be fa freddo—*cold*. He vanished from my view as we rolled out of the ward.

"Dov'e andiamo?"—*where are we going?* I looked up quizzically at Gennaro.

He didn't respond. In silence we travelled down the hall, and into a lift. They hadn't brought my other belongings, so I assumed I wasn't being moved to a room on another ward.

We turned from the lift down another hall and into a room with an open bore MRI. More scans. An attendant came over to assist my silent friend.

"Non tocca! Non tocca!"—*don't touch*—I hissed as I wagged my index finger at the attendant as he reached towards my broken side. I recoiled as best I could on the bed. They both looked at my fear-filled face and nodded they understood. Through the collaborative efforts of the three of us, my body was slowly transferred to the bench that slid into the opening of the bore.

Breath in two, three, four… and out two, three, four… In agony lying flat as my body was drawn into the bore, I cried out every protest I knew in Italian without swearing.

"Ma DAIIIIII!"—but COME ON!

"BASTA!!! BASTA!!!"—ENOUGH!!!

Dottore Russolillo entered the room as I was brought back out of the machine.

"I speak a little English, but today I have extra help," he introduced a young female Dottoressa with him who would assist with translation.

An English speaker, I felt some relief.

She explained that Dottore Russolillo was the head surgeon in ortopaedia.

"Your fracture is very complicated," the young woman began. "There is a special device they require for the surgery which is not available at this hospital."

"You will need to transfer to another hospital," the Dottore explained while chewing on the end of a cigar.

"I would have wanted to do the surgery myself, but if you wait here until we can borrow the device, it will be too long."

I felt the fear cross my face. *Device? What did they need a special device for? And change hospitals? I'm only just learning how to survive in this hospital. I need Antonio and Gennaro. They know I'm on my own.*

"You will be fine," the younger doctor gently touched my free hand as she saw the fear cross my face. "We will look after you." A new wave of terrifying uncertainty swept through me.

Returned to the relative comfort of my mobile bed, Infermiere Gennaro and I headed back out to the hallway. As we entered the cardio department, we were greeted by two female doctors. The younger of the two proceeded to cover me in electrodes, slipping some under the edges of my tight dressing where she could. They worked to record the results while I practised light conversation with them. "La grammatica italiana è molto difficile da imparare no?"— *Italian grammar is difficult to learn no?*—the older doctor smiled at me.

"Si," I sighed, "É molto difficile. Maschile e femminile... preposizioni e pronomi... " I had felt like my communication had been rapidly improving as I came to the end of my time on Elba. But here, injured, exhausted and needing terminology I just didn't have in order to handle a medical emergency, I felt like I had been flung back into the maelstrom of linguistic frustration.

Antonio was waiting when we got back. He bustled around and checked I was comfortable before he vanished to attend to the buzzer of one of the other patients.

The tops of trees across the carpark swayed lightly in the breeze outside my window. *I wish I was still on Elba. I wish I could feel the sea breeze on my face. Smell the soil as it was turned. I wish I was sitting on a mat sifting my hands through the olives, chatting with Marco in the sun.* I closed my eyes and tried to return to how life had made me feel just four days earlier.

At midday a lunch tray was left on the end of my bed. My eyes flicked open from a light doze. I waited for whoever had left it there to come back and put everything within my reach. No-one came back.

Frustrated tears stung my eyes. I couldn't reach it at all and in addition, the tray was in the way of my still throbbing leg, which I needed to adjust the position of every few minutes for comfort. As an hour passed by my frustration increased as no-one returned to help me. As I was convincing myself that I could summon the energy and bravado to knock the tray off the bed and get some attention, Patrizia and Pina appeared beside me.

"Mamma mia!" they shook their heads and waved their hands madly indicating they recognised my predicament.

"Vuoi mangiare?" Pina gently asked.

I nodded with moist eyes—*yes I wanted to eat.*

Moving the tray to the trolley beside me, Pina opened each foil sealed container and fed me a little from each. It was tepid by now but edible. They adjusted my pillows and the angle of my bed, chattering as they pottered around.

"Di dove sei?" Patrizia asked.

"Australia..."

"E che lavoro fai tu…?"

"I worked in football..."

"Tu sei non sposato…?" Pina fed me another spoon of food.

"No, I am not married... Sono divorziata... "

"Aiiii… L'UOMINI!"—Men! They exclaimed in solidarity.

Jenny arrived to check on me in the evening. With little mental capacity to focus beyond ongoing management of my pain, I realised after nearly three days in hospital and despite the conversation with the Dottore, I still didn't understand the details of my break. *Why did I need an operation? When would it happen?*

I asked Jenny to see if she could find out any more details from the staff on that night.

"È una ricostruzione dell'osso,"—*it is a reconstruction of the bone*—the infermiere who came over told us. "It is a very bad break."

I was to be transferred to l'Ospedale dei Pellegrini—*the Hospital of the Pilgrims*. Jenny's face lit up in recognition.

"This hospital is only five minutes from the hostel," she smiled reassuringly. "It will be even easier for me to pop in and check on you. He doesn't know yet when they will be moving you, but he thinks it will be soon."

In 1578 six artisan Neapolitans had established a religious congregation alongside a place to help the poor with the development of *l'Ospedale dei Pellegrini* in the Spanish Quarter. The original church and associated hospital opened in 1591 and became known as a place where pilgrims were welcomed for up to three days to recover from various illnesses which may have been afflicting them on their travels. The hospital's first department of surgery opened in 1816. I would be part of a long line of stranieri e pelligrini, who had previously passed across the same threshold of this new hospital.

I woke Friday morning feeling marginally better. Pina had tracked down a mobile hand pulley the day before. Hanging over my head, it allowed me some independent assistance so I could move my body more easily when required. It had eased some of my frustrations like trying to pull myself back to centre in the bed as needed.

Dottore Russolillo popped past after breakfast.

"You should get up," he said firmly.

"Too hard," I shook my head incredulous at the suggestion. "I can't."

"It is better. You should move," he told me firmly as he wandered on to other patients.

I looked up at the hand pulley. With a deep breath, I reached up and took the handle in my fingers and raised myself slowly into a sitting position on the bed. I winced through the pain as each part of the broken bone shifted then settled at the new angle. It wasn't great, but it wasn't as debilitating a movement as it had been. I carefully moved one leg to hang off the side of the bed as I clung to the bar of the pulley. Then the other. I paused to allow my brain to adjust to being vertical again. I saw the Dottore with one eye on me from up the hall. With immense concentration, I willed the necessary muscles to work. I waited again while my body adjusted to being upright, then slowly eased myself off the bed. Clinging to the bed... then the wall... then a rail running down the hall, I took my first independent steps in nearly seventy-two hours. To be upright and moving independently again filled me with hope.

Dottore Russollilo struck a waltz pose as I moved closer to where he stood watching my progress, "Ti piace di ballare?"—*Do you like to dance?*—he asked as he began to waltz around me.

I shook my head with a weak smile. "Oggi, non posso,"—*Today I can't.*

"Nooo... But normally you like to dance?" he insisted.

"Ma certo,"—*of course*.

He walked alongside as I edged up the hallway. He told me he used to play rugby union and loved watching the Wallabies. They had played the Azzurri in Melbourne the weekend after we had held the Socceroos match against Japan just before I finished work. He told me he had been watching the match from Italy.

"Quello che è questo parco?" I asked him about the thick grove of trees sweeping further up the hill across a road running outside the hospital, as we reached the window at the far end of the hallway.

"Ah, il parco di Capodimonte e il museo. Caravaggio, Titian, Raphael, Ribera. Important artists there. You must go when you get better," he told me over his shoulder, as he was called away.

In the midst of the forest I was looking into was a former hunting lodge built by Carlo di Borbone. The residence of the Borbone of Napoli first, then the French and eventually the House of Savoy who had led the unification of Italy. It had always been home to rich art collections and in 1950 it was established as a national museum—*il Museo di Capodimonte*. I looked longingly toward the trees hiding the lodge from view from where I stood. It had been on my list of places to visit. I hoped I would still be able to get there soon.

Back in bed after two very slow but luxurious laps of the hallway, I grasped my phone and began sifting through the functions of my basic handset. Opening something I thought was a game, I instead came across an option to access basic internet. In the three months since I bought the handset in London, I hadn't known I had the option. Glad I hadn't known about it on Elba and was able to maintain the serenity of disconnection, today I was relieved to discover I had access to the outside world.

I was trying to log-on to email, when an Infermiere I didn't recognise appeared around the partition.

"Allora, tempo per il trasferimento all'Ospedale Pelligrini."

I didn't want to go. I was settling into my hallway alcove. But it was time. He gathered my collection of belongings and re-packed my bag, before assisting me from the bed and on to a stretcher-trolley to wheel me to the ambulance. As I was wheeled out, Patrizia appeared beside me with tears in her eyes. She grasped my hand wishing me buona fortuna. Staff paused and waved as we went past. *Where is Antonio... And Gennaro?* I couldn't see them in the melee of my departure. My anxiety rose as I realised I was about to leave those who had stepped in and kept an eye on me for me for three days.

The temperature had dropped further while I had been inside. I inhaled the crisp, fresh air with new appreciation as we emerged out of the hospital. Coming to a stop beside an ambulance transfer vehicle, the infermiere indicated I needed to get up.

"Sola?" I looked at him blankly.

"Lei hai bisogno di ascendere nell'ambulanza."

Was he trying to be funny I wondered? It had taken me more than five minutes to get myself out of the bed that morning; and that was with the assistance of the hand pulley.

I lay there staring at him. *Does he seriously think I can just get up and step into an ambulance?* The driver came over and an animated conversation ensued. Together they helped get my body upright and then on to my feet.

"Tu ascendi," the infermiere gestured impatiently for me to step into the back of the waiting vehicle. The step up was at least a foot high. The frustration of not being able to communicate brought tears to my eyes again. I had no words to explain that my left leg was stiff from the bruising where the moped had hit me. Aching and barely functioning, I could neither raise it alone, nor use it to support my right leg to step up. All my upper body muscles were working overtime to simply keep me upright. We stood there staring at each other.

Why don't you understand that I can't do this! Why don't you understand how impossible this is for me to do!!! I railed in my head at them both.

I willed them to understand that they needed to help me. The standoff ended at last, and they carefully leveraged me up into the cabin of the sparse van. I sank onto the seat on offer, awkward and unable to effectively support myself as I was forced to sit up straight. No restraint was provided to ensure I was secure, and I watched in dismay as the infermiere climbed in the front so he could chat with the driver, instead of climbing in the back to support me for the trip.

The vehicle started to move. Terrified of further injury, I clung to the seat and braced for self-preservation.

Weaving down from Vomero, I took the chance to take in the

spectacular views I had been about to pursue before fate had thwarted me. Sweeping down over the old city and out across the bay, the views were as beautiful as Jenny had told me. Pain and joy swept through me as my focus fluctuated from managing the impact as our wheels bounced over cobblestones and trying to stay upright to drink in the view in the distance of Vesuvio looming over the gulf of Napoli. I was determined to see what I could of the city while I had the chance.

As we edged into the centro storico, the colour, noise and chaos of Friday lunchtime in downtown Napoli filled the streets. The sounds were barely muffled by the closed window. I peered out to catch a glimpse of life outside. Small groups of people were having animated conversations on the footpaths lined with small shops. A driver was stopped on his moped on the footpath still astride, while he participated in a conversation with one of the groups. Tight, busy streets had traffic moving at a turtle's pace. The driver resorted to putting the siren on, but it attracted nothing more than glances of indifference from the outside world. Every attempt of the driver to move forward seemed to be delayed by moped drivers who wove through any gaps between the traffic and parked vehicles. I glared through the window at them as they prolonged my painful journey.

Coming down a street lined by clothing and fresh food markets, similar to those I had walked along three days before, we turned into a dark concrete entryway, coming to a stop in what looked like a loading dock. The pain caused by sitting up for little more than twenty minutes was unbearable. I tried to express, with broken vocabulary, the urgency of receiving a fresh dose of anti-dolorifico as soon as possible to the infermiere. I was desperate to lie down.

"Si... si, si, si," he nodded at me distractedly as he wandered over to greet someone he knew before remembering he needed to help me to step down from the vehicle.

I sank into the wheelchair the driver brought over. My handbag was tucked beside me and an oversized envelope that contained my x-rays and files dropped into my lap. I clung to everything with my left hand.

We rattled up three floors in a rickety lift. Nervous about the age of the building I moderated my expectation of what the wards might be like inside. I breathed a sigh of relief, as we entered the orthopaedic ward. A wide, clean, modern hallway spanned before us.

I was parked to one side and the infermiere vanished up the hallway with my envelopes, leaving me sitting alone. Afraid in my new environment, the trauma of having to build relationships with new medical staff gripped me. While I now had the key request of 'ho bisogno di fare la pipi' under my belt, I was still without language to explain my most basic feelings, what I was experiencing or might need. It had taken three days for the staff at the last hospital to appreciate my amplified needs. Without family support and dealing with language barriers the adrenaline that had perhaps carried me this far seemed to have worn off.

The tears began to well as the fear of being alone finally consumed me.

20

Infermiera Angela arrived to take charge, greeting me with a big motherly smile. She wheeled me up the hall, then paused beside the end of an unmade bed in the hallway while she finished her handover with my transfer team. I sighed despondently. Still no proper bed for me here either.

She leant over and gave me another reassuring smile, then rolled my chair backward into a ward. Three beds lying in a row along the wall were already occupied. Opposite them though, tucked in an alcove lined by cupboards on one side, and a wall on the other a fourth bed lay neatly made and awaiting my arrival. The tears welled again. This time with relief. Consigned to the public trolley bed in the hallway of l'Ospedale C.T.O, broken and bruised I had resigned myself to my fate, but the experience had been gruelling. A proper bed, in the semi privacy of a ward seemed like heaven.

"Ho bisogno di fare la pipì," I told Angela quietly, not wanting the whole ward to hear me. "Mi puoi aiutare?"—*can you help me*—I asked.

It seemed wise to take the opportunity to go before they got me into bed. A look of concern flashed over Angela's face as she interpreted my words. She helped me out of the wheelchair, escorting me three or four metres to the ward bathroom. Lowering me on to the lavatory she pulled the door to, but remained close so she could rescue me should I teeter off.

I looked longingly at the shower cubicle in front of me. The only bed bath I had been offered was the one after I ruined my pyjama pants on my ill-fated trip to the bathroom. It was now longer than during the rains on Elba since I had last washed. At least I wasn't muddy this time.

"Hai fatto," Angela asked peeping through the door.

"Si. Ho finito," I confirmed. I had needed someone to escort me each time at l'Ospedale C.T.O. Hospital. I struggled to make it down to the seat safely alone. While I was grateful for some privacy this time, I was going to need her to get me up from the shorter than normal receptacle. Her eyes went wide with worry again, as she realised I couldn't stand of my own volition. But she quickly came in to help me up.

I begged for anti-dolorifico as she helped me over to my fresh bed. She nodded but suggested lunch first. I was exhausted from the pain but agreed to eat something.

As I lay back in my new bed and waited for the food to arrive, I studied the others in the room. Under the window, the woman from the first bed relaxed in an armchair, while a young couple slowly packed her belongings ready for departure. In the second bed a small woman lay flat, a drip in her arm. A woman in a chair beside the bed leant in to speak quietly with her, intermittently adjusting pillows and passing things to her.

In the third bed a woman in her sixties was sitting up, surrounded by pillows to support her. She greeted me with a gentle smile as our eyes met. Her face was softly framed by hair coiffed in short, light brown curls. I felt the kindness and warmth in her eyes though they were slightly hidden behind round glasses. A metal fixation protruded from the wrapping around her left arm. A young woman of around twenty with thick black curls and big dark eyes hovered near the woman's bed, chattering with everyone in the room.

"Mi chiama Fernanda," the girl said as she came over to the side of my bed to help Angela set-up my three-course lunch. "E questa é mia Zia Christina," she indicated that the kindly woman opposite was her Aunt. I introduced myself and gave Christina a little nod.

Angela gently wound the handle at the end of my bed until I was in a comfortable sitting position suitable for eating. This alone was a significant upgrade on my hallway bed where pillows were the only option to prop me up to eat. Fernanda wheeled the side table up and over my bed, opening all the lunch containers and laying them out for me. The hallway trolley had sufficed as a side table alone, forcing me to eat from containers balanced on my cast. She demonstrated how the sachet of olive oil in my cutlery packet should go over my vegetable dish, checked if I needed any help to eat, then left me to start picking at the food. I smiled humbly with my thanks.

The man assisting the lady preparing for departure approached. He spoke English quite well and asked how I came to be in hospital and alone.

"Here… it is very difficult without family members in the hospital," he looked at me apologetically. "They are important. It is the way it is in Napoli."

I slumped in the bed. I was hoping my frustrations with the sporadic attention of staff had been specific to l'Ospedale C.T.O. due to the overcrowding. I hadn't asked any friends or family to come to rescue me yet, anticipating I wouldn't be here long. I wasn't sure who could come anyway. I wasn't comfortable with the idea of my elderly parents dealing with the chaos of Napoli and had deterred them from coming over. My sisters had small children to look after. Alexis in London was a possibility. She spoke enough Italian to help too. But she had just started a new job.

God, please let me be okay, I prayed, as the man returned to help his mother-in-law finishing packing.

I bravely started to answer the questions from around the room in my broken Italian, while the English speaker translated the gaps in my vocabulary from across the room. Rapid fire questions flew about, as everyone demanded to know what had happened to me.

Fernanda came over and leant in close with deep concern in her eyes. "Se hai bisogno di qualcosa… chiama mi. Okay?"—*If you have need of something, you call me*—she insisted.

There were others like Patrizia and Pina in this hospital, who already recognised I might need a hand. I nodded gratefully.

Infermiera Angela was yet to come back with an injection of anti-dolorifico after my lunch had been cleared away. My pained expression brought Fernanda back over. She peered down at me with concern.

"Hai bisogno di un'infermiera?"

Without waiting for an answer, she pulled a red cord hanging behind my bed. Angela appeared. Pain relief was given. As the drugs swept into my system, rest came.

An elderly woman was taking up residence in the recently vacated bed by the window when I woke up. She arrived wearing pyjamas and a dressing gown, with her left arm firmly strapped in a sling. Short dark waves framed her face and when she looked up, deep brown eyes sparkled from behind gold rimmed glasses. With her free hand, she pulled items from a small bag and organised them beside her bed. More bags were brought in by another woman and unpacked into one of the cupboards beside my bed. I watched with curiosity at the organised, well-planned arrival, unlike my own chaotic admission. At least I now had my rubber flip flops with me—arriving in another survival pack with Jenny—which negated the need to have plastic bags tied to my feet if I had to step out of bed.

As the new arrival settled in, a group had gathered around Christina's bed, laughing at Fernanda as she regaled them with a story punctuated with theatrical hand gestures and dramatic facial expressions. Fernanda saw my eyes were open again and leapt up to introduce her father Cyrus, Christina's younger brother, and a young man she introduced as her fidanzato, Raffaele.

I nodded and smiled, then looked over to our new roommate now sitting comfortably in her bed. Refreshed after my nap and with a little new confidence I caught her eye.

"Come si chiama?" I asked.

"Io sono Tina," she nodded at me kindly. "Eh tu? Come ti chiama?"

Fernanda broke in to deliver an animated explanation about my accident and where I had been the preceding three days to ensure Tina had all the details.

The woman who had arrived with additional bags for Tina earlier was her sister Emilia. She returned to the ward with Tina's husband Alessandro—or Sandro as he was introduced—a distinguished looking gentleman, with wisps of white hair and sparkling blue eyes. A flurry of activity erupted with the arrival of dinner. The family set up a small table with a placemat and cutlery, then assisted Tina over to a seat. Looking quite at home despite our hospital setting, her family hovered nearby to pass her anything she needed.

A stream of in-patients came to visit Tina as the evening continued. Intrigued, I watched on as the numbers in the room increased along with the decibel level as conversations escalated. A lot of people seemed to know her. It seemed she had been moved from another ward. I felt like I was in the middle of a family gathering in someone's home rather than in a hospital ward, as crowds rolled in and around the room. I heard my story being repeated every time someone new entered the room with heads turned to stare at the bemused straniera in the corner.

As the external visitors decreased with visiting hours coming to a close, Tina shooed a short, stout woman who had arrived in pyjamas, over to meet me. "Io sono Gavina," she introduced herself.

"Gavina? Dove è quel nome da?" someone in the room asked, asked where her name was from.

"La mia nome è sardo,"—*Sardinian*—Gavina explained. Her bushy eyebrows and bright eyes were hidden behind rectangular spectacles, inquiring when my operation would be she showed me her misshapen hand. It looked like a slight deformity of the bone. I tried to understand if she was born with it or it was something that had developed. She told me it would be operated on Monday.

"Gavy! Giac-a-lee!!" Tina called out her versions of our names in her scratchy voice to get our attention. "Gavina! Giac-a-lee ha bisogno di aiuto mangiare. Domani Lei ha bisogno di ritornare ed aiutarla." She instructed Gavina to return tomorrow to help me to eat.

Gavina, rocking slightly as she shifted from one foot to the other tilted her head to one shoulder as she smiled shyly at me. Speaking slowly in Italian she said, "I am going now. Sleep well. Until tomorrow?"

I smiled, "A domani."

Lina, Fernanda's mother and Cyrus's wife, arrived later in the evening and came over to introduce herself. She would be staying the night, to ensure Christina had everything she needed. Touching my arm gently, she reiterated her daughter's offer to call if I also needed anything. I smiled in gratitude and nodded that I understood. Fernanda and Raffaele bade me farewell as they shrugged into warm coats and left for the evening.

The ward slowly emptied out. The only two guests remaining were Lina, and Mariuzzi —the daughter of Norma—who in the midst of the social chaos had remained lying quietly in the middle bed recovering from her operation the day before. Both pulled an armchair over to the bed of their family member, setting up a makeshift place to spend the night so they were on hand to help as needed.

An infermiera came past doing last rounds. I begged her reluctant assistance to be helped to the bathroom before lights went out.

I slept little. My elderly companions had quickly drifted to sleep, a cacophony of snoring erupting as they slipped into deeper unconsciousness. I stared for hours through the half-light, at shadows and shapes around the room. I wished I had my iPod, but Jenny had warned of the risk of small items of value being stolen from me in the hospital. My backpack was in a locked cupboard beside me, but my handbag remained tucked under the sheet, awkwardly pressed against my swollen leg. It was collectively deemed that this was still the safest place for it because—according to the group discussion that evening—"You never know! This is Napoli."

I looked at my phone again trying to remember how I had gained internet access just before my transfer the day before. I found a way to log in to my emails.

Hi dear Jacq, how are you? I hope that you like Napoli.
Here everything has returned as before.
We are preparing for the winter and all the jobs of maintenance...
I feel sad... without you... emptied or something.. but I am well.
Tomorrow morning I must bring the olives to the crusher... tell me your news...kisses... Marco and Simone... Rubio...

My eyes filled with tears. The message was a few days old and sent before he knew of my accident. I closed my eyes and took myself back to the farm. Able to stand up, sit down, walk, swim... shower... with the sky my only roof. To be back basking in the warmth of companionship. I had felt so healthy. So happy. And now this. Now here. I felt as daft as Napoleon for leaving. He had also chosen to leave Elba. Escaping from his exile he raised a new army back in France, only to face another crushing defeat within six months. His next exile to Saint Helena off the West Coast of Africa was one from which he would never return.

I wanted to go back. I wanted to help crush the olives. I wanted...

It didn't matter what I wanted. I wasn't going anywhere. I knew I needed to accept that I wouldn't be continuing on to the farm in the Cilento national park down near Sapri the following week. I emailed my host Sebastiano, and apologised first for changing my dates, and now not being able to come at all.

Gavina returned before breakfast on Saturday, tipping a pile of biscotti from a box onto my bedside table for me to snack on. Her other hand unfurled to reveal another small packet for me. Unwrapping it she showed me a bracelet of plastic turquoise beads.

"Hai fatto!?"—*You made it?*—I exclaimed. Nodding proudly, she clipped it around my left wrist. "Grazie Gavy," I smiled, touched by the gift from my new friend.

Mariuzzi was preparing Norma to be discharged when Jenny arrived. She handed me my iPod. "Ahhh... Thank you!" I smiled. After my long sleepless night, I was willing to take the risk of it going astray for the sake of some calming music.

Chatting with Tina, Jenny asked what her injury was. She had had una caduta and broken her arm in two places.

"During her first admission only one break was initially detected," Jenny translated, "but she returned complaining of pain further up the arm that wasn't resolving. Now she needs to have an operation."

"Una caduta!" I nodded in recognition, "Everyone uses that word when they talk about what happened to me," I explained.

Jenny laughed, "It means 'to fall'. A common word I'm sure in the ortopaedia ward."

Norma was able to go home today and she and Mariuzzi came over to my bed to say goodbye. Norma's kind face, which I could see for the first time now she was upright, was framed by black hair brushed back into a ponytail. She placed a hand near my face on the pillow as she leant in. She said something about Dio. Jenny explained that Norma wanted to pray for me. I nodded and smiled gratefully at my gentle roommate. Squeezing her eyes shut she muttered some words over me quietly. Then gently touching my head she said farewell.

The doctor doing morning rounds was quickly accosted by Tina as he entered the room. As she chatted to him at length I saw her nod in my direction and say my name. I tried to understand the conversation. Something, something, operazione, something, martedì. I gazed back quizzically.

"La Sua operazione sarà martedì," the dottore repeated looking directly at me. My operation was to happen Tuesday. I nodded, relieved to have an update but at the same time, feeling my stomach sink. It had been four days already. Another three until the operation. I wondered what was going on under the bandaging that was holding my broken limb together. I was slowly gaining some control of my pain, using re-directed tension in the other muscles throughout my body. But despite this progress and the regular doses of anti-dolorifico, I was in an indiscriminate state of agony most of the time.

Tina's son Raffaele and his wife arrived with Sandro late morning. Tina held court with her family from an armchair under the window. As lunchtime approached a lively conversation erupted from their corner before Raffaele approached my bed, "Vuoi una pizza?" he asked.

Nodding at me encouragingly from her armchair Tina demanded, "Si! Si! Vuoi mangiare una pizza!"

I didn't need encouragement. "Si per favore," I accepted with delight.

Infermiera Angela walked in with the hospital lunch but Sandro and Tina waved at her to take it away. With great excitement they explained that today they would be feeding me pizza. With a smile of approval, Infermiere Angela took the unopened meals away. My table was positioned and set. Tina sent over a tea towel from her selection of cloths, ordering they drape it over me like a bib.

Raffaele returned half an hour later and presented me with a box containing a perfect Margherita pizza. "Tutto per me?"—*all for me*—I asked in surprise.

Laughing and nodding at me encouragingly Tina yelled, "Mangia! Mangia!"—*Eat! Eat!*

In honour of a visit to Naples by Queen Margherita in 1889, a local baker called Esposito designed the pizza to feature the colours of the Italian flag. Tomatoes for the red, basil for the green and mozzarella for the white. I plunged in. The thin base oozed with the flavours of local produce. Despite the restrictive tautness of my wrappings that surrounded my waist, I managed to eat half of the pizza before I paused. Raffaele came over to check if I had had enough. I watched it go as he cleared it away, wishing I could fit more in. But lunch wasn't over yet. Tina sent her sister Emilia over to me next brandishing a small box with fresh arancini. Tina nodded encouragingly at me from the corner as Emilia insisted I take one. The waft of one of my favourite foods centimetres away was too much. Concentrating intensely, I negotiated with my stomach to make room for the deep-fried balls of rice covered in breadcrumbs, with a centre filled with meat ragu.

I was overwhelmed by the families who had brought their table to me. As Marco had said to me on Elba, the taste of food improves when shared with others.

As I finished, Fernanda rushed to liberate me from the table. Relaxed against the pillows, I was uncomfortably full but my digestive reprieve would be short lived. Sandro came over with a fresh sfogliatella wrapped in a napkin. I eyed with desire the delicious treat—made from a dough like phyllo pastry, cut into discs and formed into a sort of pocket filled with citrus and ricotta—but also feeling quite overwhelmed by food. I patted the dressings banded around my waist to indicate I was full and made a sad face to indicate my regret. With a laugh and an encouraging "piu tardi... piu tardi"—for later, Sandro placed the delectable pastry on my side table.

As I emerged from a light doze later that afternoon, a deep throaty voice, croaked through my sub-conscious. I attempted to open my sleep heavy eyes and began to make out the figure of a slight woman with silvery hair and ruby red rimmed glasses, unpacking her overnight bag into the bedside drawer Norma had vacated. The woman, who introduced herself as Assunta, began chattering to me as she packed her belongings into a cupboard. I smiled at her blankly as she glanced up at my lack of response. Tina called out from the corner and Assunta went over to sit on the edge of Tina's bed to hear my story. She threw sympathetic looks over her shoulder in my direction as she listened intently, interjecting with the obligatory head shakes and gasps as Tina spoke. I wondered how many of the details of my story were being further exaggerated with each telling.

Ciro and Lina arrived to visit Christina. The sound levels grew as stories were shared amongst family members from the day past, with laughter erupting regularly at the more dramatic exposés of the narrators. Assunta moved to sit quietly on a chair beside her bed as Tina returned to conversing with family members who had returned for the evening. Unlike the vivacious arrival of Tina, with her flourish of bags and a never-ending trail of visitors, Assunta seemed very alone. We made eye contact and smiled at each other in silence, unsure how else to connect. Then I watched with relief as Assunta was eventually drawn into the raucous embrace of the two families on either side of her.

As my three roommates finished their dinner, Tina shooed Assunta over to help me. She had no obvious injury. Perhaps, I wondered, she was here for some sort of elective surgery which would make her the most capable of my three roommates. She talked away at me in a local dialect, laughing at my blank smile, shaking her head, smiling and muttering at my lack of comprehension as she cleared away my semi empty containers and reset my table back to the side.

I fell asleep with the voices of the families still rumbling around me, waking only as the infermieri on last rounds came in to administer an anti-dolorifico injection late in the evening. The small television, in a wall rack above Christina's bed hummed quietly.

As the lights and television went off, silence in the ward descended. I heard the last roll of the wheels of the infermieri trolley as it was parked for the day. An orange glow filtered through the frosted glass window, propped ajar to allow fresh air. The sounds of the city floated in. Mopeds roaring past, footsteps, people yelling and calling out to each other.

Listening to the gentle rumble of snoring from across the room and the heavy breathing of deep sleep, I wished for the same simple escape from my discomfort as I stared into the dim light. I seemed able to sleep through Italian family life roaring around me during the day—somehow comforted by their presence—but in the silence of the night hours, sleep did not come.

Before first light, the door was pushed open. Ciro, the refreshment vendor entered in his neat uniform reminiscent of a 1950s cinema attendant. He bore a large tray covered in foil with a smaller tray full of plastic espresso cups with a small piece of foil covering each.

Tina gestured at him to bring a warm cornetto from the covered tray to me. He placed a fresh pastry beside me with one of the foil covered plastic cups containing espresso. I struggled to reach under the sheet for my bag.

"Tutto bene Giac-a-lee," Tina batted her hand at me at my attempts to pay. She was insistent that my breakfast would be looked after as well. As I gulped the hot, sweet espresso down, the infermiere dropped off my morning milk drink and dry biscotti. Ignoring the delivery, I picked up the warm pastry Ciro had left. Warm chocolate oozed out as I pulled it apart. I smiled gratefully at Tina as she nodded approvingly at me from her bed.

"É buona no?" she asked without needing a response.

Gavy was visiting with us mid-morning when a Padre in brown robes, thick glasses and sporting a long black and grey flecked beard, came to the door to advise it was time for Sunday mass in the ancient church across the courtyard. She followed him out to participate. I wished I had the energy to join them.

Instead, I took another slow and steady—gloriously independent—trip to the bathroom. After the exhaustion of the transfer I had regained enough strength to get myself out of bed and was enjoying the dignity of being able to go to the loo alone again. I paused on my way to look out the window and spotted Gavy walking up the stairs of the church with some other pyjama clad patients. The sky above was blue and scattered with soft clouds with the sun draping warm rays over the metal cross atop the chiesa rising up as a centre piece in the grey courtyard I was looking down into.

Under the cross the triangular roof displayed a stone carving. A distinctive triangle with a dot at the centre, from which carved light radiated. Amidst the rays were cherubs and below in Latin the inscription…

TEMPLUM.UNI.TRINOQUE.DEO.DICATUM.

A church consecrated to God, one in three. A reference to the trinity of Father, Son and Holy Spirit. God in one. The faith base of the founders of the church and associated charitable health service developed through the hospital.

Four large ornate stone pillars supported the front wall, two each side framed a large stained-glass window installed above large green doors at the top of the stairs, which ascended from both left and right. As the doors opened and Gavy vanished inside, light escaped from within indicating a brighter interior than the grey outer walls.

On each side of the pillars a statue rested in an alcove. One was draped in magnificent robes and carrying a shepherd's crook. The other dressed more simply, had a halo above his head. The drab walls of the hospital extended out from either side of the renaissance church.

Gavy returned a few hours later clutching her digital camera with photos to show me the interior of marble floors, bright white ceilings, ornate walls trimmed with gold, and magnificent paintings lining the alcoves. The inside was pristine.

She told me she had a friend coming to visit her this afternoon who spoke a little English. Promising to return with her later, she vanished for lunch.

Only a few relatives arrived at lunchtime. The table in the corner was set for all three of my roommates this time. As Tina and Assunta came over to help set my meal up, my mobile rang. Taking the call, chaos erupted as Tina and Assunta simultaneously demanded I "mangia! mangia!"—*eat! eat!*—while the food was hot, instead of answering.

"Scuzi a sec Jess," I said into the phone as I answered.

"È mia sorrella in Australia,"—I justified the lunch interruption telling them it was my sister Jessica, calling from Hervey Bay. I couldn't help but laugh at the looks of concern prompted by my phone call taking more priority than my food.

The women reticently accepted my excuse and left me to my conversation, though continued to throw looks of concern my way with occasional hand signals indicating that I should still "mangia! mangia!" Jessica overhearing the interaction chuckled as I flicked between Italian and English, and explained to her what was causing such a ruckus in the background

"So, Jacq you're still in hospital. Nearly a week is quite a long time. Are you okay?"

I told her of my trials, but also the relief that had come from the warmth and kindness of the nonne—as I had taken to affectionately referring to my elderly roommates—and their families.

As I came off the call and finished picking at my lukewarm lunch, Assunta approach. "Ti piace mozzarrella?" she asked brightly.

A plastic plate with a large ball of fresh buffalo mozzarella was promptly delivered to me, part of a food delivery which had just arrived in the hands of a man with a little girl one of Assunta's relatives.

I savoured the texture and flavour of this local specialty with delight.

"Tre cose importante lo so di Napoli,"—*three things that I know are important about Napoli*—I told Tina and Assunta. "Buffalo Mozarella! Pizza Margherita! E Sfogliatella!"

Laughing in delight and clapping their hands, I could see their pride knowing they had arranged these three local delicacies to be brought to my hospital bed. "Ahhh… anche prosciutto!" exclaimed Assunta mid-clap. "Ti piace il prosciutto?"

A pile of the thinly sliced meat was piled next to my buffalo mozzarella. I dutifully started chewing my way through.

No longer hungry but seeing how much seeing me eat seemed to please everyone, I picked up the *sfogliatella* from yesterday to finish.

"Aspetta! Aspetta!" Tina shouted, waving her uninjured arm at me. What had I done?

Opening another patisserie box sitting on the table a fresh, a still warm sfogliatella was brought over to me and the old one confiscated.

The results of hard work and healthy eating on Elba will be quickly undone here, I thought cheerfully as I savoured the fresh citrus and ricotta flavours, as pastry flakes scattered over my dressings.

A steady stream of visitors continued to come through all afternoon. I rested quietly in my corner, watching the moving picture of Italian family life in motion swirl around me.

Gavy reappeared late afternoon with her English speaking friend Karina. A tall woman with reddish brown hair and a soft smile, came and sat down on the corner of my bed as we smiled shyly at each other in greeting. In broken but quite clear English, Karina explained she worked with a relative of Gavina's, who was unable to visit today, so she had offered to come and check on her.

"I will give you my details in case you need anything," she told me. Handing her my open diary where there was still a little space to write, she wrote all her details down. Gavina took the opportunity to write all her details down as well. She pointed to her town as she finished writing, explaining that she lived much further south in an area called Maratea. "Puoi venire a trovarmi lì quando stai di nuovo bene,"—*you can come and visit me there when you are better*—Gavina said shyly, before wandering over to talk to Tina.

Karina and I chatted quietly about my accident and how I was feeling. I bemoaned the fact I was unable to shower and how awful my hair felt and smelt. It had been six days since it had been washed. While my natural curls were looking better than they ever had, the smell of my long locks was not good.

"I can wash your hair Jacqui," she smiled softly. "Tomorrow when I come back, I will bring everything we need so we can wash your hair at the bed." I looked at her nervously wondering how that was possible. "I am a nurse. I have done it before. It will be okay."

I leveraged myself out of the bed. Walking was still difficult with my bruised leg, but I stepped out of the ward for the first time in two days to see Karina out. Taking my first steps into the hallway was a powerful feeling.

"I was not sure if you would want to meet me," Karina told me shyly as she waited for the lift, "but now that I know you are here on your own, I will come back to see you again. Maybe I can practice my English." She kissed me on both cheeks before she vanished behind the doors with a little wave.

Only Christina's family were in for dinner that night. Small tablecloths with patterns of giant lemons, green leaves, blue and yellow flowers, and green checks, brightened up the nondescript, grey hospital room. The containers of hospital food were opened and served onto plastic plates. Tina, Assunta and Christina gathered around the table for the evening feast, all wrapped up in snug pyjamas and dressing gowns. Sitting upright on a normal chair was still too challenging for me, but having noticed that I was moving around the ward now, Fernanda came over to assist me into an armchair near the table so I could be close to the group. Lina and Cyrus hovered close to assist with anything the nonne needed while Fernanda stayed next to me so she could pass me the food and drinks. The chatter in the room was loud and cheerful. Another important discussion about the food had everyone talking at once.

Cyrus stood in the background laughing at my bemused expression. With facial expressions and hand gestures he explained to me that meal-time was always the same. As I broke into laughter, for a few moments the hospital setting faded away. It was dinner time in

Napoli. And I was wrapped in the warm embrace of family.

21

Settled in an armchair at the end of Tina's bed with a light blanket that Fernanda had draped around me, a doctor appeared at the door the following morning. His eyes paused briefly on my empty bed before he scanned the room. His eyes rested on me tucked in the chair and he beckoned for me to follow him. He walked back out to the hall without pause.

"Professore Russo," the ladies hissed and gestured at me frantically. He was apparently very important. I eased myself to my feet and hobbled out into the hall. The Professore had vanished from sight before I managed to exit the room. As I looked each way trying to work out where he had gone, his face appeared around a doorway further down the hall looking for me. I walked slowly towards him while he waited.

The serious looking doctor was standing behind his desk by the time I entered his office.

"Your fracture is very complicated Jacqueline," he said in English as he put my x-rays up on a backlight. "The bone. It is broken in three, four... maybe more places," he pointed to the scan.

Three, four... maybe more? No wonder the pain was so severe.

As he pointed out the shattered area I began to comprehend why my injury had attracted so much attention.

"This top part of the bone connecting into your shoulder," he continued, "it is your proximal humerus that you smashed."

Smashed? Did he say smashed? I remembered the way my arm had felt disconnected from my body the day they scraped me off the cobblestones and into the ambulance. I felt the blood rushing from my face. I could interpret what I was looking at now. I felt hot, then nauseous, as the extent of the injury became clear. Shrugging off the light sweater draped over my shoulders, I leant more heavily on the back of the chair I was leaning on.

"You are still quite young, so we do not want to put in a prosthetic device," the surgeon said matter-of-factly.

I began having heart palpitations. "A prosthetic?" My voice petered out as he pulled up an x-ray of a similar injury he had repaired for someone else a week ago. He pointed to where they had instead inserted a plate and pins.

He paused and turned around to look at me intently.

"Jacqueline... we maybe have to take some bone from your hip to repair it."

Time to sit down. I eased myself into the chair I had been leaning on.

"Bone from... from my hip?" I whispered weakly. "Why?"

I could hear his voice continue... something about the biological benefits of a bone graft for the healing process. I nodded blankly, willing myself not to cry as fear wrapped its icy fingers around my previously courageous spirit. I was really hurt. Really, really hurt. Ignorance had been my bliss. This wasn't a simple operation. It needed a special device. They needed to take bone from my hip and put it in my arm. All efforts to stay positive and optimistic over the previous week began to crumble. I was terrified as I took in the information.

"We will only do that if we have to Jacqueline," he attempted to reassure me. "We have to see when we operate and know more what has happened from inside."

Another surgeon entered with a query for the Professore. Waiting for them to finish their conversation, I tried to process the new information. *What was I thinking not asking for anyone to come from home to be with me.*

I caught both dottori looking at me with concern as their conversation finished. The tears had welled up. Digging deep to find my false bravado, I quickly wiped the evidence away and smiled weakly at them.

"Do you have any more questions?" Professore Russo asked gently.

"How long... will the operation take?" I wasn't sure what else to ask.

"We think maybe four hours."

I limped back to my ward the weight of the news heavy. Four hours... I had never had a broken bone before. I had only ever been to hospital once as a child—suspected appendicitis at the age of ten had turned out to be merely a bad bout of constipation.

How could this have happened?

Infermiere Giovanni was chatting with my roommates when I returned. I slipped quietly back onto my bed trying not to attract attention. As I settled under the sheets, the tears started flowing. I wanted to sob but couldn't. The vibration through my body would send me into paralysing agony. But I had no bravery left. Salty tears streamed down my face.

As Infermiere Giovanni walked towards the door to leave, he caught sight of my tear-stained face, awash with despair.

"Uh, uh, uh, ahh!" he exclaimed urgently gesticulating at Tina and Assunta to head my way. He stayed at a distance, watching on protectively as the two nonne came alongside my bed.

"No, no, no... non tu piangi," they exclaimed.

No crying? I thought hotly. I thought Italians were all about dramatic shows of pain and emotion. *First, I was told to remain calm when brought into emergency by the paramedic, and now not to cry when I am battling sheer terror!*

"Ho paura,"—*I have fear*—I cried. "Mi voglio mia madre,"—I want my mother. It didn't matter how old I was. I wished my parents were here. "É fa male,"—*it's bad*—I wept.

Assunta took my hand as Tina stroked my hair.

"Tutto andrà bene. Hai noi,"—*everything will be okay. You have us*— Tina soothed.

"Tua madre non è qui ma noi siamo. Oggi noi siamo Tua madre," *Your mother is not here but we are. Today we are your mother*— Assunta rasped in her throaty voice.

I smiled gratefully through the tears.

I picked up my camera and scrolled through to a photo of my parents that I still had on there and showed them. They peered over their glasses at the small picture and smiled approvingly.

"Quanti anni ha tua madre?" Tina asked how old my mother was as she studied the picture. Both she and my mum were seventy-three years old. Their birthdays just four days apart. I wiped my eyes again and studied the proxy mother God had sent me. Tina even had brown curls and brown eyes like my own mum. Blowing my nose gently, I winced with the pain caused by directing much needed energy to my facial muscles.

Christina walked into the ward with Fernanda. Having had her last consult, they had been to collect her supply of post-operative medicine and instructions as she prepared to depart. They quickly joined Tina and Assunta at my bedside, adding their reassurances that I would not be alone.

By the time mum and dad made their daily call I had composed myself again. I explained the details I now had about the operation. I decided not to mention the possible bone graft.

He only said maybe, I thought anxiously to myself.

I was watching Italian daytime television from my bed late morning when a man peered around the door asking for me. The nonne waved him over to me. I looked at him curiously as he came over to the end of my bed. Tim Faulkner, with a strong American accent, explained that he was a pastor at a local Church.

My Aunt in England, Dad's youngest sister, had been busy searching the internet trying to find details of protestant churches in Italy and reaching out to find some expats who might be able to come and check on me. She had found someone with a connection to il Faro—*the Lighthouse*—International Baptist Church, and they had forwarded her email to Tim.

"So how you doin' Jac-a-lyn?" Tim asked.

I told him of the kindness of the other patients and their families and the visit from Karina.

"But I'm afraid of tomorrow," I told him.

I tried not to look as panicked as I felt. I was terrified of coming out of the operation, something not being okay and being unable to communicate that. With a little more movement possible in the past day or two I had felt more competent in managing my basic needs, but I was about to have a major operation. One that would leave me completely reliant on strangers. How would I find the strength to work around the language barriers when I was coming out of anaesthetic and in the hours after.

"My wife has come to sit with patients after operations before," Tim told me, "I will ask Jacki to come and sit with you tomorrow when you come out of the theatre," he reassured me.

I paused, "Your church isn't located on the trainline into the city is it?" I asked, remembering a sign for an evangelical church I had seen as my train had slipped through the outskirts of the city a week earlier when I had arrived. I remembered thinking the sign 'Chiesa Evangelico' was an unusual sight in a predominantly Catholic country.

"No, not us," he mused for a moment as to which church it might be, "We are located northwest of the city in an area called Castel Volturno," he described the area on the northern outskirts.

He paused to pray with me, asking that God would provide for all my needs and for the operation to go well. I felt my spirit grow more peaceful.

"Is there anything practical you need?" Tim asked as he paused at the door preparing to take his leave.

""Slippers maybe?" I suggested. Something warmer than my flip flops when getting out of bed would be a treat at this point. He nodded with a smile before vanishing out into the hall.

My roommates looked at me curiously wondering who he was. I

didn't have enough words to explain.

Karina returned that afternoon bearing a small tub, a big plastic bag in lieu of a hairdresser's protective wrap, shampoo, conditioner and a hairdryer. Unable to lean over or sit up at the basin to have my hair washed, she instead helped me into a position lying across the bed. Most of my body was supported by strategically placed pillows, a chair placed under my feet on the other side, while my head hung over the other edge with the bucket on a chair underneath.

She poured warm water over my hair with a plastic cup, adding shampoo and gently massaging out the grime and grease. The nonne watched on approvingly.

Karina giggled as she took the bucket away, "È una buona cosa noi lavammo i Tuoi capelli!"—*it is a good thing we washed your hair!*—she said, "L'acqua è MOLTO sporca!"—*The water is VERY dirty!*

A week since my last shower, having clean hair again was as exciting as going to a beauty salon.

Infermiere Mario came by just as Karina finished settling me in the bed with my freshly blow-dried hair. He asked Karina if I had been to my pre-operation appointments. I shook my head.

"Would you like me to come with you?" Karina asked as she helped me back out of the bed.

After an x-ray to see where everything was sitting prior to surgery we crossed a hall to the cardiologist's office. Karina gently assisted me onto a bed. Infermiere Mario approached me bearing a pair of scissors and a sympathetic expression.

"They need to cut open the bandages to allow them to put the monitoring devices on," Karina explained to me.

I reverted to my careful breathing techniques to manage the discomfort of lying completely flat and clutched my right hand, trying to stabilise the injured arm as Mario's scissors cut through the top of my wrappings, loosening the firm support they had given me for a week. As the Dottoressa began sticking the round circles and wires on my chest and torso, two more Dottori came in. I lay there trying to ignore how exposed I felt with so many people in the room.

As we began our slow return to the ward, Karina explained that one of the doctors had asked if she would like to observe the operation. "If he was serious Jacqueline, would you like me to be there," she asked.

"Si! Si si... assolutamente!" I agreed gratefully. To have someone there to tell me afterwards how the surgery went gave me some reassurance.

Soon after we returned, a new patient was wheeled in on a stretcher trolley and transferred into Christina's recently vacated bed. Maria was in her mid-sixties. A barrage of enquiries after her condition from the fashionable young couple who followed her in, erupted in the room. As Karina interpreted I contributed my own appalled shake of the head this time, muttering sympathetically, "È terribile! Ai ai, molto terribile!" Apparently she had been hit by a car and the driver had sped off. She was okay but her arm was broken.

Karina stayed to assist me with my dinner. We were chattering like old friends as the trolley arrived. She unpacked the meal and explained what was on the menu.

"No no..." Tina was waving at us from her bed as I prepared to eat. Sandro, Emilia and her husband had arrived with more food parcels.

"Would you like some frittata?" Karina translated tonight's offer for me. I was happy to have the choice made for me as the hospital food was pushed aside to make room for a plastic plate sent over with a large slice of warm vegetable frittata.

Tina offered some to Karina also. She politely declined.

"Saying no to food is not well understood in this ward," I warned her with a laugh knowing the form of my adopted Italian mama. The words had barely left my mouth, when a plate was thrust into Karina's hands. She looked up at me, startled. With a smile that told me she was secretly pleased, she whispered, "It is true!"

Marco had continued sending me daily messages from Elba. When I told him, I had to have an operazione he had asked me again if I wanted him to come.

I wanted to say yes. I paused, my thumb hovering over the buttons, wondering how to respond. Of course I wanted him to come. But it felt too much to ask. We barely knew each other. I couldn't expect it of him.

I told him I would be okay.

Then you come and stay with me to recover afterwards...?

I wasn't sure if that would even be possible, but I told him I would like to.

Another message came through from him during dinner. I couldn't understand what he was asking and showed it to Karina.

Vuoi che io ti corte?

"Chi é Marcoooo???" Karina giggled as she read it.

"Che ha detto?"—I blushed wondering what he had said.

"He wants to know if you would like him to 'court' you!"

I blushed as she demanded to know more. I told her wistfully of the friendship that had developed while on Elba.

I sat starring at my phone after she left. Marco wanted to court me? Did men actually exist with the courtesy to ask if they can court you? I had joked with friends about wanting to meet a man who didn't want to just drift into a relationship and 'see what happened' but was bold enough to make his intentions clear. My pain and the anxiety about my operation momentarily forgotten, I messaged him back.

Siiiiiii! Si! Si! Bacio x

As the ward emptied for the evening and the lights went down, I waited for sleep to sweep over me. The evening serenade of my snoring nonne was piqued with the groans of Maria, who had moved to rest in an armchair beside her bed. I was horrified to see a large area of bruising enveloping the right cheek of the elderly woman. Her right arm was strapped to her body in a cocoon similar to mine. She seemed intent on ensuring everyone knew how much pain she was in.

"Mama mi... oh mama mi," I heard her groaning under her breath, "OH mama MI... mamaaaaa MIII," the volume increased.

My roommates, while prone to being loud, and in some cases bossy, all seemed to have gentle souls underneath their verbose demeanours. Maria however seemed more agitated. I watched her struggling to get comfortable as the injuries hindered her both in bed and when she tried to sit in the chair instead. Barking at her daughter and later her husband, who had arrived after dinner, they seemed reticent to respond unlike Tina's family who were always at the ready to help her.

In the dark of the night, her loud, continuous expressions of discomfort increased my own anxiety. I slipped my earphones in to try and close out her pain. I had enough of my own to deal with. I empathised with her pain. Really, I did. But my own desperation for at least a little sleep before my operation, was quickly wearing down my patience.

I opened the new Hillsong album to listen to. I had picked up the CD in Florence in a bookshop across from the Galleria where Michaelangelo's statue of David was housed, and had finally loaded it into my library. As I thought about what was ahead of me in the morning, my attention was suddenly arrested by the words of the song in my ears.

'Because You're with me, because You're with me, I will not fear.'

I smiled quietly. Peace transcended the anxiety in my spirit. The day had started off full of fear, but then miraculously Tim had appeared. And in an unexplainable turn, Karina would be back first thing and with me throughout the operation. And Jacki would be here afterward. My nonne and their families had their eyes on me. I wasn't alone. God was with me in those who had stepped in to care for me.

22

I crept past my sleeping roommates and into the bathroom before dawn. My clean hair fell softly around my shoulders as I ran a comb through it. I wet a paper towel in the sink and gave myself a mini sponge bath. I stared back at my pale reflection in the mirror. That would have to do.

Out in the hallway I pensively limped up and down in the half light of dawn. *How long will it be until I regain even this level of movement and independence post operation*, I wondered sadly.

As the first rays of sun slipped through the windows I returned to the ward.

"Ecco la!"—*here she is*—my ward mates welcomed me with relief, perplexed by the sight of my empty bed as they had begun to stir.

Karina walked in just before eight with a warm smile and kiss on each cheek, followed by a doctor who was to escort us down to the operating theatre. In the hallway entry of the operating suites sat trolleys with dark green covers over them. Karina was handed a dark green cap in similar fabric to tie over my hair.

"Per favore scali su," an infermiere instructed me to climb on to one of the trolleys. Karina helped me settle, then vanished to change into scrubs as I was wheeled into the operating theatre.

My eyes flicked around the sterile environment as I was rolled to a stop. I was transfixed by the enormous lights above me that would serve to illuminate the work of the surgeon. Staff moved quickly around the room. The infermiere draped a green sheet over me, then gently wriggled my pyjama pants and underwear off.

"Good morning Jacqueline. Come stai?" Professore Russo appeared beside me.

"Non c'è male, grazie,"—*not too bad*—I smiled up at him calmly.

My left arm was stretched out. I turned to see the anaesthetist quickly working to insert a cannula to feed the drugs through. I watched all the activity bustling around me in the room. It served to distract me from the fact they were about to knock me out and slice open my arm.

*Because You're with me, I will not fear…*the song drifted back to mind.

God, please let everything go okay today. Please don't let me have a bad reaction to the anaesthetic or let anything go wrong. If my time is up for any reason though, I understand. Please accept me in heaven just as I am… I prayed pragmatically.

Professore Russo hovered over me while preparations continued.

"Ho fede in te,"—*I have faith in you*—I whispered as I looked up at him.

For the first time, a gentle smile creased his cheeks.

My eyelids drooped, the figures in the room became waxy and distorted. Karina's voice pierced through the last of my consciousness, "I am here Jacqui. Tutto bene?"

"Ciao… bella…" I murmured as everything faded to black.

"Wake up Jacqueline," Professore Russo's voice broke through the fog, "You need to wake up now."

I felt the rush of air in my lungs as I inhaled suddenly and was wrenched back into agonising consciousness. Pain flooded through me. My body and mind wrestled to come back from the depths of anaesthesia. I felt them raising me into a sitting position, multiple hands and arms supporting me.

"Ciao Jacqui," I heard Karina in front of me. "It is all okay now."

Pushing through the haze, I tried to see her, "Ciao! Ciao Karina! Finito?"

"Yes Jacqueline. Tutto bene."

I was still in the operating theatre. *What was wrong?* I knew coming out of a general anaesthetic was supposed to be bad, but I had expected it to be gradual. I felt panicked by the activity around me. The team was working quickly to re-wrap my torso dressings while still in the sterile environment.

I could hear Karina's reassuring voice still speaking words of encouragement from somewhere behind the frantic movement of the doctors. They lay me down again. My body immediately convulsed with tremors.

"Fa freddo, fa freddo," I muttered, feeling icy cold.

"É normale Jacqueline," Professor Russo soothed gently as he moved in front of me so I could see his face. Extra coverings were pulled over me, the weight of the fabric providing interim comfort and a greater sense of security as I was wheeled out into the hallway.

"It is okay Jacqui, I am here. I am here. It is all finished now," Karina hovered beside me. *Dear, dear Karina*, I thought looking up into her calm eyes as I lay shaking uncontrollably. She couldn't solve my physical distress, but the presence of my new friend soothed my emotional anxiety as my level of consciousness increased.

The pain rattled through me from head to toe. I wished the shaking would stop. The vibrations increased the pain in my arm and... 'No!' Deep seeded pain pierced my left side. They had definitely taken bone from my pelvis to graft into my proximal humerus.

"La dolore!" I sobbed, "è fa male." It hurts!

Professor Russo appeared beside me.

"Brava Jacqueline. Tutto okay," he said quietly looking down at me. He waved someone over. An infermiere appeared, who checked and adjusted the container that was drip feeding drugs into my left arm. Professor Russo lifted the tube into my line of sight, "It should be better now."

The tremors gradually eased. The sharp edge of pain softened ever so slightly.

An orderly appeared at the end of the bed. Taking off the brake, he began wheeling me up the hallway. Wild-eyed I looked for Karina. "I need more drugs Karina," I pleaded as she followed after me. "It hurts too much. I am not ready to be moved," I cried. The new movement sent fresh shockwaves through my body.

"It has been one hour," she soothed. "You have to be patient while the drugs take effect."

I glared with fury at the impassive face of the orderly at the foot of my trolley. He carefully kept his eyes away from meeting mine.

A radiologist awkwardly slid a board under the relevant parts of my body to take post-operative scans. Karina helped the orderly to wheel me back out to the lift. We rattled up in the small cabin, only long enough to fit the length of the trolley bed, with my companions squeezed awkwardly on either side. I stared at the metal roof, trying to find something to focus on to distract me from the pain.

An enormous group had gathered outside my room. Sandro and Raffaele's worried faces stood out in the crowd as they watched me go by.

"Ciao," I bleated out to the familiar and non-familiar faces alike.

All the family members visiting that afternoon had been sent out of the room while I was brought back in. Patients and visitors from the room across the hallway had also come out to witness my return, bulking up the numbers of my hallway welcoming party.

"Uno, duo, tre," before I understood what was happening, a surrounding group of infermiere quickly transferred my body using the sheet underneath me, back onto my bed. I cried out. A flurry of activity erupted as they worked to get all the tubes and containers attached to me in the right place.

"Would you like your pillow adjusted?" a voice asked me in English. Delirious from the movement of my broken body, I whimpered, "Non lo so, non lo so."

"Aspettiamo. Forse piu tardi,"—*maybe later*—I heard.

A new face appeared above me.

The stranger took my hand in hers. I held on tight.

"We thought you would be out by lunchtime," she told me in her American accent.

"What time is it now?" I whispered through dry lips.

"After four in the afternoon."

My operation had taken six and a half hours. With the time left in recovery and being x-rayed, I had been gone for eight hours. Interest in my well-being seemed to have spread like wildfire in Ortopaedia as everyone awaited my return.

"Thank you for coming," I tried to smile at Tim's wife Jacki, "I'm sorry I can't sit up to meet you."

Karina came over and introduced herself to Jacki before she left. She leant in and gently stroked my face as her eyes met mine reassuringly. "I am glad you have someone here now. I'll see you soon," she smiled at me as she left the room.

I tried some weak chatter with Jacki to distract me from the pain.

"Tell me more about what brought you and your family to Napoli?" I croaked out. As she spoke, Jacki took a tissue and dipped it in water to wipe my dry lips, occasionally allowing one or two tiny drops into my mouth to provide slight relief to my parched tongue.

Tina had also been to the operating theatre that day. Not requiring such a complicated procedure as I had needed, she was already sitting up in bed, just out of my line of sight. Her sister came to the end of my bed. She held up a set of soft pink pyjamas and bed socks where I could see them.

"They are a gift for you from Tina and her family," Jacki smiled down at me. She thanked them on my behalf, then stored them in my cupboard for when I was ready to be dressed.

I whispered through my parched lips and told her about the overwhelming kindness of all the family members who had kept watch over me. "Did they look after you today?" I asked hoarsely.

"They made sure I had lunch while I waited and they told me all about you," she smiled.

Sandro and Raffaele came to the end of my bed, standing so I could see their kind faces while they got an update from Jacki. Tina had proudly told me all about their three sons the day before. One worked in the police force in the north, another lived and worked in

China. And Raffaele and his wife ran a local sporting goods store. I looked into Sandro's kind blue eyes as he watched over me while chatting quietly with Jacki. As well as Tina being a similar age to mum and looking a little like her, Sandro shared the same bright blue eyes and fairer features of my father. Seeing his face amidst the crowd in the hallway had felt like I had family waiting for me. As I lay there in silent struggle—my body fighting its way back from the trauma of surgery to begin healing—I felt at peace under his concerned gaze.

I drifted through the night never completely unconscious. A dull and ever-present pain emerged as morning broke. With the repaired arm cocooned, the other was connected to a drip. I could do nothing but lie and wait.

Ciro came in quietly before 6am putting his tray down on the table, ready to make deliveries.

"Qualcosa da bere?"—*something to drink?*—Rosetta came over quietly to ask. I nodded gratefully looking forward to a sip of water. My throat felt raw after having the ventilation tube down it for so long during the operation.

"Buono per lo stomaco," she nodded reassuringly at me as she poured an espresso from Ciro's tray into my mouth.

"Forse un'po l'acqu anche?"—*Maybe a little water too?*—I asked, wondering what effect the strong, sweet coffee alone would have after having not eaten for thirty-six hours.

She poured a little water into a cup and held it to my lips. I savoured each tiny sip of fresh cool water as it re-hydrated my lips, mouth and throat.

A warm, cherry and cream cornetto was fed to me piece by piece. I gazed into Rosetta's eyes with gratitude, too weak to find words.

Tina was quieter than usual this morning as she managed the pain after her own operation, but I could see her smiling from her bed, content that I was being looked after, even though she wasn't able to help herself.

Two doctors came in during morning rounds. With one on each side of the bed they asked me to sit up. I looked back at them blankly wondering if they were on more drugs than me.

"Quando era la Tua operazione?—*When was your operation?*" one asked.

"Ieri," I croaked out.

He pulled the covers back as if to get me up. I had no clothing below the waist still. He quickly flicked the covers back over me. They wound the bed up to a slight angle then awkwardly held me up to unwrap my cocoon as they needed to change the dressings on my surgery sites. I was relieved that somehow in the melee after the operation, someone had slipped one of my singlet tops on me before I was re-wrapped providing me with some modesty. They cleaned my wounds and changed the dressings as quickly as possible. Secure again in my cocoon they wound my bed back down.

"Rest and we will see you tomorrow," they told me.

I stared after them as they left the room. With both arms still incapacitated—the drip still yet to be removed—I was too weak to work out how to ask when I might be liberated. Tina came over to my bed after the doctors had left. She inspected my sallow features with concern as she leant in to look at me.

"Oggi…" she paused, "Me ne andrò a casa." My eyes welled up

with tears as she told me she would be going home today.

"Ho felice per te."

I was happy for her but didn't know how I would survive without the deep source of strength and warmth that Tina and her family had brought to my bedside in the past five days. I was devastated they would no longer be there.

"Assunta will still be here," she acknowledged my other mother as she came over to the side of the bed and gazed protectively at me. I met Assunta's eyes with gratitude.

Three women in white coats came into the room at that moment. A cousin of Tina's who worked at the hospital with the Assistiente Sociale, and two other colleagues.

Tina had told them I was here on my own and would need assistance when I left the hospital. An animated discussion erupted over my bed. I was getting used to conversations happening over me that I couldn't understand. Sandro came into my line of sight.

"Quando sarai pronto a lasciare l'ospedale, verrò a prenderti in macchina"—when I was ready to be discharged, he told me, he could come and pick me up in his car.

Did that mean they want me to come and stay with them? That sounds nice. I couldn't think beyond today but nodded gratefully.

The group had not long dispersed when two more women and a man arrived looking for me. It took me a moment to recognize Norma, the fellow patient who had left after my first night in l'Ospedale dei Pellegrini.

"I am Patrizio Zucchetto," the man introduced himself with an odd Irish lilt to his Italian accent. He was Norma's pastor from the evangelical protestant church she attended. Patrizio introduced the second woman with them as his mother Pina.

"We have brought Norma in for her check-up," he explained, "but we wanted to check if there was anything that you need."

I told him about Tim from *il Faro* International Baptist Church coming to see me prior to my operation, and how Jacki had sat with me the day before when I came out of surgery.

"Do you know them?" I asked.

"Yes of course," Patrizio smiled in surprise at the connection. "Sometimes our church communities do shared activities together."

Promising to stay in touch he offered to ask his wife Jennifer to check on me again later in the week. Jennifer he told me, was Irish. "I wondered why your English accent had such a distinct Gaelic lilt." I smiled.

I watched sadly as Tina and her family gathered her belongings. She left her telefinino number with me, giving my hand one last squeeze before she left. The ward fell silent in the wake of their departure.

It was mid-afternoon when a tall, broad shouldered woman, half limped, half bounded into our ward. She was younger than my previous roommates—perhaps the same age as my older sisters who were in their mid-forties. Dropping a small bag down on the bed that Tina had vacated, she came close to the side of my bed to put her bags away. I felt myself shrink into the mattress, nervous she would bump the bed, not aware of the fragile state I was in.

"Eh! Ciao!" she exclaimed cheerfully as I watched her carefully edging around the corner of my bed.

"Ciao!" I warmed to her friendly smile instantly. "Io sono Jacqueline. Come ti chiami?"

"Io?"—*Me?*—"Sono Antonina," she threw over her shoulder as she unpacked. Assunta jumped in on cue to explain my story.

Antonina's face softened, as she gazed down at me sympathetically while listening. As the story ended her face broke into another big smile.

"Allora," she thumped her chest with her fist and leant in a little closer to look me right in the eye, "Se hai bisogno di qualcosa… ti chiami me!"

I nodded obediently with a smile and promised to call her over if I needed anything.

Karina, who worked in a nearby clinic in the mornings, came by to check on me in the early evening. She checked I was comfortable and had everything I needed, then fed me some dinner before taking her leave before it got any darker. "The hospital is not in the safest area at night," she apologised, "I don't like to catch the train home too late from Montesanto," she referred to the nearby funicular station on the edge of Quartieri Spagnola where the hospital was located.

Antonina was up early the next day. She hobbled energetically over to my side. "Un caffé?" she asked brightly holding up the espresso that Ciro had left beside my bed. She poured the espresso down my throat and fed me bite sized pieces of a cornetto. *Who had paid for breakfast* I wondered, now that Tina had left?

A woman popped her head around the door.

"Hai bisogno di aiuto mangiare?" she asked.

I studied her, wondering why she looked familiar. Antonina confirmed that she had fed me already. As I tried to listen in to their conversation, I realised she was a family member of a patient across the hall. She had been in the hall when I had been brought up from surgery and had apparently offered to take over from Tina, to ensure I received a coffee and cornetto each morning. She smiled over at me and told me that the breakfast was a gift from her mother.

Overwhelmed at the kindness of another stranger, tears welled up as I thanked her. She patted my hand as she waved my gratitude off.

Maria and Antonina were resting quietly in their beds when Jacki returned to see me mid-morning. Assunta had left for the operation on her shoulder.

"Well now... you're looking a bit brighter," she smiled, pleased to see me raised up slightly in the bed.

She retrieved some underwear along with the soft pink pyjama pants given to me by Tina from the cupboard. She slipped them over my legs, then carefully re-directed the catheter tube to exit over my waist band. We chattered quietly, getting to know each other as she helped me to brush my hair and handed me wipes and moisturiser to refresh my face.

Dottore Corduas appeared with Infermiere Mario who pulled an equipment trolley behind them and over to my bed. I wasn't sure if I had met this doctor though again, his kindly face looked familiar. Jacki explained that he had been part of my surgical team.

"Il Dottore wants to know if you think you might be able to sit up for the dressing change today," Jacki translated for me.

I gazed at him fearfully.

"Possiamo provare?"—*can we try?*—he encouraged me.

"Okay," I said hesitantly. "Proviamo."

With the doctor in front, an infermiere on either side and Jacki hovering nearby, they gently lifted my legs to angle my body so I could hang them over the side of the bed. I winced in pain as the movement triggered the surgery site on my hip.

I took a deep breath, then allowed them to raise my upper body gently into an upright position on the edge of the bed.

"Aspetta... aspetta..."—*wait... wait*—I breathed out as I assessed how being upright made me feel after more than forty-eight hours lying flat.

"How do I tell them that I feel faint or dizzy?" I asked Jacki.

"Giro di testa."

She told them to wait a moment while I took some more slow, deep breaths to try and find my vertical equilibrium.

"Okay. Va bene," I let them start.

Gently Dottore Corduas cut off the wrappings. Feeling them peel away the dressing from the incision in my arm made me wince not from pain, but rather vulnerability around the exposed surgery site. He cleaned it with hygienic swabs, then quickly applied a new dressing.

With the help of Infermiere Mario they wrapped the layers of padding around me again preparing to return me to my cocoon.

"Jacqueline, possiamo provare qualcosa?"—*can we try something else?* Dottore Corduas asked before they had finished. He demonstrated that he would like me to move off the bed and try and stand on my feet for the last stage of my wrapping.

"Si, provo,"—*yes, I can try*—I agreed.

Jacki pulled out the pair of slippers she had bought for me and slipped them on to my feet.

With the physical assistance of the infermiere and the encouraging smiles of Dottore Corduas and Jacki in front of me, I slowly edged off the bed. I rested my feet on the ground, then gingerly took the last of my weight off the bed.

The dizziness became more insistent. I felt ill as the three pairs of hands held me. I never got the words out in time. I awoke to find myself flat on my back on the bed, with my feet on the warm chest of the Dottore. Jacki fanned me as the infermiere tried to adjust the rest of my body into a better position on the bed.

The rush of the faint had left me chilled out in another endorphin fed happy place. For a few moments pain was forgotten, I felt safe on the bed with the Dottore holding my feet. While rapid chatter swirled above me between the three, he periodically made sure to give me direct eye contact and a warm smile and nod, to reassure me that everything was okay despite the language barrier.

"Jacqui, they think you have post-operative anaemia. You are going to need a blood transfusion," Jacki leant down to explain.

The medical staff disappeared to make the arrangements.

The post fainting rush vanished as quickly as it had appeared. Jacki did what she could to make me comfortable before she had to leave.

I lay awkwardly on the bed waiting. Another infermiere came in to take a blood sample while Dottore Corduas and Infermiere Mario finished their rounds. They returned to finish the final layer of my dressing that had been interrupted by my faint, gently working around my limp body rather than trying to get me to sit up again.

I wasn't permitted to eat or drink while I waited to receive blood. I ignored everyone while they ate lunch, lying in the dark isolation of my new misery. Despondent, I waited. I had no energy to communicate what I needed. I was crushed by frustration. I had no energy even to respond to Antonina's cheery calls from across the room, checking on me.

A familiar face appeared at the door as the taunting smells of lunch were cleared away. Cristina's brother and Fernanda's father Cyrus. He slipped over to my bed and sat down on the chair beside me. It felt like an old friend had come to visit. I felt a flicker of joy lift me a little from my morose mood.

"Come stai Jacqueline," he enquired.

"Non, stai bene," I told him sadly, "Ho l'anaemia e ho bisogno di trasfusione."

He nodded his understanding. He sat with me a while, saying very little. I looked into his kind face as he held eye contact with me. Restricted by our lack of shared words, the wordless compassion in his eyes reached deep into my soul.

He finally broke the silence, explaining that he was in the area for work, and had wanted to check on me to see how I was after the operation. He clasped his hands together to shake them in a typically Neapolitan gesture of concern. He took his leave with a gentle pat of my hand, promising to update Christina, Lina and Fernanda. My eyes filled with tears as I watched him go, overwhelmed by the kindness of someone I had met so briefly, but had taken a pause from their daily life to check on mine.

The infermiere arrived with the blood supply as my ward mates began their evening meal. Restrained again by tubes and needles going into my left arm, I waited quietly for the red blood cells to slide into my veins.

My mind drifted back to my arrival in Siena. Miriam and I on our way back from our first shopping trip loaded with Italian staples like basil, tomatoes, cheese and pasta. For a moment in time, residents of a medieval Italian town, we had relished being just a little Italian. I had wanted to become Italian. I had dreamed of etching out some sort of life here—even if only for a short time. I could now say with some authenticity at least, that I had Italian blood running in my veins.

23

"Un caffè?" Antonina limped over to my bed at 6.30am, the familiar little plastic cup covered in alfoil clasped between her fingers. "Hmmm... controllerò se ti è permesso mangiare..." she let me have the espresso but paused before feeding me my daily cornetto to go and check with the infermiere if I was permitted to eat yet, after the transfusion had suspended all meals the day before.

Infermiere Pasquale followed her back into the room with a smile and shake of his head as I looked eagerly at the packet containing my proposed breakfast in Antonina's hand. Pasquale turned my left arm over to find a vein to take a blood sample before he would let Antonina raise my sugar levels. He shook his head sympathetically as he examined the state of my inner elbow where the same veins had offered passage for blood tests, anaesthetic, post-operative pain relief and finally the blood transfusion last night. I followed his gaze to see the light bruising and the skin looking angry and irritated in reaction to all the needles that had pierced the same area over the past ten days. It looked like I had been shooting up in an alley. He turned my arm back over and found a vein in my hand to take this morning's bloods from instead.

Fernanda's smiling face appeared around the door mid-morning. She had brought Christina in to have her dressings checked.

Kissing Assunta in greeting, she came over to fuss around my bed, check I was comfortable and had what I needed. Christina joined us after she had been for her check-up. Brighter and more relaxed after a few days at home, she sat beside me for a few minutes enquiring after my health. Like her brother the day before, she sat quietly and communicated by keeping eye contact, nodding at me encouragingly. Fernanda told me of her upcoming wedding plans and how I must return to Napoli so I could attend. I smiled wistfully unsure of where I would be heading next week let alone next year.

After the blood transfusion, the need to return home to Australia for my longer-term recovery now seemed inevitable. From the moment of the accident I had refused to believe that I would have to return home. I was determined that this was not going to be how my trip ended. I hadn't even been away four months. I still hadn't worked out who I was other than that which I already knew myself to be. And while I had a fledgling love interest in Marco, that spark would surely never survive if I was to go back home.

I continued to hope I might be able to stay with Sandro and Tina or go and stay with Marco. I also had the option of heading to England to stay with family there. But as I lay awake in the early hours of the morning, I slowly began to accept that I was in need of the comfort of my own family and the familiarity and security of home.

An elderly nun entered the ward as Cristina and Fernanda left. Cloaked in a faded grey habit, she stood in the centre of the room and stared hard at me, as Assunta explained that I had needed a blood transfusion the day before. She came over to my bed, leant in close and lifted my eyelids to check the colour. I hoped there was evidence that the blood transfusion was doing its job. She seemed satisfied, giving me a gruff nod. She tied a piece of pale blue string around my wrist with a tiny pendant with the Virgin Mary on it. Making the sign of the cross over me, she said a quick well-rehearsed prayer then left. The religiosity of her routine struck me as rather dry and ritualistic compared to the spontaneous and fervent prayers Norma had delivered, but I appreciated the intent.

I could hear Karina chatting with Antonina over by the window as I began to stir in the afternoon.

She wandered over when she saw my eyes open.

"Has Antonina been looking after you?" I asked sleepily.

"I like her Jacqui. She is true, not false," she nodded back with a smile toward my roommate.

Antonina had told me of the pizzeria she ran in a small town called Masse Lubrense on the Sorrentine Peninsula.

"Quando Tu è migliore, Tu devi venire al pizzeria,"—*when you are better, you have to visit the pizzeria*—she had told me emphatically. I felt it was a non-negotiable suggestion. I could imagine her whipping up magnificent meals and riling up the locals with her banter. Experiencing her hospitality in her own space was a grand idea to look forward to. I knew I would have to come back one day.

Despite the language barrier, I knew my gregarious roommate to be all heart. True not false summed up her authenticity well.

Too weary for much conversation, I encouraged Karina to practice her English and tell me more about her life. I listened as she spoke of growing up in Romania, the daughter of a Romanian mother and German father but raised as an only child by her mother. She spent four years at a boarding school from the age of fourteen, where she shared a dormitory with twenty-one other girls and they only had hot water to shower with twice a week. She told me of summer holidays swimming in the Black Sea. After finishing school, she moved to Germany where her father lived. She spoke very little German when she arrived and told me how difficult it was to communicate. She started working as a nanny, then entered into nursing. After a long-term relationship ended, she moved to Napoli, learnt another language and steadily increased her nursing qualifications.

She had been thinking about returning to live in Germany after nine years in Napoli. But recently Giancarlo had entered her life. He was based in Rome but travelled extensively as tour manager for a popular Italian singer. It was early days in the relationship, but she wanted to see where it went, so for now she had put her plans to move back to Germany on hold.

'Life happens while you are busy making other plans,' John Lennon once said. The interruption to her plans seemed to hold more promise than the interruption to mine. But I still hoped that for whatever reason my journey had been so significantly upended, this bend in the road I had thought I was on, would still lead me to where I was supposed to be going.

Karina was out of the room taking a call when dinner arrived. As she returned to the room she saw me struggling to embrace any opportunity for independence and open the containers myself. She rushed over to help.

"Tutto okay," I said, desperate to be able to be able to do things for myself again.

"I know Jacqui, but when I am here you should let me help."

Relaxing back against my pillow, I allowed her to feed me. I was frustrated by the ongoing need to be dependent, but even trying to open my food had drained the small reserves of energy I had. I couldn't force my recovery to move faster.

An infermiera dropped a meal off for her also. She ate a little from one of the containers but left the others unopened.

"Jacqui do you mind if I take these?" she asked pointing to the unopened food trays that I hadn't wanted tonight.

"Si, certo," I confirmed, wondering why she wanted them.

"There are people I walk past on the way to the train who would be grateful of these meals," she explained as she placed them in a plastic bag. She crossed the room and also collected the unopened trays of my roommates.

Effortless compassion towards me, but also thinking of the needy on the streets. I stared at her astounded. She really was an angel.

Jenny popped in on Saturday afternoon with Alyn. They were on their way to the cinema. Karina arrived before they left and my two most consistent visitors met for the first time. She and Jenny chatted in Italian across the bed while I lay there too weak to concentrate on the conversation. Karina leapt straight onto the small, but many varied tasks that assisted my daily comfort as they talked. Adjusting my pillows, straightening my bedside table, making sure I could reach my water, checking my shoulder bag (still kept under the sheets beside me) wasn't bumping the surgery site on my hip. As she vanished into the hallway to speak to one of the infermiere about when my next dose of pain relief was due, Jenny leant in and said, "I feel terrible, but I wouldn't think to do half the things she has just done for you."

"I don't think many people would automatically think of all

those little things," I smiled.

I told her also about the food parcels she had taken out to people on the street the night before.

But you have done so much for me too Jenny," I reminded her, "Considering I was just a passing guest in your hostel!" She shrugged off my thanks.

"Naples is a big city, but it's a small community," she said, "Mostly this is good... except EVERYONE knows your business," she laughed.

After Jenny and Alyn had departed for their film, Karina told me she had been speaking with infermiere Pasquale.

"La come me per aiutarLa con una lavata Jacqui?"—*would you like my help with a wash*—she asked. Desperate for a wash three days after the operation I had been making enquiries that morning from the infermieri about anyone who might be able to help me in lieu of family. I had been thinking a staff member. I couldn't bear to let Karina do yet more for me. One week ago we were strangers, and again she was stepping in for my family. But desperate to feel clean, I humbled myself and accepted her help.

"Grazie Karina," I blinked away my tears of affection as she cleared away the tub and towels after helping me freshen up in the bed.

Placing her hand gently on my cheek she leant in and said, "Di niente Jacqui di niente," —*it is nothing*.

Antonina changed from her pyjamas into daywear the next morning. As she held my morning espresso up to my lips, she told me that she had a day pass to leave the hospital today. Her family would be here soon to take her out.

Her husband and daughter arrived, along with her sister and brother-in-law mid-morning. Thirteen-year-old Francesca sprawled across Antonina's bed, the delighted mother wrapping her arms around her after nearly a week apart.

"Ciao," I smiled at the group. "Io sono Jacqueline. Non parlo Italiano molto bene," I quickly warned before they all started trying to talk to me.

Antonina roared with laughter. She explained to them that I was Australian and detailed my accident along with an update on my current condition. Her sister Carmella came over to the side of my bed. Speaking more slowly and using more Italian than the local dialect that Antonina often slipped into, she told me they had family in Sydney, but had never been to visit.

"Tu hai visitato Sorrento?" she asked if I had visited Sorrento.

"Si…Io ricordo l'odorato dei limoni che vengono dai negozi,"—I remember the smell of the lemons coming from the shops—I told her wistfully, as I reminisced back to the two nights our tour group had stayed there the year before. She looked at me with a smile and slight tilt of her head.

She went over to a bag she had left near Antonina's bed and began rummaging. She returned to my side holding a large, bright yellow lemon in her hand. "Per te Jacqueline," she said with a smile as she placed it on the table beside me, "da Massa Lubrense".

In the quiet that fell over the room with their departure for the day, I picked up the lemon and inhaled the refreshing scent of the robust fruit. I may not have made it down to the lemon groves of Sorrento and the Amalfi Coast this time, but it seemed they had at least come to me. I thought of the little bottle of limoncello I had bought from one of those Sorrentine stores and used to toast my year ahead from my Sydney balcony, now nearly a year earlier. To wherever the road may lead I had toasted, as the potential of my adventure lay open wide before me. I had had the chance to take control for the briefest few months, but now life was reasserting itself and the freedom to go and do as I pleased for a time, had been wrenched away.

The Dottore who had escorted me down to my operation was on rounds that morning.

"Come stai Jacqueline?" he asked as he came over.

"Meglio,"—*better*—I proudly used the useful new word Infermiere Gianni had taught me the day before. He pulled back the sheets and rolled the top of my pyjamas down. As he felt around the surgery site on my hip, I grimaced at the firm pressure from his fingers.

He returned a few minutes later with Infermieri Pasquale and Infermiere Nina, wheeling a trolley bed between them. They worked together to slide me over onto the mobile trolley bed, then tucked blankets around me.

After five full days bed and ward bound, I was grateful for a change of scenery, though I had no idea where we were off to. Infermiere Pasquale gave me a smile of reassurance as he wheeled me into the shaky lift. My companions smiled as my face lit up at the sight of sunlight cascading between the cool stone walls, splashing onto the cobblestoned ground as we emerged into the courtyard that I had only seen from above since arriving. I inhaled the fresh air with delight as my cabin fever from days indoors broke.

It was momentary, but enough sensory stimulation to lift my spirits before I was wheeled through another door and we were back inside. Our destination was less appealing. They were to take an ultrasound around my hip area and needed to cut open my cast again to allow the radiographer access. Nina held my hand and kept eye contact as I braced for the pain that would inevitably follow as my arm was released from its cocoon.

We returned upstairs and I was wheeled into a treatment room at the end of the hall back in the Ortopaedia ward to be re-cocooned. Karina's face peeked around the door as my trolley came to a stop. She was in early today and had been looking for me.

She began to help Infermiera Nina carefully remove all the remaining strapping from my arm and chest. The two women wiped the skin of my arms and torso clean with soft warm cloths before the Dottore and Infermiere Pasquale returned to reapply my dressings.

Karina stood in front of me watching my face carefully, "Hai giro di testa Jacqui?" she asked as the men eased my body into a sitting position for the first time since the faint three days earlier.

"Tutto bene," I replied cheerfully as I took deep breathes to ensure oxygen was travelling where it needed to. I was desperate to see my body making some progress towards recovery. I felt weak but not faint and was again cheered by the simple act of being upright. As I felt the Dottore pull the dressing off the wound on my arm I turned my head, curious to see how impressive my scar was.

"No, no," he waved a finger at me then placed it under my chin to gently turn my face away. Perhaps he didn't want me breathing germs on the area. Or perhaps he thought the sight of it may cause me to faint again. I felt the cool of the disinfectant swabs sweep over the area before the surgery site was covered up again.

Emboldened after managing to stay upright during my dressing change, I asked Karina if they would let me sit in an armchair for lunch. With all four surrounding me, they eased me from the trolley bed on to my feet and into an armchair they had placed beside my bed. Assunta and Maria nodded and clucked in encouragement from across the room, pleased to see some progress.

Karina sat on the edge of the bed. "Today you must have a little of everything. For strength," she insisted as she opened my lunch. I managed for an hour to sit vertical for the first time in six days. The *giro di testa* of three days earlier, didn't return.

I was back in bed when Antonina burst back through the door just after dinner. We all cheered at the return of our boisterous friend. With a large, white rectangular, cake box in her hands she raised it up triumphantly to present it to the room.

She lumbered over to me first, placed the box on my lap and lifted the lid. A spread of luscious sweet treats were revealed including sfogliatella and another popular local delicacy called babá, a type of sponge soaked in rum.

I pored over the selection as I inhaled the sweetness. Assunta and Maria loudly barked out their recommendations from across the room. I selected a mini babá, knowing my choice of the local specialty would win approval from the crowd. A cheer erupted as my choice gave a nod to local culture. Antonina advised I should also take another for later. I wrapped a mini strawberry flan into a napkin and placed it on my bedside table and I set to work devouring my first choice, as Antonina worked her way around the room sharing the treats with the others.

Antonina leapt into action to create a lounge room for television viewing that evening. She pulled all the armchairs into a semi-circle at the end of my bed so I felt a part of the action. Once she had Maria and Assunta settled comfortably, she came over to make sure I could reach anything I needed.

"Per favore mi puoi alzare il letto?"

Antonina nodded impressed with my articulation and wound my bed up so I was in a semi-sitting position. Karina had written down some key phrases so I knew how to ask people to wind my bed up or down. As Antonina took her seat, I gazed over the eclectic but companionable ensemble with their backs to me at the end of my bed. I felt warm with affection.

Assunta had taken me on as her confidant in the past few days. Against doctors' orders she had been sneaking into the bathroom for a smoke a couple of times a day. Waving the cigarette between her fingers at me, she would give me a wink and lift a finger to her lips requesting my secrecy as she projected the image of a naughty grey-haired schoolgirl making her way to the bathroom wrapped in her red dressing gown. From there she would lean out the window exhaling her contraband into the Neapolitan skies.

Maria, I had discovered, had six children. All adults now. She often looked sad and cranky. But earlier today when we were again alone for a few minutes, I asked her if I could take her photo. Using my left hand, I zoomed in on her face with my compact camera from my bed six metres away. As I clicked the shutter, her face had lit up the screen with the biggest smile I had received from her. She came over to see the photo and was clearly pleased with it. She had spent the afternoon sending everyone who came through the door to see me, so I could show them her portrait. With every complimenti received her face had lit up with the same smile that I had unearthed from her, in our brief moment of wordless connection.

24

My roommates were quietly coming to the end of their overnight concerto of snoring as the first hint of light seeped into the room.

I examined the bed to work out how to get myself up without assistance. I tucked the toes of my right foot under the bar at the end of the bed, to give myself a counterbalance as I eased my body up with my left arm. I got as far as being propped up on my elbow then paused for a rest. I focused on the muscles that weren't hindered by my injury sites.

I can do this, I coaxed myself.

I slid my legs to the edge of the bed and spotted my slippers below. I slid carefully off the mattress and dropped my feet into the warm footwear. I took a small pause to check my equilibrium before I crept to the door and let myself out.

As I limped along the hall, I passed the night shift infermieri as they prepared for early morning rounds. Startled to see me up and about their faces broke into big smiles, "Brava Jacqueline, brava!" they exclaimed.

A pretty woman in her thirties with long mousy hair and blue eyes was standing beside her bed which was parked in the hall outside our room. Her left arm was wrapped to her torso like mine and she was trying to put on a dressing gown.

"Buongiorno," I smiled tentatively. "Io sono Jacqueline."

"Sono Natalia," she responded with a slight smile.

"Hai bisogno di aiuto per questa?" I offered to help. She shook her head as she looked at my own strapping and acknowledged my own limitations.

"Ho uno mano, anche te. Insieme abbiamo due mani."—*I have one hand, also you. Together we have two hands*—I suggested.

"Va bene," she nodded gratefully as I helped her into her dressing gown.

A warm welcome awaited me on return after my roommates had woken, shocked to see my bed empty.

By the time Ciro arrived, I had been to the bathroom to add a touch of make-up to lift my pallor and pushed a bright red head band over my brushed hair. Baby steps towards feeling normal. Busy with his deliveries Ciro brought my espresso over without looking up.

"Buongiorno," I smiled. "Io sono Jacqueline."

His eyes flicked up as I spoke to him for the first time. A slight crinkle lifted the corners of his mouth as he nodded in acknowledgement, "Sono Ciro."

I nodded. He placed the espresso and the cornetto on the table beside me. He gave my hand a squeeze before he continued on with his morning deliveries.

Forty-eight hours had made an enormous difference. I winced with every step as my hip railed against the pain in the bone that had been grafted for my arm. But I pushed past it happy to be liberated from my bed. I paused by the window and let the fresh morning air fill my lungs as I leant on the sill for support. While imprisoned I had had no knowledge of whether the sun was shining, unless glimpses of sunlight slipped across the room. Or if it was raining, unless I could hear the water landing on the dome of the chiesa, a roll of thunder shuddering through the air, or see the lightning flashes of an early morning storm.

I gazed wistfully into the grey courtyard, desperate to go outside. Desperate to feel healed and whole. I wanted to escape. I drifted back to Elba again. Hoeing the asparagus field with the sun on my back. Plunging into the sea with the cool water refreshing my tired body. Walking through the olive grove and reaching up to drag off that last handful of fruit we had somehow missed. Feeling the silvery leaves in my hand as the olives collected in my palms. Up in Capolieveri with Marco enjoying a glass of wine with the bougainvillea vines wrapped around the picturesque architecture and an inky blue, star filled sky above. I wanted to be on a hydrofoil heading over to one of the islands in the bay of Napoli, climbing Mt Vesuvius, exploring the museums and historical castles in the city, taking in a performance at Teatro San Carlo. I wanted to be on the farm that I should have arrived at by now in the Cilento National Park, harvesting chestnuts and learning to milk a goat. I wanted to continue my journey down the coast and work on a farm on the slopes of Mt Etna. And maybe just maybe, eventually head back to Elba to see Marco, who was continuing to send me messages checking in on me. But I wouldn't be doing any of that. I would be going home. Not to Sydney but to Brisbane where I hadn't lived in over ten years. And I would be staying with my parents.

Jenny was off to Berlin for a long weekend to mark the twentieth anniversary of the Berlin Wall coming down. Karina had come to see me the day before, but she was off on a mini break with Giancarlo on Ischia, the larger of the islands in the bay of Napoli for a few days now. I had walked with her down the hallway as she left.

"I'm glad you can get out of bed again Jacqui," she said earnestly, "I don't think I could have gone away if you were not able to look after yourself a little. I teared up, thanking her for everything she had done for me in the past week.

"Jacqui di niente. You do not need to thank me. I like you. I liked to help you."

Leaning in she kissed both my cheeks and said quietly, "Ti voglio bene."—*I wish the best for you.*

Though I was on the mend, I felt anxious as I faced the absence of my two most consistent visitors, translators and helpers. I watched her vanish into the lift, hoping I would see her again before I left Napoli. I was still not fit to fly, but planning was in progress with my travel insurer to get me home. After all the effort it had taken to leave my job, my home, my life in Australia, my struggle to come to terms with my trip ending was brutal. I was in disbelief that it had come to this. I refused to consider that this was the end. I was determined to come back and somehow complete the journey I had set out on.

Maria's husband had collected her the afternoon before. She had already called twice to check in on me. It was even harder to understand her on the phone, but the message still got through that she was there if I needed her.

Assunta, after a final check with the Dottore was cleared for departure. We made our heartfelt farewells as she left with her nephew after lunch.

Antonina remained on her bed that morning, resting quietly. I sensed she was nervous about the operation on her knee which was due to happen the next day. With some Italian women's magazines that I had found on the table, I settled awkwardly into the armchair at the end of her bed so we could keep a companionable silence without anyone else around. I was comfortably ensconced in my soft pink pyjamas from Tina, with a light blanket over my knees when the door opened. Norma and Mariuzzi, along with Patrizio's parents, appeared. Their eyes briefly rested on my empty bed, before they spotted me tucked in the armchair. Norma and Pina's faces lit up with delight at my transformation since their visit the day after my operation a week ago.

Norma was back for another check-up. She handed me a box of chocolate biscotti. I studied the woman who I had only been in hospital with for one night, while she was recovering from her own operation no-less, who had been back to visit me twice. She had taken note that I was on my own. I had found out from Patrizio the week before that she was from Venezuela originally. I wondered if she knew what it was to be a stranger in need in a country not her own.

My face lit up as Tina and Sandro appeared around the door. Also, at the hospital for Tina's one-week check-up, they came in bearing a jar of freshly preserved peaches. Tina handed me a large plastic shopping bag, nodding and gesturing that I open it. I pulled out some white tracksuit pants, two oversized zip-up sweaters that would fit beautifully over my cast and some giant t-shirts. They had carefully chosen some items from Raffaele's sporting goods store for me.

As the new arrivals sat down, Norma squeezed her eyes tight.

Clasping my left hand, she stood beside me praying intensely out loud. Sandro, Tina, Patrizio, Mariuzzi, Pino and Pina all sat around me nodding in affirmation at what she was saying.

I felt the lump rising at the back of my throat as emotion swept through me as words from the gospel of Matthew began filtering through my mind.

> *I was hungry and you gave me something to eat,*
> *I was thirsty and you gave me something to drink,*
> *I was a stranger and you invited me in,*
> *I needed clothes and you clothed me,*
> *I was sick and you looked after me,*
> *I was in prison and you came to visit me.*

My eyes had filled with tears by the time she finished her prayers. With the strength returning to my body, my mind found capacity to begin processing the number of people from this city who had taken an interest in my well-being. Whether they held a personal Christian faith or not, Jesus' instruction on how we should care for strangers in need had been exemplified through almost everyone I had come in contact with since landing in hospital.

After Norma had finished praying, she and Mariuzzi, Pino and Pina said their goodbyes and took their leave. Tina went over to put my new clothes into my locker, while Sandro settled into a nearby chair for a chat. The door opened again. My seventh and eighth visitors for the morning arrived. Maria and her husband had popped back to check on me. The language barriers kept the visits short but sweet, but each left me basking in the kindness of a city that had taken me in.

As the room emptied out, I glanced over at Antonina. She looked at me perplexed by the trail of diverse visitors I had spent the morning hosting. I stuttered out a phrase I had been working on in my notebook.

"La gente di Napoli mi ha abbracciato.," I started slowly. "Due settimane fa ero sola. Ora ho molti nuovi amici!"—*The people of Napoli have embraced me. Two weeks ago I was alone. Now I have many new friends!*

She nodded thoughtfully as she gazed at me, before returning to the magazine she had been pretending to read.

I was on my way across the room when Ciro came through with his espresso deliveries in the afternoon. Towering at least half a foot above the small man, he raised his eyebrows at seeing me on my feet. He chattered away to me in dialect and as he made to leave the room, indicated I could follow him if I wanted to. I assumed it was an invite to join him on his delivery round. We walked down the hall to the bottom of some stairs. I paused as he started to climb to the next floor. He turned around beckoning me to follow. One step at a time and clinging to the rail, I ignored the ever-present piercing pain in my hip. I liked the idea of going beyond the hall but wondered if I should go back. The stairs turned a corner halfway up and I found Ciro waiting. Standing on the stair above me brought him to my height. He reached out and took my hand. Raising it to his lips he kissed it. I looked at him warily. With a sudden movement he leant in with lips poised to kiss mine. I withdrew slightly as I burst out laughing. Beaten up and unwashed and still an Italian man could be opportunistic. "No, no no!" I exclaimed, waving my finger at him in admonishment. *'Never say yes to an Italian man if you aren't certain what they are asking,'* I recalled Nicole's words on Elba.

He looked briefly taken aback.

"Va bene," he shrugged, "A domani,"—*until tomorrow.*

Antonina was taken away for surgery the following morning, as was Anna—a quiet girl who had taken Maria's bed late in the afternoon the day before and kept quietly to herself. Assunta's bed still lay empty. The ward was lonely as I waited for their safe return from the operating theatre.

After a light siesta post lunch, I woke to see a pretty woman not much older than me, moving around the ward on crutches. In a bright velour tracksuit, she paused to show her friend some other similarly bright tracksuits, before she stored them in her cupboard. She appeared to be well prepared with comfortable clothes for her hospital stay. It seemed she expected to be here for a while.

I eased out of bed to commence a slow journey to the bathroom. I paused to introduce myself and explained my language barrier. Anastasia's face radiated with warmth as she introduced herself and her best friend Elena.

At dinner time Anastasia was joined by her husband Miguel—a short, distinguished looking man with grey hair—and their two beautiful teenage daughters Marina and Sabrina. Leaning down, he kissed Anastasia tenderly on the lips. I was taken by the tender love I could see between them. Sixteen-year-old Sabrina came over to say hello to me. She was learning English at school and communicated quite clearly. We were muddling our way through my story between my broken Italian and her broken English, when I heard Antonina weakly interjecting from where she lay in bed with a drip in her arm recovering from surgery. She instructed her sister Carmella—who was staying the night to attend to her post-operative care—to explain to everyone how I had come to be there. It had been a few days since I had experienced the empathetic head shaking of someone hearing my story for the first time. This time the operation and blood transfusion details included. I smiled weakly. I was reminded it had been a tough two weeks.

Anastasia was warm and friendly, a quieter soul than most of the others who had come through so far. We steadily became acquainted through small conversations from across the divide of the room.

Antonina bounced back from her surgery and was up and about with the help of crutches within two days. On Thursday morning she came over to tell me it was time for her to leave. My eyes filled with tears.

She nodded reassuringly towards Anastasia "Lei guarderà dopo tu. Tutto sarà va bene."—*She will look after you. Everything will be okay.*

Another changing of the guard. With telefonino numbers and email addresses exchanged, and a promise from me to return to visit the pizzeria one day, we said farewell.

Four women appeared at the door asking for me after lunch.

"Are you Jacqui?" a woman with a strong American accent asked. I nodded, curious as to who the women were.

"I'm Marcia Monahan," the pretty blonde-haired woman in her mid-fifties introduced herself. "Jacki hasn't been able to get back in to see you so we said we would come in," she explained. Marcia and her husband were also Pastors with Il Faro, the International Baptist Church. The church had a lot of attendees from the NATO and American military bases located in Napoli as well as the local community. She introduced Erica from New Jersey, Shirl from Hawaii and Georgia from Australia who all had husbands who worked at the military base.

"Married an American," Georgia shrugged with a smile in response to my question about her Australian accent. "My sister visited recently and I thought you might need a packet of these," she said holding up some Tim Tams. My face lit up at the sight of the treat from home. "And also, these," she put a small pile of Australian women's magazines down.

"And I made cupcakes," Shirl sang out, presenting me with a plate of treats.

"You look much better than I expected after all Jacki told us,"" Marcia smiled, noting the fact that I was even sitting up.

"It's been a rough few weeks," I admitted.

"I hardly ever dare come into the city," Shirl told me, "I get nervous hearing all the stories about the petty thefts."

"I was nervous when I first arrived," I smiled as I thought about all the things I had been alert to when coming to stay in Napoli. "This however wasn't a situation I had expected!" I laughed as I acknowledged what a ridiculous few weeks it had turned out to be.

The girls stayed chatting for about an hour. It was re-invigorating to be able to chat with several people fluent in my own language. I told them of my journey from Siena, to Elba, to Napoli.

"Can you speak Italian now?" Erica asked me incredulous.

"Not really," I laughed. "I struggled through language school, improved a little on Elba, but here in hospital I had none of the vocabulary I needed." I pulled out my notebook where I had begun writing down new words as I heard them, practicing my ambidexterity.

Frattura—*fracture*. Osso—*bone*. Rotto—*broken*. Transfusione—*transfusion*.

"And you were working on a farm before you came here?" Marcia asked.

"Fresh food, outdoor work, sunshine, sea... and then I ended up here," I rolled my eyes. I pulled up my pyjama pants to show the bruising I had noticed on my feet and lower legs, caused by rolling on the cobblestones after I landed. I was glad to see my skin still had some of its sun kissed glow from the days on Elba.

Erica, a trained nurse, offered to come back and wash my hair on Saturday along with Marcia. I accepted gratefully as I ran my fingers through my again increasingly greasy locks, self-conscious after another long stretch without being washed.

The beds on either side of Anastasia were filled later that afternoon. A tiny woman—another Maria—took up Antonina's bed, and a lady called Theresa moved in opposite me.

The doctors had told me I would need to stay in hospital at least another week until I was allowed to fly following the operation. I woke up despondent on Friday. I thanked God for all the people who had come to me and prayed for help to cope as I prepared for a day alone with no guests expected.

My phone beeped. A message from Antonina. It beeped again. Alexis in London. Antonina again. A message from Debbie in Brisbane. Then my sister Trish. Then Antonina again. Then Marco. Then Antonina. Then Georgia. And so, it continued through the morning.

As my phone fell silent, the door opened and Gavy walked in. She had been discharged not long after Tina, but because she lived down in Maratea further south in the region of Basilicata, this was her first chance to return for a check-up. I impressed her by getting out of bed to welcome her. We chatted quietly for a few minutes and I asked Anastasia to take some photos of us together. An invitation to come south and visit her was left open as Gavy closed the door behind her.

Jennifer, the wife of Patrizio, arrived for a visit after lunch. Quietly spoken with her lilting Irish accent, she offered to give me a manicure on my free hand while we sat and chatted about how she had come to Italy, met Patrizio and ended up staying. The joys and challenges of that decision, life in Ireland growing up, and life now on the outskirts of Napoli.

Like Antonina, Anastasia watched on curiously as I welcomed the flow of visitors. She chatted briefly with Jennifer asking how I knew so many people. Jennifer explained how word had got out that there was an Australian in hospital with a terrible injury who needed people to check on her. But that was the explanation amongst the expat community. I was still at a loss to comprehend the generosity from the many who had kept me in their thoughts, who were themselves patients recovering from surgery or a trauma themselves. All my new friends were unknown to each other and yet each day someone had been there when I needed them, providing for my needs in each of their own ways.

I had wanted to get to know the heart of Napoli—a city I had seen as dark and dangerous. It was not lost on me that in the most profound way, I had been given the opportunity to see her true self.

I was imbued with such love and kindness. I found myself overwhelmed.

On Sunday morning, Anastasia sought permission for her, Theresa and Maria to take me down to mass in the hospital church. With my hair freshly washed by Erica and Marcia the day before, my new slippers from Jacki complimenting my pyjamas and sweater from Tina, my fellow ward mates surrounded me protectively as we began my most challenging journey in weeks. The sun and fresh air made my head spin as we emerged from the rickety lift. With small steps, we moved as one across the courtyard. Theresa and Maria, both in for elective surgery, stayed close and encouraged me to pause whenever I needed to. Anastasia swung beside us on her crutches.

We ascended the stairs with a pause on each. I hoped we had left early enough to get to the service on time. Such a short journey was taking a while. At last, I entered the nave of Chiesa di Santissima Trinita dei Pellegrini, greeted by the bright white walls and arches and a host of angels sculpted into the half dome above us. Theresa and Maria helped me to a seat to rest a few minutes while they went to look at the artwork. A marble altar at the front was crowned with a white and gold sculpture. I studied it intently. The Christ. God the Father. Angels.

Raising myself gently to my feet with the help of the back of a pew, I wandered over to see what Anastasia was looking at. She pointed into the locked cabinet. Relics of saints. I tried not to recoil at the sight of the bones. The use of relics still didn't sit well with me, but I didn't want to offend. We limped around the church together looking at the paintings lining the walls. Other people wearing day wear (unlike the four of us in bathrobes and pyjamas) began entering for the service. The women hustled me into a seat.

Clergy wearing red robes entered soon after and the service commenced. The hard, straight-backed pew proved a difficult angle to sit in. My head periodically spun as I tried to focus on the rituals going on around me. Anastasia and Theresa's watchful eyes checked over me every few minutes. As everyone stood at the end of the mass to honour the departing clergy, I was without strength to rise. I felt a gentle hand on my shoulder. An elderly man with bowed head stood praying over me. Maria caught my eye and nodded encouragingly at me from behind Theresa. Maria's husband I had discovered was an evangelical protestant minister from another local church. She also knew of the churches that Marcia, Jacki and Tim, and Patrizio, Jennifer and Norma were a part of.

My roommates had arranged a special Sunday evening meal. We set the small table up for four this time and sat down for birra and pizza. I relished sitting at a table with others to share a meal.

I noticed the table shaking slightly, ripples rolling across the surface of my beer mid-way through our dinner. Seeing the alarm cross my face Teresa asked what was wrong.

I nodded at the now settling liquid. "Vesuvio?" I asked nervously. Was this a sign of the long overdue eruption? Bursting into kind laughter they all shook their heads.

"Il metro, Jacqueline," Anastasia explained stroking my hand reassuringly, "la stazione è vicina."—the station is nearby. I sighed with relief as I joined the laughter.

I sat up on the edge of my bed to await the day to begin before dawn the next morning. Anastasia seeing me awake, crept over to sit beside me. As the sun slowly rose, filling the ward with rosy hues, we sat whispering and giggling quietly like sisters waiting for our parents to wake up. She told me of her fears about her operation. The last time they operated, they only anaesthetised the area while they operated on her broken femur, to improve her recovery time. She remembered the sounds and smells that haunted her from the operating theatre.

After breakfast, Anastasia let out a cheer as a familiar face to her entered the room. Gennaro, the regular cleaner who she knew from her last stay, had just returned from holiday. Anastasia quickly briefed him on who I was. His bright smile immediately brought fresh joviality to the ward as he strode over to my bed. Handing his phone to me, he proudly showed me pictures of his grandchildren. He clicked through to press play on some music. He left the phone in my hands as he moved away to start work. He began waltzing demonstratively around the ward with his mop singing 'Volare'. He paused at the end of my bed, dipping the pole like he would a dance partner, before popping up with a mischievous smile. Two more voices joined in for the chorus as Infermieri Mario and Lelo pushed their trolleys into the room for morning rounds.

The memory of my second night on Elba flashed into my mind. As we sat on the beach singing the same song. Two months later, it seemed I had a lot more courage than I could ever have expected to need to draw on.

Dottore Corduous put his head around the door, to see what was going on. Breaking into laughter at the sight of the singers, he came over to see me.

"Oggi, noi prendiamo i Tuoi punti," he told me demonstrating what was about to happen with scissors. They were taking my stitches out today. I scrunched up my nose at the thought but was curious to know how many stitches I had received. Gennaro finished mopping the room, as the song faded to an end. He took his phone from me and headed to the next ward.

Infermiere Mario came over to assist Dottore Corduas to cut off my wrappings. Anastasia sat alongside the bed, holding and stroking my hand as my cast was loosened. Dottore Corduas nodded towards her as the bulky dressings were taken away, "Ora vai con questa bella signora,"—he told me to go with Anastasia to the bathroom.

"Una lavata prima?"—*a wash first*—she offered as she helped me to stand. Sitting me on a chair in the bathroom, she limped to the sink. With wet hand towels she gently cleaned the skin of my torso with warm water. She had found a clean singlet top in my bag and gently slipped it over my injured arm before stretching it over my head. I watched her balancing carefully without her crutches, fighting her own physical battle but there to help me.

I lay back down as Professore Russo came past to check the wound and assess movement in my arm. I winced fearing the level of pain would rise again as he lifted it gently a little each way. While it ached, to my relief the pain was nothing compared to what it had been. "Buono," he nodded at me before indicating Dottore Corduas could proceed.

"Uno," I winced as he began counting the stitches as he pulled them out.

"Due. Tre. Quattro. Cinque. Sei."

Sixteen removed from my arm. Eight from my hip. Washed,

un-stitched, re-wrapped, and cheered by the morning of song and laughter, healing had begun.

"In the final analysis, Naples, like all great cities, is better defined by its citizens than by its buildings and monuments."

~ Jordan Lancaster ~

25

May 2011

The five-hundred-year-old church of Pio Monte della Misericordia on via Tribunale—the same east-west thoroughfare the Greeks marked out as the Decumanas Maggiore—was undergoing renovations the day I walked in eighteen months after being flown back home to Australia. I clambered under the scaffolding, the noise of workmen clanging tools and banging hammers above, to find a spot where I could take in the 500-year-old masterpiece looming behind the main altar.

Napoli, at the beginning of the seventeenth century was the capital of the Kingdom of the Two Sicilies and under Spanish rule. It was the largest city in Europe, with a population three times that of Rome, with continued growth due to a flood of migrants from land and sea. Social structures were in flux after a succession of autocratic Spanish Vice Roys had broken down the power of the Neapolitan aristocracy, compensating the former ruling classes— barons and landowners—with hedonistic rewards at the court of the Spanish Viceroy, in lieu of reduced power. A new class of professionals and entrepreneurs were emerging in the city: lawyers, tax advisers, importers and exporters of grain, moneylenders, and traders in luxury goods. The city was flourishing financially, however there was only enough work for a small percent of the population. Rural migrants had flooded to the city to escape the uncertainty of life as small landholders; though they had been ultimately driven off their land by the punitive royal taxes the Spanish had imposed on the rural peasantry. As the population rapidly expanded the people faced mass unemployment and grim poverty. The crowds of beggars were called lazzaroni—literally meaning lepers—but in fact it encompassed a whole sub-class of the poorest of the poor, who crowded the streets suffering from starvation and malnutrition.

Amidst this increasing need in the city, the Pio Monte della Misericordia was founded in 1602, by seven Neapolitan nobles who, aware of a population in need of help and solidarity, decided to share their possessions and committed to works of charity. Dissatisfied with the narrowness and superficiality of life at the court of the Spanish Viceroy and moved by the plight of the lazarri they began to meet on Friday nights at the Hospital of the Incurables to feed the needy. The confraternity grew and they extended their activities to extend to all, the works of mercy through the hands-on-charity described by Jesus in the book of Matthew.

> *I was hungry, and you gave me something to eat,*
> *I was thirsty and you gave me something to drink,*
> *I was a stranger and you invited me in*
> *I needed clothes and you clothed me*
> *I was sick and you looked after me*
> *I was in prison and you came to visit me.*

By 1606 they had built and consecrated a church, just as a roguish painter known as Caravaggio arrived in Napoli, having fled Rome after killing a man during a brawl. Seeking a visual expression of their charter they commissioned the passionate painter who—perhaps even more than they realised at the time—knew well the brutality of life on the streets outside the homes of his wealthy patrons.

The painting and biblical passage was brought to life at this seminal moment in the city.

When the verses from the book of Matthew had come to mind eighteen months earlier as Norma prayed over me, I had had no knowledge of the painting I now stood in front of, Caravaggio's *Le Sette Opere di Misericordia*—The Seven Acts of Mercy. But from my own experience, it was clear that the painting evidently sat firmly within the city's psyche five-hundred years later, continuing to demand her citizens respond to strangers in need.

I was hungry and they fed me. I was thirsty and they gave me drink. I was a stranger, and they took me in. I needed clothes and they clothed me. I was sick and they came to visit. I was trapped in a prison of sorts, and they came to me. The only thing I hadn't needed—thankfully —was the seventh spiritual act: to be buried.

They say, 'See Naples and Die'. I had barely seen the city that fateful day. Instead, I had discovered her true heart as I experienced the intrinsic beauty that had shaped the city for me through the warmth of her people, who had cared for me in my own infirmity as a stranger in their care.

From the moment I was wheeled through the airport in Rome to my flight home, I knew I had to return.

Regaining full use of my arm took ten months of hard work with the support of physiotherapists back in Brisbane and then later Sydney where I returned. With the open arms and practical and emotional support of family and friends I found work while I continued with rehabilitation three times a week. I began deconstructing the notes I had made on my phone while in hospital, as I sought to understand the shadow and light of the experience that I had been through. I returned to Italian classes through the language school at the University of New South Wales to continue to build on my language skills as I prepared to return to Napoli and be reunited with those I met in hospital. And finally, eighteen months to the day that I had been flown out, I landed back in Rome.

I stepped through the arrivals gate into the waiting arms of Karina and Giancarlo who had since moved northeast of Rome to a rural area near Lago di Bracciano. They dropped me to my bed and breakfast in the city centre where Alexis was waiting. She joined me from London for my first weekend. Then I spent a week back in language school in the Italian capital, immersing myself completely in the language as I made final preparations for my anticipated return south. As I walked through the streets of the eternal city, the hair on my neck rose every time I heard the engine or felt the wind of a moped as they zipped by.

Karina and Giancarlo returned to take me for dinner in their local community the night before I headed south. I would return to stay with them again for a few days at the end of my planned two-month trip.

The steady rhythm of the tracks beneath my train carriage helped soothe my nerves as I wound my way back down to Campania from Rome.

I stayed first with Marcia and her husband Tim, north in Castel Voltorno on the outskirts of the city where they lived in the heart of Camorra territory. I visited il Faro Baptist Church where I was reunited with Jacki and Tim as well as Erica. I met many for the first time —both Americans and Italians—who knew me from the time they had spent praying for my well-being while I was in hospital. I caught a train out to Patrizio and Jennifer's home in Quarto and got to know their young family over lunch.

A week with Tina and Sandro northeast in Successo gave me the chance to again feel the depth of the love of my adopted Italian parents. I spent time at the kitchen table with Tina, where she showed me how to make limoncello and biscotti, and took me to see the buckets of olives they had marinating in a spare room from the last harvest. Sandro took me below ground under the palazzo—his family home for over one hundred years—to show me their cantina, a large cave like space down a hundred steps under the home where they kept their wine. And in their rustic white Fiat 500, he drove me to the station to do day trips into the city.

Anastasia and I had become close in my last week in hospital. Kindred spirits that found each other despite our language barrier. It was like reuniting with an old friend despite the brief tenure of our initial friendship. I shared a room with her daughters—now aged eighteen and twenty-two years old—in their apartment in central Napoli, and reunited with her husband, mother and Aunties, as well as other extended family who I had met when they had visited her in hospital.

Her daughters practised their English on me as we walked the streets linked arm in arm, explaining the architecture, pointing out where the ghosts of past history lived and sharing with me their favourite parts of the city they were born to. We ate pizza and sipped espressos, explored the Duomo where the faithful gather three times a year to witness the liquefaction of what is claimed to be a sample of Napoli's patron Saint Gennaro's blood.

Anastasia's best friend Elena, I discovered, was a cook for the brothers at the ancient church of San Lorenzo Maggiore located on the corner of San Gregorio Armeno, famous for artisan presepe stalls—the traditional Neapolitan Christmas Nativities. She slipped me through a side door during the siesta hours when it was closed to the public for a private tour of the church. She pointed out the spot from where a legendary Napolitano love affair is said to have commenced in 1336, when Giovanni Boccaccio (one of the Three Crowns of Italian literature along with Dante Alighieri and Francesco Petrarch) first laid eyes on his muse Fiammetta. We explored the museo beside the church, before we went below ground to see ruins of the ancient Roman marketplace still laid out underneath.

I returned to the same church with Anastasia on Saturday afternoon to meet children who lived in the local area, who gathered together for community activities each week. Children rushed into her arms as we approached, flinging themselves on me also, before realising I was a new face. With the other volunteers we herded the rampaging bambini out into via Tribunal and shepherded them along one side keeping a wary eye on the mopeds and cars continually squeezing through the narrow inner-city passage until we reached a scout hall, resplendent with crumbling frescos. The children entered into a foray of activities with the vibrant young group leaders, later enjoying platters of food waiting under clothes on a table nearby.

Over dinner back in their home her husband told me about his life as a Carabinieri police officer as Anastasia interjected with how worried she became when she didn't see him for a few days at a time when he was out on assignment.

At the end of my week with them, they drove me south to stay with Antonina and her family at the pizzeria in Masse Lubrense. She fed me so much each day I had to avoid public transport and offers of lifts as I explored the Sorrentine peninsula, instead taking a forty-five-minute walk through the lemon and olive groves to the bay each day to keep making room for more food. Along with her daughter Francesca she drove me to Positano to wander down the steep streets, visit the iconic Church of Santa Maria Assunta, and walk the volcanic black sand before we headed up high on the cliff for a lavish lunch cooked by a fellow local restaurateur.

Returning north of the city I stayed with Erica and her family in Monte di Procida on the most north-western tip of the bay of Napoli. She had offered me a place to stay, giving me the chance to get to know her and find out more about the lives of American military families based in the region. Their home afforded views across the bay to Mount Vesuvius, and I enjoyed everyday adventures with the local expat, from attending her daughter's swimming lesson in a pool up high on Capo Miseno—where Pliny the Younger had documented the AD79 eruption of Vesuvius that had consumed Pompeii—to sweating it out together in a spin class instructed in Italian. We took trips to the mysterious Solfatara di Pozzuoli within the volcanic Phlegraean Fields, (once an obligatory stop of the Grand Tour of the eighteenth century) and explored the archaeology park of the ancient Greek settlement of Cumae. Treading along a path of giant stones, we found the cave of the Cumaean Sibyl, an ancient pagan priestess who was thought to have prophesied the birth of the Messiah that Christians identify as Jesus. Her image, along with three other Sibyls who had similar prophecies, are found within Michelangelo's biblical fresco in the Sistine Chapel.

I sat under the orange trees in the garden of the home of Dottore Corduas in the cool of an early summer evening and got to know his wife Anna, a lawyer, as well as other friends and family over dinner. I returned to the halls of l'Ospedale dei Pellegrini to see if I could find any of the other dotteri and infermieri who had cared for me, before exploring the hospital church, this time on a guided tour by Sabrina and her classmates, whose latest school assignment coincided with my visit, providing me with a guided tour of the ancient landmark.

I looked into the crater of Mount Vesuvius and walked the streets of Pompeii and Herculaneum, ate true Neapolitani pizza—this time in a pizzeria—and ate the olives and lemons that fall from the trees on the Sorrentine Peninsula. I smelt the buffalo cattle from which the milk for the mozzarella comes, as well as being reviled by the scent of the piles of rubbish which were mounting up in the streets of the city as the disposal crisis again escalated during my stay.

I wandered through castles and palaces and gazed upon magnificent works of art in the solitude of museums not oft enough frequented by other tourists. The parklands surrounding the galleries of Capodimonte were far more beautiful than I could have imagined from the window in the hall of l'Ospedale CTO. The

Museo di Capodimonte was quiet and captivating as I wandered her halls exploring the shadow and light in other works by Caravaggio. I found myself obsessed with the artist's work, after discovering my own deep personal connection with his work at the Pio Monte della Misericordia. I discovered the works of Titian, Raphael, and Ribera, before landing on the most arresting painting in the building. The dramatic work of ground-breaking female baroque artist Artemisia Gentileschi in 'Judith Slaying Holofernes'.

I was awestruck in the Capella di Sansevero as I gazed on the Cristo Velato—the Veiled Christ—one of the most emotive sculptures in the world: and equally horrified to discover the alchemical experiments of Raimondo di Sangro, Prince of Sansevero in the museo below.

I entered the halls of the Museo Archeologico to see the Farnese collection and mosaics and murals brought from Pompeii. One day, I returned to the scene of the accident just around the corner from the Museo entrance. Just to see if I could make any more sense of what had happened.

There was a street sign beside the traffic lights that I had stepped out to cross at on that fateful day. I had been following one of the directional signs on it pointing to Vomero. But it seemed I had had another path to follow. There was another sign on the same pole.

It pointed to l'Ospedale CTO.

EPILOGUE

"It is indeed an arduous task, and one beyond my strength, that I embark on, trusting not so much in my own powers as in the light of that Giver who giveth to all men liberally, and upbraideth not".

~ Canto I - Dante ~

As I waited for my flight out of Rome after leaving hospital, Marco's final text message had been in English.

"I love you."

Despite all that had befallen me, I had still somehow finished my trip with a romance with a man on an Italian island. And it had been beautiful. We stayed in touch through brief emails, the occasional text and Facebook for about a year. It was hard to let go of the idea of running away to live on Elba to create the fresh start I still craved, but my time in hospital had reminded me of the importance of having more than a romantic love in my life. I needed more than one love to fulfil my emotional needs.

After experiencing the support of the Italian families and going through the trauma of a marriage breakdown away from home and then a major accident, the importance of being present with my own family had come back into focus after so long living away from them. Not only for what I needed from them, but also for the role I wanted to play in their lives. All the loves in our lives shape us and strengthen us. As much as I still held to the fairy-tale of finding that one great love again, having fallen for that idea before, I knew I needed the other loves of my life—friends and family—in balance to fulfil me also.

The decision to move back to Brisbane permanently was hard and wouldn't come until two years after the accident. I had strong professional connections and opportunities still in Sydney and held some good roles in the time I spent back down there before my return trip to Italy. It had been my home for most of adult life. But despite the embrace of my urban family on return, the pull to move home to my own family was ever-present. I realised I had missed enough Sunday lunches at my parents' place, and cups of tea and homemade biscuits while chit-chatting with my ageing mother. My ten nieces and nephews were growing up without me around.

In Siena I had begun to understand that the direction I needed to take next had to offer me more than just a career with financial reward, but a vocation as well. I needed a sense of purpose.

Disconnecting from everyday life on Elba had re-connected me with simplicity and taken me back to my centre as I dwelt in the basic joys in my life before the clutter of adulting. It re-established my desire for balance in how I used my time and invested my energy as well as engaged with those around me.

Then Napoli. The dominant use of the colour red in Napoli is said to represent the heart of a city, built on love, blood and passion. I left the city with all three infused into me in some way, shape or form. With the courage gained from my experiences, I began to pursue my passions and seek a life, different to, but as big and beautiful as the one I had once imagined before all those original dreams of youth had been swept away.

My journey didn't end in a hospital bed. Nor did it end after I returned to Campania to spend two months travelling through Napoli and her surrounds to better get to know the people and city, that had created a fork in my anticipated road when I set off. With my desire to discover who I was other than which I already knew myself to be, I tapped into the sparks ignited along my journey and then relentlessly pursued them. I made a deliberate choice to continue travelling, though it turned out that my onward journey was in my own country. And the road I was on would eventually lead me back home.

I returned to university to get my first degree, gaining a Bachelor of Photography at the Queensland College of Arts. My Monday mornings went from writing reports about football games I had worked on over the weekend, to sinking into a seat in a lecture theatre to indulge in classes on art history and theory. I began to draw on my experiences in Italy for assignments—Caravaggio's work being an excellent study for a budding photographer—as I continued to explore ideas around the shadows and light that filter through the different chapters of our lives and the spiritual dimension that shapes the interior of our soul.

Everyday life continued to ebb and flow with highs and lows. As it does for all. In the shadow and light of my life, my faith remains my balancer, sustaining the core of who I am and inspiring me to pursue becoming the person I still long to be.

L'amore di Dio è al centro della mia vita—The love of God is at the centre of my life.

It has never left since I learnt of it as a child. But, the love of the people of Napoli reinforced the knowledge that no matter the roads I travelled in this life, there would always be a much bigger love than all the others. One that has held me close and kept me, through joy and pain, triumph and failure.

I set out in search of some sort of definitive answer for my life. Nothing happens overnight. Instead, I learnt that the beauty of life is in the pilgrimage. My loss of control following the accident ultimately spurred me on to continue to explore what I was capable of, dream about where those capabilities might take me, and discover the most unexpected landing points along the way.

Life is a journey, not a destination. Or as Ralph Waldo Emerson actually put it, *"To finish the moment, to find the journey's end in every step of the road, to live the greatest number of good hours, is wisdom."*

Con ringrazie ...

Australia

Mum and Dad, Patricia and Jessica for always being there.

To my BFF...E (best friend forever... and ever) Debbie. Thank you for walking by my side both physically and emotionally through life's phases, geographic changes and emotional shifts, and saving me a fortune in counselling with that ever ready listening ear and your gentle encouragement.

To my Sydney urban family Kris, Laura, Elise, Jane, Helen, Pete and Amie, for your love, kindness, encouragement, friendship and commitment to the dance floor of life (not to mention the provision of places to stay, a car and all manner of practical help on return to Sydney), and encouragement to keep writing. An extra special thank you to Kris for being an inspiration and motivator by your own example, to keep growing and stepping out creatively.

To my travel buddy and fellow adventurer, Alexis – so many roads walked together despite geographical distances. Here's to more fun in the years to come!

To TJ, for your gentle friendship alongside a willingness to do the hard edit on my manuscript (in fact pushing me to hand it over), then taking your impression of my journey and using your visual communication skills to bring the story to life on the cover.

To Lisa, whose desire to see people empowered to be all that they can be weaves so authentically throughout all areas of your life, with not just words but practical and generous action.

To Rosanne, Kate and Tracey for your love, encouragement, generosity, and faith in me over a lifetime of friendship.

Italia

To the staff of Ortopaedia dal'Ospedale Pellegrini specialamente Professore Russo, Dottore Corduas e Infermieri Giovanni, Giuseppe, Angela, Pasquale, Mario and the lovely blonde nurse, whose name I can't remember but will never forget the depth of your compassion.

To Karina, la mia angel, e Gavina who introduced us; Carissima Signora Tina (1936 – 2020)—sempre nel mio cuore—e caro Signor Sandro. Alla famiglia di Signora Christina e Fernanda, Lina e Cyrus; Signora Assunta e Emma; Antonina e la tua familigia; Anastasia e la tua familigia; Marcia and Tim Monahan; Jacki and Tim Faulkner; Erica and family; Georgia and Shirl; Norma and Mariuzzi; Patrizio and Jennifer Zucchetto; Pino e Pina Zucchetto. Jenny and Alyn from Six Small Rooms.

And the myriad of strangers and new friends who showed me kindness in both l'Ospedale C.T.O. and l'Ospedale dei Pellegrini.

Per mio caro amico Marco… La fortuna aiuta gli audici!

E a Gesù, grazie per la vostra vita, l'amore e gli insegnamenti a cui fare riferimento come cerco di essere la migliore versione di me stesso.

ABOUT THE AUTHOR

JACQUELINE BAWTREE was born in Jimbour on the Southern Darling Downs of Queensland and grew up in Brisbane, Australia.

She lived in Sydney and Melbourne for ten years, before taking time to travel.

Her first book, Coming Home, recounts her decision to take a career break and spend a year in Italy, only to land in hospital four months into her journey after a run in with a moped on the streets of Naples. Forced to confront all she had left behind, she eventually found herself... **Coming Home.**

Jacqueline now lives in Brisbane and works as a writer and photographer, exploring the stories of her hometown and surrounds.

www.ingramcontent.com/pod-product-compliance
Lightning Source LLC
Chambersburg PA
CBHW010244010526
44107CB00063B/2675